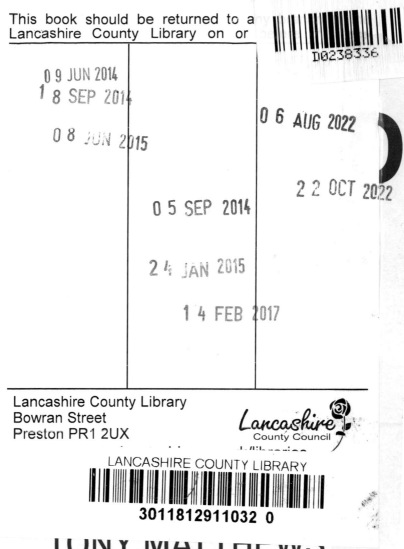

TONY MATTHEWS

Foreword by Bryan Robson OBE

AMBERLEY

First published 2014

Amberley Publishing
The Hill, Stroud
Gloucestershire, GL5 4EP

www.amberley-books.com

British Library Cataloguing in Publication Data.
A catalogue record for this book is available from the British Library.

ISBN 978 1 4456 1948 4 (print)
ISBN 978 1 4456 1966 8 (ebook)

Typesetting and Origination by Amberley Publishing.
Printed in the UK.

Contents

Foreword

It was a great honour to be asked by Tony to write the foreword to his latest book covering the England football team in the World Cup.

Anyone will tell you that being involved in this tournament is, to a certain degree, the pinnacle of a player's career, whatever the outcome.

To be able to pit your skills against the world's greatest footballers is something special. I had the pleasure of appearing in three World Cups, in Spain 1982, in Mexico four years later and in Italy in 1990. And I was also privileged to captain my country in the latter two tournaments.

Unfortunately, England failed to deliver the ultimate prize, but we did give it a good go in Mexico and also in Italy, being eliminated in the quarter-finals by Argentina and the hand of a certain Diego Maradona in 1986, and then by West Germany, agonisingly on penalties, in 1990.

I will never forget the look, and anguish, on manager Bobby Robson's face after that shoot-out defeat in Turin. That was a horrible moment for us all – players, management and supporters alike. I sincerely believed we were good enough to win the World Cup in Italy. Sadly, it was not to be.

As all serious football supporters know full well, the World Cup started in 1930, but it was twenty years later before England entered, and it wasn't the greatest of baptisms – going out to the outsiders, the United States. Better displays would follow, none moreso than in 1966 when Bobby Moore led us to victory over the West Germans at Wembley. And if the truth be known, although I was only a youngster still at school, we should have retained the trophy in Mexico in 1970.

Since then, England's overall performances, in what I believe is the greatest sporting event on Earth, have been hit and miss. As mentioned earlier, we came close on a couple of occasions, so why can't we win the star prize again in Brazil?

Roy Hodgson will be hoping to have all his key players available, and will be praying that they all remain fit.

I know that injuries can play a huge part in the manager's plans. I suffered badly in 1986 when my hopes of glory were crushed after I re-aggravated an existing shoulder injury in our second game of the group stages against Morocco. It prevented me from participating further in the tournament. And four years later I was injured again, playing in only the first two games. That was tortuous.

I just hope and pray that no one suffers in Brazil. Having said that, winning a major tournament, such as the World Cup, is not just about the handful of truly great players available – and believe me, England have quite a few – it's about the entire squad.

Team spirit will play a huge part. One or two players will never get a game, others will be relied upon to defend, create and score goals. Whatever transpires, England, as always, will fight to the end ... and going back in time, there have been many who have produced outstanding performances for their country, and there will be, I'm sure, a few more in the years to come.

Bryan Robson OBE

Introduction

The World Cup Ball Starts Rolling

Having withdrawn in 1928, England rejoined FIFA in the summer of 1946. Stanley Rous, who was secretary of the Football Association at the time, persuaded the council members to appoint Walter Winterbottom as the FA's first director of coaching, suggesting he also take on the responsibility of being England's first team manager.

A Lancastrian, born in Oldham in 1914, Winterbottom was the only son of a ring frame fitter in a textile machine works. At the age of twelve, he was awarded a scholarship to Oldham High School and later won a bursary to Chester Diocesan Training College, graduating as the top student in 1933. He took a teaching post at the Alexander Rhodes School, Oldham, and while there played football for Royton Amateurs, Mossley FC and as an amateur for Manchester City.

However, it was City's archrivals from Old Trafford who secured his services as a part-time professional in 1936. While continuing with his teaching, Winterbottom, playing as a wing-half and centre-half, made twenty-three League and FA Cup appearances in his first season at Manchester United (1936/37). But he was called into action only four times during the next two campaigns before a spinal disease, later diagnosed as ankylosing spondylitis, eventually brought his career to an end – although he did play for Chelsea as a guest, and was named as a reserve for wartime internationals.

In the summer of 1939, he left his teaching position to study at Carnegie College of Physical Education, Leeds, and on graduating was appointed as a lecturer. During the Second World War, he served as an officer in the RAF, attaining the rank of wing commander and working at the Air Ministry with overall responsibility for training PE instructors at home and overseas. He also organised coaching courses for the FA at grammar schools in London. And then, in 1946, when League football resumed after a break of seven years, he started his job as manager of England's national team, his teaching plans being turned upside down!

Although Winterbottom was to manage the England team, head man Rous announced that not all of the FA's councillors were happy with the decision. Nevertheless, it was stated that the FA committee would retain sufficient power with regards to coaching and to a certain extent team selection.

Winterbottom got to work immediately. He introduced the idea of having both youth and under-23 teams, so that his coaching staff could nurture young footballers through the system while also giving them international status at a relatively young age. With the help of experienced managers, coaches, and scouts from around the county, and also from his own personal knowledge, he quickly sorted out the best players available for international duty with England.

First Game in Charge

Winterbottom's first game in charge was a Home International Championship encounter against Northern Ireland at Windsor Park, Belfast, on 28 September 1946. The line-up he chose was: goalkeeper Frank Swift (Manchester City), full-backs Laurie Scott (Arsenal) and George Hardwick (Middlesbrough), a middle line of Billy Wright (Wolves), Neil Franklin (Stoke City) and Henry Cockburn (Manchester United), and a front line comprising right-winger Tom Finney (Preston North End), inside-right Raich Carter (Derby County), centre-forward Tommy Lawton (Chelsea), Wilf Mannion (Middlesbrough) and Bobby Langton (Blackburn Rovers).

A crowd of 57,111 saw England win in style by 7-2, with all five forwards scoring goals, and Mannion netting a hat-trick.

Over the next four years – before the 1950 World Cup in Brazil – Winterbottom used a further thirty-one players (making it forty-two overall) as he slowly but surely assembled a squad he believed was strong enough and good enough to win the Jules Rimet Trophy.

England qualified for the 1950 tournament by winning the Home International Championship of 1949/50. In effect, the four home countries had agreed, in principle, to take part in the World Cup, and FIFA stated that the four internationals between the countries should act as a qualifying competition, with the top two going through to Brazil. However, Scotland announced that they would only go if they won the Home Championship.

1

The 1950 World Cup Qualifying Matches

15 October 1949
Ninian Park, Cardiff

Wales 1 England 4
Attendance 61,079

England Team: B. Williams (Wolverhampton Wanderers), B. Mozley (Derby County), J. Aston (Manchester United), W. Wright (Wolverhampton Wanderers), N. Franklin (Stoke City), J. Dickinson (Portsmouth), T. Finney (Preston North End), S. Mortensen (Blackpool), J. Milburn (Newcastle United), L. Shackleton (Sunderland), J. Hancocks (Wolverhampton Wanderers).

This was the first-ever World Cup qualifying match in which England and Wales had taken part. England dominated for long periods despite having Wolves skipper Billy Wright struggling on the left wing for most of the second-half with a torn thigh muscle. Star of the show was Newcastle United centre-forward Jackie Milburn, who scored a hat-trick.

The game was virtually over inside the first thirty-five minutes as a rampant England scored three times in five worthy attacks, starting with an opener from Blackpool's inside-right Stan Mortensen midway through the half. Soon after, in the twenty-ninth minute, Milburn bagged his first and, five minutes later, the raven-haired striker made it 3-0 as the home defence was torn apart by some precise wing play by Preston North End's right wing plumber Tom Finney.

'Wor Jackie' duly completed his hat-trick in the sixty-sixth minute, at a time when Wales were momentarily on top. Mal Griffiths' late strike on eighty minutes, after Bert Williams had pulled off a quite stunning diving save from Trevor Ford, was all the principality could manage.

Although a 'walking passenger', Wright continued to have an influence on the match with quiet but encouraging words to his colleagues.

16 November 1949   England 9 Ireland 2
Maine Road, Manchester   Attendance 69,742

England Team: B. Streten (Luton Town), B. Mozley, J. Aston, W. Watson (Sunderland), N. Franklin, W. Wright, T. Finney, S. Mortensen, J. Rowley (Manchester United), S. Pearson (Manchester United), J. Froggatt (Portsmouth).

Manager Walter Winterbottom was without Cardiff hero Milburn for this encounter. Six weeks earlier, the Irish had been battered 8-2 by Scotland in Belfast. He brought in Manchester United's Jack Rowley for his fourth cap as his replacement, while also handing international debuts to the Luton Town goalkeeper Bernard Streten, Sunderland wing-half and Yorkshire cricketer Willie Watson, and Portsmouth left-winger Jack Frogg. Wright had recovered from injury and took his place at the heart of the defence, alongside Stoke's Franklin.

The game was rather one-sided as England virtually ran the show from the first to the last whistle, although Ireland did score twice courtesy of some indifferent defending! Although Froggatt scored on his debut, the star of the show was Rowley, who fired in a four-timer. His Manchester United teammate Stan Pearson and Mortensen both scored twice.

Rowley started the ball rolling with England's opening goal on five minutes. Froggatt made it 2-0 on twenty-eight and Pearson netted a third just past the half-hour mark. Ten minutes from half-time, Mortensen powered in a fourth goal, Rowley made it 5-0 on forty-seven minutes, and 'Morty' was there again three minutes later to bring up the half-dozen.

Sammy Smyth reduced the deficit on fifty-two minutes, but further goals by Rowley (fifty-five and fifty-eight minutes) and Pearson, with quarter of an hour remaining, took the score to 9-1 before Bobby Brennan netted Ireland's second five minutes from time.

Spare a thought for Ireland's 'keeper Hugh Kelly (Fulham), who was making his international debut. He conceded another ten goals in his next three internationals, making it ninteen in four. Nevertheless, with a smile on his face, he still enjoyed playing football.

NB: This was the last time an all-Ireland team played together at senior level.

15 April 1950   Scotland 0 England 1
Hampden Park   Attendance 133,250

England Team: B. Williams, A. Ramsey (Tottenham Hotspur), J. Aston, W. Wright, N. Franklin, J. Dickinson, T. Finney, W. Mannion (Middlesbrough), S. Mortenson, R. Bentley (Chelsea), R. Langton (Bolton Wanderers).

England duly clinched a place in the World Cup, and also won the Home International Championship, with this narrow victory over the Scots in Glasgow.

'The game fell short of being a great one,' wrote Clifford Webb in the *Daily Herald*. 'There was grand approach work by the England forwards and half-backs, typically dour defence by the Scots, and occasional spasms of Scottish genius in attack, which actually gave them more scoring chances than their opponents.'

As an experiment, Winterbottom and his fellow selectors chose Chelsea's Roy Bentley at inside-left for his international debut. Stan Mortensen of Blackpool appeared alongside him at centre-forward to form the first post-war spearhead partnership. With Wilf Mannion and Tom Finney playing together on the right wing in the absence of Stanley Matthews, England's attack had a good look about it, but it was the Scots who looked the more threatening overall.

All credit to England's defence: it was faultless and restricted the Scots to just four worthwhile efforts on goal. Bert Williams of Wolves dealt with them all with a safe pair of hands. At the other end, Mannion (2), Bentley and left-winger Bobby Langton went close before Bentley, interchanging passes with Mortensen, scored the deciding goal at sixty-eight minutes.

Billy Wright and Neil Franklin were outstanding in England's back division. Soon after this match, the latter announced that he did not want to be considered for the World Cup because he was joining Independiente Santa Fe, an outlawed club in Bogotà, Colombia, who had offered him – and other English club players – 'a lot of money' and a good living. Like Wright, he had played in all twenty-seven England matches since 1946 and the pair had developed a tremendous understanding together on the pitch. So England had lost their lynchpin with the World Cup due to start in just six weeks' time. Winterbottom had to sit down and choose a reliable replacement for Rio.

Losing Franklin came as a shock to a lot of England stars, including Stanley Matthews, who said, 'I didn't at the time think Neil was unwise not to go to Colombia, if he wanted to. It was going to earn big money, but he realised afterwards what a mistake he made. In fact, those who went to Bogota soon got homesick.'

Pre-World Cup Action

Before the start of the World Cup, England played two friendly matches, beating Portugal 5-3 in Lisbon and Belgium 4-1 in Brussels. Jimmy Mullen (Wolves) became the first substitute to be used by England when he came on for Jackie Milburn against the Belgians. And in both of these games, Wright's centre-back partner was Bill Jones of Liverpool. Jones was a late replacement for his clubmate Laurie Hughes, who had been the initial choice to fill the gap left by Franklin, but had withdrawn through injury. But in conceding four goals, there were worrying signs that Wright was missing his favourite partner, and Jones was given a tough time in Lisbon by Portugal's African-born centre-forward David, who scored twice. Jones was also severely tested in Belgium and there was no doubt that England had major problems ahead of their opening World Cup match against Chile.

Winterbottom's twenty-one-man squad for England's first-ever taste of World Cup finals action featured some big names, most of whom had played at full international level since the war. There were, however, five uncapped players, which, to some purists, was something of a shock. The average age of the squad was 28.2 years, and the average experience was 9.5 caps. Captain Billy Wright was the most capped player with 30, followed by Tom Finney (26), Wilf Mannion (20) and Stan Mortensen (19).

Winterbottom's England squad for the 1950 World Cup was:

Goalkeepers: Ted Ditchburn (Tottenham Hotspur), Bert Williams (Wolves). Full-backs: Johnny Aston (Manchester United), Alf Ramsey (Tottenham Hotspur), Laurie Scott (Arsenal), Bill Eckersley* (Blackburn Rovers). Half-backs: Henry Cockburn (Manchester United), Jimmy Dickinson (Portsmouth), Laurie Hughes* (Liverpool), Bill Nicholson* (Tottenham Hotspur), Jim Taylor* (Fulham), Willie Watson (Sunderland), Billy Wright (Wolves). Forwards: Eddie Baily* (Tottenham Hotspur), Roy Bentley (Chelsea), Tom Finney (Preston North End), Jackie Milburn (Newcastle United), Wilf Mannion (Middlesbrough), Stanley Matthews (Blackpool), Stan Mortensen (Blackpool), Jimmy Mullen (Wolves).

NB: Stand-by reserves were full-back Bert Mozley (Derby County), defender Bill Jones (Liverpool) and winger Johnny Hancocks (Wolverhampton Wanderers).

*Uncapped players.

2

The 1950 World Cup in Brazil

Only thirteen countries took part in the 1950 World Cup. England (seeded) competed in Pool 2, along with Chile, Spain and the USA.

25 June 1950	Chile 0 England 2
Estádio do Maracanã, Rio de Janeiro	Attendance 29,703*

England Team: B. Williams, A. Ramsey, J. Aston, W. Wright, L. Hughes, J. Dickinson, T. Finney, W. Mannion, R. Bentley, S. Mortensen, J. Mullen.

In the official opening match, hosts Brazil beat a lacklustre Mexico 4-0 inside the rather tatty-looking Estádio do Maracanã in Rio. Twenty-four hours later, England started their campaign, and things began well enough for Winterbottom's men. Most sources, including the FIFA match report, list the official attendance* as under 30,000 (as stated above). However, many commentators and reporters believe it was much higher, with estimates ranging from 45,000 to 60,000.

Liverpool's Laurie Hughes took over at centre-half and Jimmy Mullen was selected at outside-left. In fact, it was the Wolves' winger who crossed for Mortensen to head home England's first goal on twenty-seven minutes, albeit against the run of play. Wilf Mannion secured victory six minutes into the second-half, finding the net with a crisp, low, right-footed drive from the edge of the area. Mortensen made a surging run past three defenders before passing to Tom Finney, who laid the ball back for the Middlesbrough man to score. Chile's Newcastle United forward George Robledo struck the England crossbar on the hour mark, and after that the South Americans forced Bert Williams into three fine diving saves to maintain his side's two-goal lead. This, though, was a far from impressive start to England's World Cup campaign. Finney recalled that during the second half, several players struggled for breath in the oppressive atmosphere.

Stanley Matthews, who around this time was not the FA's favourite son, missed the first game. He flew into Rio sometime after the official party, having been sent on a totally meaningless trip to Canada as a footballing ambassador by the FA in early June! Matthews sat in the stand and watched the Chile match, and would unfortunately do exactly the same thing four days later, when England took on the USA.

NB: The times given for the goals scored against Chile vary widely between several newspapers. Therefore, I have used the times stated in the FIFA match report, which are the same, or within a minute or so of those given in the vast majority of press reports.

29 June 1950	England 0 USA 1
Belo Horizonte	Attendance 10,151

England Team: B. Williams, A. Ramsey, J. Aston, W. Wright, L. Hughes, J. Dickinson, T. Finney, W. Mannion, R. Bentley, S. Mortensen, J. Mullen.

Four days after beating Chile, England's next match was against the rank outsiders, the United States of America – makeweights in the minds of virtually every neutral in Brazil and, indeed, in world football. The venue was 300 miles from Rio, in the mountainous region of Belo Horizonte, where the heat was far was less oppressive, although the pitch was rather bumpy, with patchy grass surrounded by a cinder track. Not too far away, around 2,000 British workers were employed at the Morro Velho gold mine, ensuring the team would have decent support.

Before the game, Scotsman Bill Jeffrey, manager of the USA, said publicly, 'We ain't got a chance, but we're gonna fight to keep down any cricket score.' A group of Americans, after a stiff training session and an early evening meal, were so relaxed and unperturbed that they went out revelling until the early hours on the eve of the match. 'We're having the time of our lives and we want to enjoy every minute of our time in Brazil,' said defender Harry Keough. The USA had lost 3-1 to Spain in their previous game, and to them this encounter with England was effectively a mini cup final. But what transpired out on the pitch stunned the entire footballing world, and the rumblings could have been measured on the Richter scale.

Winterbottom, along with skipper Billy Wright and sole selector Arthur Drewry, a Grimsby fish merchant, decided unanimously to field the same eleven players who had struggled in the main against Chile, although Drewry had the final say. His decision was a surprise to many, but as he said, 'My policy is that I never change a winning team.'

Stanley Rous, then secretary of the Football Association, thought there was a danger of England taking America too lightly and hinted that Stanley Matthews should have been included in the team. He actually went to see Drewry personally and urged him to play Matthews. Nothing happened and once again the Blackpool wing-wizard was given a seat in the main stand, and in the thirty-seventh minute he saw French-speaking Haitian immigrant Joe Gaetjens score the match-winning goal to produce the biggest shock (up to that point) in world football. Gaetjens was later reported to have died in a Haitian prison after helping organise a guerrilla attack against the island's dictator, François 'Papa Doc' Duvalier, but his name lives on in football history – a legend in the States!

The game was played on a cramped, narrow pitch, meaning that England couldn't use their tightly marked wingers as they wished. England put in over twenty efforts on goal during the course of the game, and America just one, which was decisive. Four minutes after Finney had struck a post, the USA attacked down the right. With all defenders in position, goalkeeper Bert Williams seemed to have an innocuous cross from Walter Bahr covered, only for Gaetjens to dart forward and divert the ball into the net with the back of his head. Absolutely amazing.

After that it was all England. In fact, 85 per cent of the game was played in the American half of the field. Throughout the second half, the crowd saw wave after wave of England attacks. Finney (2), Mannion, Bentley, Mortensen and left-half Jimmy Dickinson had shots saved by USA 'keeper Frank Borghi, who was a professional baseball catcher! And with time running out, right-back Alf Ramsey thought he had salvaged a point with a late free-kick, only for Borghi to pull off a stunning save. Indeed, it was the brilliant form of Borghi, and some amazingly good luck, that produced the unimaginable scoreline.

Surprisingly, several newspapers around the world printed the result as an England victory by 11-1 or 10-0, believing that a typographical error had occurred in the transmission 'US 1-0 England'. It was obviously a huge result for the Americans, but also a huge result for England as well. And suddenly, Winterbottom's men, who in some quarters were regarded as favourites to win the tournament, were in total shock. The so-called 'kings of world football', so confident of victory, had been brought down to earth with an almighty bump. Later, a disillusioned Stanley Matthews stated publicly, 'I blame the defeat by the USA on the manager's prematch talk on playing tactics that had been introduced for the first time.' Preston winger Tom Finney wrote in his autobiography, 'The game against the USA should have been a formality. It turned out to be a fiasco.'

That shock defeat against the USA – and it was a shock – was followed by a further 1-0 reverse, this time against Spain in the giant Estádio do Maracanã in Rio. England *had* to beat the Spaniards to stay in the competition. They played very well at times but failed to find a way past the brilliant Barcelona goalkeeper Antoni Ramallets. England exited in the first round in their first-ever World Cup.

2 July 1950	England 0 Spain 1
Estádio do Maracanã, Rio de Janeiro	Attendance 74,462

England Team: B. Williams, A. Ramsey, W. Eckersley, W. Wright, L. Hughes, J. Dickinson, S. Matthews, T. Finney, S. Mortensen, J. Milburn, J. Mullen.

At last England decided to play Stanley Matthews on the right wing – a prospect the Blackpool star hardly relished. Tom Finney was switched to the opposite flank and Jackie Milburn was introduced at centre-forward in place of Roy Bentley. Bill Eckersley, who came in to partner Alf Ramsey at full-back, and inside-left Eddie Baily were both handed their first caps.

England dominated the game for long periods. Finney was twice tripped inside the penalty area, but each time the referee waved play on. Mortensen and Milburn saw efforts brilliantly saved, Milburn also had a headed goal wrongly ruled out for offside as early as the fourteenth minute. Baily, probably the best outfield player on the pitch, came close with a wonderful long-range effort. Defensively, England looked sound enough, but the overall composure was missing, due no doubt to the absence of the Stoke City centre-half Neil Franklin.

The only goal of the game arrived three minutes into the second half, when right winger Telmo Zarraonandia scored from close range after a deep cross from the right had been headed back into the danger zone by Silvestre Igoa and was missed by Laurie Hughes. After this, the Spaniards dropped back and defended in depth, sometimes having all eleven players behind the ball. England became frustrated and, in the last fifteen minutes, resorted to pumping long balls into the opposition box, hoping for a break, a lucky bounce, which never came.

Spain finished top of the group with six points, England were second with two points and two goals from three games. Not the sort of return people had predicted.

After the disappointment in Brazil, manager Walter Winterbottom made it quite clear that there was an awful lot of work to be done before England could rank among the best football teams in the world, saying, 'Before the War, most of the South Americans and the best European sides were quite unknown. We went to Rio pretty well prepared, but simply failed to produce the goods ... and we now know what needs to be done.'

1950 World Cup Fact File

- Countries taking part: 13 (divided into four groups, each comprising 4, 4, 3 and 2 teams respectively).
- Egypt withdrew from the competition, against the rule that required all participating players to wear football boots.
- Final: Uruguay 2, Brazil 1.
- Final venue: Estádio do Maracanã, Rio de Janeiro (attendance 199,854). Some sources say the attendance was nearer 205,000.
- Leading scorer: Ademir Marques de Menezes (Brazil), 8 goals.
- Mexican goalkeeper Antonio Carbajal appeared in the first of his record five World Cups.
- The referee for the final was Englishman George Reader from Southampton.

Back To Basics

In their first full game after returning from the 1950 World Cup, England played Northern Ireland at Windsor Park, Belfast, in the Home International Championship before a 50,000-strong crowd. Allenby Chilton of Manchester United came into the defence, alongside Billy Wright, for his first cap. Jackie Lee of Derby County was also given his debut at centre-forward. Indeed, he celebrated the occasion with a goal in a 4-1 victory.

Six weeks later, in mid-November, two Arsenal players – Lionel Smith at right-back and thirty-eight-year-old Leslie Compton at centre-half (the oldest player to win his first England cap) – and the Spurs winger Les Medley were handed their senior debuts by

Winterbottom for the home game against Wales at Roker Park, Sunderland. All three did well in a 4-2 victory before 59,137 fans; Eddie Baily scored twice, along with Wilf Mannion and Milburn.

There followed over the next twelve months a 2-2 draw with Yugoslavia at Highbury, when Nat Lofthouse netted twice on his debut, a 3-2 defeat by Scotland at Wembley, 2-1 and 5-2 home victories over Argentina and Portugal, a 2-2 stalemate with France, a 1-1 scoreline with Wales in Cardiff, a 2-0 win over Northern Ireland at Villa Park and a 2-2 draw with Austria at Wembley.

A total of fifteen players made their first appearance for the full England team between November 1950 and November 1951, among them Fulham's Jim Taylor, who had actually been a member of the 1950 World Cup squad, and Bill Nicholson of Spurs, who scored with his first kick in international football against Portugal. Also, goalkeeper Gil Merrick from Birmingham City and the Manchester City inside-forward Ivor Broadis were also handed their first caps, and both would play in the next World Cup in Switzerland.

However, before the 1954 tournament in Scandinavia was even talked about, manager Winterbottom and his coaching staff knew full well they had a lot of work to do with so many players to choose from, some of whom were not getting any younger. Twelve more internationals were fulfilled before the World Cup qualifiers began. These included 5-2 and 5-0 home victories over Wales and Belgium, a 6-3 win over the USA in New York and a 3-0 defeat of Switzerland in Zurich. Another six players were also given baptisms, including the Manchester United duo of Johnny Berry and Tommy Taylor.

England started their 1954 World Cup qualifying campaign with Home International matches against Wales and Northern Ireland in October/November 1953. England won both fixtures, beating the Welsh 4-1 and the Irish 3-1. In between, Winterbottom's side drew 4-4 with the Rest of Europe at Wembley. This game was a friendly to celebrate the ninetieth anniversary of the Football Association.

The 1954 World Cup Qualifying Matches

10 October 1953
Ninian Park, Cardiff

England 4 Wales 1
Attendance 60,879

England Team: G. Merrick (Birmingham City), T. Garrett (Blackpool), W. Eckersley (Blackburn Rovers), W. Wright, H. Johnston (Blackpool), J. Dickinson, T. Finney, A. Quixall (Sheffield Wednesday), N. Lofthouse (Bolton Wanderers), D. Wilshaw (Wolverhampton Wanderers), J. Mullen.
Dennis Wilshaw (Wolves) celebrated his first senior cap with two well-taken goals. Bolton's centre-forward Nat Lofthouse also netted twice for the second successive match. England, after a moderate start, eased to a comfortable victory after Welsh full-back Alf Sherwood was shepherded out to the left wing with concussion.

England's four goals came in the space of ten minutes either side of half-time, after the hosts had deservedly taken the lead midway through the first half through Ivor Allchurch. In fact, John Charles may well have bagged a hat-trick before England had equalised. Only some superb saves by Gil Merrick prevented the Leeds United player from achieving this feat. England handed a senior debut to Sheffield Wednesday's twenty-year-old inside-forward Albert Quixall, who would later play for Manchester United.

11 November 1953
Goodison Park

England 3 Northern Ireland 1
Attendance 39,775

England Team: G. Merrick, S. Rickaby (West Bromwich Albion), W. Eckersley, W. Wright, H. Johnston, J. Dickinson, S. Matthews, A. Quixall, N. Lofthouse, H. Hassall (Bolton Wanderers), J. Mullen.
A goal by Harold Hassall (Bolton Wanderers) after just thirty-one seconds gave England the perfect start, but they didn't capitalise on this and, in truth, were second-best for the remainder of the first-half. Ireland, responding well, came close to equalising several times before finally drawing level through Eddie McMorran nine minutes after half-time, with goalkeeper Gil Merrick fumbling the low shot down to his left.

England regrouped, settling back into a routine and, on the hour mark, following a mazy Stan Matthews dribble, Billy Wright set up Hassall for his second goal. The lively Lofthouse wrapped up the victory fifteen minutes later when he rose superbly to head in a left-winger cross by Jimmy Mullen of Wolves. In fact, Lofthouse collided full on with goalkeeper Smyth as he powered the ball into the net. The Bolton player limped off while Smyth suffered a broken nose but continued between the posts. Stan Rickaby (West Bromwich Albion) made his only England appearance in place of Alf Ramsey at right-back.

In November 1953, Winterbottom's men were shown a lesson on how to play football as they were thumped 6-3 by Hungary at Wembley before a crowd of 104,000. The 'Galloping Major' Ferenc Puskás (2), Nándor Hidegkuti (3) and captain Józef Bozsik scored for the Magyars. This was England's first-ever defeat by an overseas country at Wembley. That hammering hurt, but after weeks and even months of hard graft, a place in the 1954 World Cup finals was secured with a well-executed and thoroughly deserved 4-2 win over Scotland at Hampden Park.

3 April 1954   **Scotland 2 England 4**
Hampden Park   **Attendance 134,544**

England Team: G. Merrick, R. Staniforth (Huddersfield Town), R. Byrne (Manchester United), W. Wright, H. Clarke (Tottenham Hotspur), J. Dickinson, T. Finney, I. Broadis (Manchester City), R. Allen (West Bromwich Albion), J. Nicholls (West Bromwich Albion), J. Mullen.

Manager Winterbottom made eight changes to the team beaten hands down by Hungary six months earlier, with right and left full-backs Ron Staniforth (Huddersfield Town) and Roger Byrne (Manchester United), centre-half Harry Clarke (Spurs) and inside-forward Johnny Nicholls (West Bromwich Albion) all making their senior debuts against the Scots.

Backed by the majority of the huge crowd, Scotland took the lead on seven minutes through Blackpool's Allan Brown. Ivor Broadis equalised eight minutes later after some smart approach work involving Billy Wright and Tom Finney, and this same combination set up birthday boy Nicholls to score with a diving header five minutes into the second-half. Well-taken goals by Ronnie Allen (West Bromwich Albion) and Jimmy Mullen pushed England 4-1 ahead before the Scots netted a strange second goal in the very last minute when Willie Ormond's high cross suddenly dipped and swerved into the net past a bemused Gil Merrick.

So, after three solid wins in the Home International Championship, England duly booked their place in the 1954 World Cup finals. Did the team ease off after that? I don't know, but a month before flying to Switzerland for the World Cup, England lost 1-0 in Belgrade against a useful Yugoslavian team and were thrashed again by Ferenc Puskás and his wonderful Magyars, this time by 7-1 in Budapest. One reporter wrote, 'The Hungarians were a world apart, they carved England to pieces in ruthless fashion.'

Another wrote, 'There was only one team in it – Hungary – they played magnificent football.'

Syd Owen (Luton Town) became the eleventh centre-half used by Winterbottom in Yugoslavia when the only goal of the game came in the eighty-seventh minute when the ball deflected off debutant Owen into the path of Rajko Mitic, who scored from close range. Winterbottom, though, was philosophical, and at a news conference after the game said, 'We are well prepared for the World Cup and will give it our best shot. I'm confident we can do well.'

Winterbottom's England squad for the 1954 World Cup was:

Goalkeepers: Ted Burgin* (Sheffield United), Gil Merrick (Birmingham City). Full-backs: Ken Green* (Birmingham City), Ron Staniforth (Huddersfield Town), Roger Byrne (Manchester United). Half-backs: Jimmy Dickinson (Portsmouth), Bill McGarry* (Huddersfield Town), Syd Owen (Luton Town), Billy Wright (Wolverhampton Wanderers). Forwards: Ivor Broadis (Newcastle United), Tom Finney (Preston North End), Nat Lofthouse (Bolton Wanderers), Stanley Matthews (Blackpool), Jimmy Mullen (Wolverhampton Wanderers), Albert Quixall* (Sheffield Wednesday), Tommy Taylor (Manchester United), Dennis Wilshaw (Wolverhampton Wanderers).

NB: *Several other players – wing-half Ken Armstrong (Chelsea), centre-halves Allenby Chilton (Manchester United) and Joe Kennedy (West Bromwich Albion), inside-forward Johnny Haynes (Fulham), winger Harry Hooper (West Ham United) and centre-forwards Ronnie Allen (West Bromwich Albion) and Bedford Jezzard (Fulham) – were put on reserve status and remained at home awaiting a call if the need arose.*

* *Uncapped players.*

The 1954 World Cup in Switzerland

The 1954 World Cup competition itself was arranged on a convoluted, almost perverse basis. The sixteen participating countries were divided into pools, with the two best teams in each pool seeded. Football writer Brian Glanville said, in so many words, 'It was haphazard, complete chaos reigned throughout the tournament, stadia were hardly adequate, officials lacked experience in dealing with large crowds and the excess of the Swiss police sometimes unpleasant.' England (seeded) entered pool 4 alongside Belgium, Italy (also seeded) and Switzerland, meaning that the seeded pair did not have to play each other.

17 June 1954 Basle	England 4 Belgium 4 (after extra time) Attendance 39,221

England Team: G. Merrick, R. Staniforth, R. Byrne, W. Wright, S. Owen, J. Dickinson, S. Matthews, I. Broadis, N. Lofthouse, T. Taylor, T. Finney.
England played Belgium first and looked set for victory when they led 3-1 early in the second half. But defensive lapses handed their opponents two simple goals, which took the game into extra time. Nat Lofthouse then edged England back in front before an unlucky headed own goal by Jimmy Dickinson handed the Belgians a draw.

One down after just five minutes, England recovered and produced some enterprising and purposeful football. They went in at half-time leading 2-1 with goals by Ivor Broadis and Lofthouse, whose strike was a real cracker – a stunning diving header from Tom Finney's precise cross. Broadis then added a third goal before some sloppy play in front of stranded goalkeeper Gil Merrick denied Winterbottom's men victory. Syd Owen was injured late on, allowing Billy Wright to switch to centre-half, a position he then held, virtually unchallenged, until his retirement in 1959.

After the game, *The Times* correspondant wrote these words on England's inept performance: 'The eleven players were like those rare children of light who can pass through any experience protected by a sheath of impenetrable innocence.'

20 June 1954   England 2 Switzerland 0
Berne   Attendance 49,895

England Team: G. Merrick, R. Staniforth, R. Byrne, W. McGarry, W. Wright, J. Dickinson, T. Finney, I. Broadis, T. Taylor, D. Wilshaw, J. Mullen.
For England's second pool 4 game against the host nation, manager Winterbottom made several changes. He introduced Bill McGarry at right-half and switched Billy Wright to centre-half in place of the injured Owen. Taylor moved to centre-forward in place of Lofthouse (injured) and the Wolves duo of Wilshaw and Mullen were selected together on the left wing, with Finney taking over on the right flank from Matthews, who was also sidelined through injured.

   In sweltering heat, the hosts proved mediocre opponents and posed little threat as England eased to victory with goals by Mullen (forty-two minutes) and Wilshaw (sixty-eight), the latter's strike being a fine individual effort that saw him glide past three defenders before netting with a low, crisp drive from 15 yards. Taylor (twice) and Finney also came close to scoring in this rather one-sided, disjointed and sluggish contest in which Wright was the star performer at the heart of England's defence. A quarter-final place awaited Winterbottom's team and, with confidence high, many were talking of greater things, perhaps a place in the semis, even making the final itself!

26 June 1954   England 2 Uruguay 4
Basel   Attendance 34,773

England Team: G. Merrick, R. Staniforth, R. Byrne, W. McGarry, W. Wright, J. Dickinson, S. Matthews, I. Broadis, N. Lofthouse, D. Wilshaw, T. Finney.
The now fit duo of Stanley Matthews and Nat Lofthouse both returned to action in the quarter-finals against the 1930 World Champions Uruguay. Tommy Taylor and Jimmy Mullen were the two players who dropped out. With the afternoon temperature in the low thirties, England, as a unit, played pretty well. They looked supremely fit and mobile, tackled hard, strong and fair (most of the time), passed precisely and attacked with force. But Uruguay were just that little bit better, more committed and, in the end, deserved their 4-2 victory. England played with pride and passion, but two mistakes by goalkeeper Gil Merrick proved to be their downfall.

   One down to Carlos Borges' fifth-minute goal, England hit back strongly. Lofthouse equalised after a smart manoeuvre by Matthews in the sixteenth minute and they certainly looked in control. But after Dennis Wilshaw had lobbed narrowly wide, Merrick allowed a speculative long-range drive from Uruguay's captain and centre-half Guillermo Varela to find the net and make it 2-1 seconds before half-time. That became 3-1 shortly after the interval when Juan Alberto Schiaffino scored from inside the box, only for plucky England to hit back again. After two near misses, Tom Finney cut the deficit to one in the sixty-seventh minute and, soon afterwards, 'Man of the Match' Matthews struck a post and had another effort brilliantly saved by the diving Roque Máspoli. But with twelve minutes remaining, a free-flowing move ended with Javier Ambrois' fierce drive finding the net to give Uruguay victory. England were out but they had shown great commitment and the future looked bright, especially with the introduction of an under-23 team, whereby up-and-coming youngsters could be monitored in full, with the future in mind.

1954 World Cup Fact File

- Countries taking part: 16 (divided into four groups of 4).
- Final: West Germany 3, Hungary 2.
- Final venue: Wankdorf Stadium, Berne (attendance: 59,453).
- Leading scorer: Sándor Kocsis (Hungary) 11 goals.
- West Germany were 2-0 down in the final.
- Hungary scored a record 27 goals in their 1954 World Cup matches.
- Sándor Kocsis (Hungary) netted two hat-tricks.
- The Walter brothers, Fritz and Ottmar, played for West Germany in the final.

Looking Ahead to 1958

After returning from World Cup duty, England comfortably won the 1954/55 Home International Championship, beating Northern Ireland 2-0, Wales 3-2 (with a hat-trick for Chelsea's Roy Bentley), and Scotland 7-2 (when Dennis Wilshaw netted four times, becoming the first player to score that many times in a Wembley international). Six friendlies were also fulfilled between December 1954 and November 1955, as well as two more Home Internationals against Wales and Northern Ireland.

West Germany were defeated 3-1 at Wembley and Denmark 5-1 in Copenhagen, Spain were held 1-1 in front of 125,000 fans in Madrid and lost 4-1 at Wembley six months later. France triumphed 1-0 in Paris, and Portugal 3-1 in Lisbon. In the two 'local' games England drew 1-1 with Wales in Cardiff and beat the Irish 3-0 at Wembley.

Since losing to Uruguay in Basel in the 1954 World Cup, manager Winterbottom had handed senior debuts to twenty players: goalkeepers Ron Baynham (Luton Town), Reg Matthews (Coventry City) and Ray Wood (Manchester United); full-backs Jeff Hall (Birmingham City), Jimmy Meadows (Manchester City), Bill Foulkes (Manchester United) and Peter Sillett (Chelsea); wing-halves Ken Armstrong (Chelsea), Ray Barlow (West Bromwich Albion), Ronnie Clayton (Blackburn Rovers), Duncan Edwards (Manchester United) and Ron Flowers and Bill Slater (both of Wolves); inside-forwards John Atyeo (Bristol City), Geoff Bradford (Bristol Rovers), Johnny Haynes (Fulham) and Don Revie (Manchester City); and left-wingers Bill Perry (Blackpool), Brian Pilkington (Burnley) and Frank Blunstone (Chelsea).

In the third Home International of 1955/56, England drew 1-1 with Scotland before a huge audience of 132,817 spectators at Hampden Park. There followed four more friendly matches in May 1956, England beating Brazil 4-2 at home, Finland 5-1 and West

Germany 3-1 away, and drawing 0-0 with Sweden in Stockholm. These were followed by the 1956/57 Home International matches against Northern Ireland (1-1) and Wales (won 3-1), before Yugoslavia were eclipsed 3-0 ahead of important (home and away) 1958 World Cup qualifiers against Denmark and the Republic of Ireland. England won a third Home International Championship encounter against Scotland at Wembley 2-1, with debutant striker Derek Kevan (West Bromwich Albion) scoring with a terrific header, along with a beauty from 'Red Devil' Duncan Edwards. Sheffield United goalkeeper Alan Hodgkinson also won his first cap against the Scots.

England, full of confidence, did the business in the World Cup qualifiers, winning three and drawing one of their four games to top Group 1 with seven points out of a possible eight, and so clinch a place in the finals in Sweden.

The 1958 World Cup Qualifying Matches

5 December 1956
Molineux, Wolverhampton

England 5 Denmark 2
Attendance 54,083

England Team: E. Ditchburn (Tottenham Hotspur), J. Hall (Birmingham City), R. Byrne, R. Clayton (Blackburn Rovers), W. Wright, J. Dickinson, S. Matthews, J. Brooks (Tottenham Hotspur), T. Taylor, D. Edwards (Manchester United), T. Finney.
Fielding four vastly experienced players – home skipper Billy Wright (with 80 caps to his credit), left-half Jimmy Dickinson (48) and wingers Stanley Matthews (51) and Tom Finney (63) – England comfortably beat a plucky Danish team under the Molineux floodlights. This was the first international at the ground since February 1936.

The game against the Danes was distinguished by Tommy Taylor's hat-trick and two quite stunning strikes by his Manchester United teammate Duncan Edwards, who played at inside-left in place of the injured Johnny Haynes. Indeed, Edwards, all strength and muscle, had another terrific shot saved and almost uprooted a post with a thunderous free-kick. Taylor also came close to adding to his total, while Finney and inside-right Johnny Brooks both missed easy chances. Matthews, however, was perhaps 'Man of the Match', after he gave Jørgen Hansen and his fellow defenders a real roasting. Taylor scored in the eighteenth and twentieth minutes to put England in control. Ove Bech Nielsen reduced the deficit on twenty-eight minutes before Taylor completed his treble early in the second-half. Nielsen netted again for the Danes in the fifty-second minute (after some slack marking at the back) before Edwards set the stadium alight with goals in the fifty-sixth and seventy-seventh minutes.

8 May 1957
Wembley

England 5 Republic of Ireland 1
Attendance 51,340

England Team: A. Hodgkinson (Sheffield United), J. Hall, R. Byrne, R. Clayton (Blackburn Rovers), W. Wright, D. Edwards, S. Matthews, J. Atyeo (Bristol City), T. Taylor, J. Haynes (Fulham), T. Finney.

Tommy Taylor once again stole the headlines with another superb hat-trick as the Irish were blitzed with a wonderful attacking display by England. Bristol City's John Atyeo bagged the other two as Walter Winterbottom's team made it ten goals in two World Cup qualifiers. Taylor's treble was scored in the first half as the visitors were brushed aside. He first struck in the tenth minute, cutting inside from the right before driving the ball hard and low past goalkeeper Alan Kelly.

The Manchester United centre-forward grabbed his second goal on nineteen minutes with a crashing right-footed drive from just inside the arc on the edge of the penalty area. Atyeo found the net in the thirty-eighth minute, heading home from point-blank range after a smart build-up and cross from the left. Ninety seconds later, Taylor completed a wonderful hat-trick with a towering header from Tom Finney's flighted left-wing corner.

The Irish, inspired by Johnny Carey, were much better in the second half and gave England plenty to think about after Dermot Curtis had reduced the arrears in the fifty-sixth minute. England perhaps had more of the play, but they had to wait until the very last minute for their fifth and final goal, when Atyeo converted Finney's left-wing pull-back in style with a fierce shot from 20 yards.

15 May 1957   **Denmark 1 England 4**
Copenhagen   **Attendance 34,941**

England Team: A. Hodgkinson, J. Hall, R. Byrne, R. Clayton, W. Wright, D. Edwards, S. Matthews, J. Atyeo, T. Taylor, J. Haynes, T. Finney.
This World Cup qualifier proved to be the swansong for 'Mr Football' Stanley Matthews, who retired from the international scene at the age of forty-two, having gained a total of fifty-four full caps over a period of twenty-two years.

Tommy Taylor once again rattled the Danes with two more well-taken goals – this after England had fallen behind in the twenty-seventh minute when John Jensen scored from inside the area. Johnny Haynes equalised less than two minutes later, but it wasn't until the last quarter of the game that England took control. Taylor made it 2-1 in the seventy-first minute, John Atyeo headed in Haynes' tempting cross five minutes later and Taylor scored his second goal of the game in the eighty-sixth minute, at a time when the hosts had effectively given up. German referee Albert Dusch could and should have awarded each side a penalty, and the Danish goalkeeper Theil Drengsgaard pulled off four excellent saves to keep his side in the game until England edged in front at 2-1.

19 May 1957   **Republic of Ireland 1 England 1**
Dalymount Park, Dublin   **Attendance 47,605**

England Team: A. Hodgkinson, J. Hall, R. Byrne, R. Clayton, W. Wright, D. Edwards, T. Finney, J. Atyeo, T. Taylor, J. Haynes, D. Pegg (Manchester United).

The Irish stunned England by taking a third-minute lead through Sheffield United star Alf Ringstead. And, in fact, the hosts had several chances to increase their advantage before John Atyeo stepped up with a last-ditch equaliser. One of Old Trafford's Busby Babes, David Pegg, made his debut on England's left wing.

England didn't play at all well in Dublin. The three main centre-forwards never got going, the wingers had spasmodic periods of good fortune and the wing-halves failed to get to grips in midfield. The defence, on the other hand, did quite well, with goalkeeper Alan Hodgkinson pulling off three excellent saves. Wright, winning his eighty-fifth cap, was once again the stand out player in the England's team.

Before England left for Sweden, they played three Home International Championship matches – beating both Wales and Scotland 4-0, but losing, surprisingly at home to Northern Ireland by 3-2 – and five friendlies, defeating France, also 4-0, Portugal 2-1, drawing 1-1 with the USSR but losing, dramatically, 5-0 in Yugoslavia.

Ten players were handed their full debuts; among them the West Bromwich Albion duo of right-back Don Howe and inside-right Bobby Robson (who netted twice on his debut against France), the Blackburn Rovers winger Bryan Douglas and Manchester United's utility forward Bobby Charlton, who thankfully had escaped the Munich air crash. He also scored on his debut against the Scots in front of 127,874 fans at Hampden Park.

For the 1958 World Cup tournament in Sweden, England were drawn in Group 4, along with Austria, the favourites Brazil and the USSR, and the purists clearly expected them to qualify for the knockout stages!

Walter Winterbottom's twenty-man squad for Sweden was:

Goalkeepers: Eddie Hopkinson (Bolton Wanderers), Colin McDonald (Burnley). Full-backs: Tommy Banks (Bolton Wanderers), Don Howe (West Bromwich Albion), Peter Sillett (Chelsea). Half-backs: Eddie Clamp (Wolverhampton Wanderers), Ronnie Clayton (Blackburn Rovers), Maurice Norman (Tottenham Hotspur), Bill Slater (Wolverhampton Wanderers), Billy Wright (Wolverhampton Wanderers). Forwards: Alan A'Court (Liverpool), Peter Brabrook* (Chelsea), Peter Broadbent* (Wolverhampton Wanderers), Bobby Charlton (Manchester United), Bryan Douglas (Blackburn Rovers), Tom Finney (Preston North End), Johnny Haynes (Fulham), Derek Kevan (West Bromwich Albion), Bobby Smith* (Tottenham Hotspur), Bobby Robson (West Bromwich Albion).

NB: *You will note that Stanley Matthews and Jimmy Greaves were both left behind, yet FIFA's official World Cup records show that goalkeeper Alan Hodgkinson (Sheffield United) and wing-half Maurice Setters (West Bromwich Albion) were actually named in the England squad but did not travel to Sweden. Other 'reserves', placed on standby effectively, were full-back Jim Langley (Fulham) and forward John Atyeo (Bristol City). In fact, England took only twenty players to Sweden when the rules stated they could have taken twenty-two.*

* Uncapped players.

The 1958 World Cup in Sweden

It transpired that England unfortunately did not perform well in Sweden. They never won a game, drawing all of their three group matches – against the USSR, the eventual tournament winners Brazil, and Austria – before losing 1-0 to the USSR in a play-off after both countries had finished level on points (3) and goal-average (4-4).

8 June 1958   England 2 USSR 2
Gothenburg   Attendance 49,348

England Team: C. McDonald, D. Howe, T. Banks, E. Clamp, W. Wright, W. Slater, B. Douglas, R. Robson, D. Kevan, J. Haynes, T. Finney.
England, trailing 2-0 going into the final quarter of their opening game, hit back strongly to earn a draw and a point against a very physical Russian outfit, with wingers Bryan Douglas and Tom Finney continuously being clattered with late tackles and obvious body checks. Quicker out of the blocks, the Russians took the lead in the thirteenth minute through Nikita Simonyan and went close on three other occasions before Aleksandr Ivanov made it 2-0 ten minutes into the second half. At this juncture, England decided to wake up, after efforts by Derek Kevan and Finney had been saved by the 'Man in Black', goalkeeper Lev Yashin. A long free-kick by Billy Wright was flicked on by Douglas to Kevan, who headed home on sixty-six minutes to bring England back into the game.

Then, with just six minutes remaining – soon after Bobby Robson had been denied a goal because of a foul by Kevan on Yashin – a limping Finney stepped up to fire home a dubious penalty past the Russian 'keeper. Yashin was so disgusted with the referee's decision to award a spot-kick when Johnny Haynes was brought down seemingly a foot outside the area, that he spun the official completely round, yet stayed on the pitch. Right at the death, one of the many crunching tackles on Finney resulted in him being stretchered off, and out of the tournament. This was not the greatest of starts by England, but a point was better than nothing, as they say.

11 June 1958   Brazil 0 England 0
Gothenburg   Attendance 40,895

England Team: C. McDonald, D. Howe, T. Banks, E. Clamp, W. Wright, W. Slater,
B. Douglas, R. Robson, D. Kevan, J. Haynes, A. A'Court.
This was the only match in the entire tournament in which eventual winners Brazil failed
to score. This was down to the defensive tactics worked out by manager Winterbottom
and his assistant Bill Nicholson, who had watched the South Americans' opening 3-0
group victory over Austria.

From the start, the Brazilians were never allowed to get into their smooth rhythm,
the nearest they came to breaking the deadlock was when a vicious 20-yard drive from
Vavá (Edvaldo Izidio Neto) struck the crossbar. Bill Slater completely mastered the skilful
Didi. Wright, commanding as ever, always got the better of Mazzola, while Pelé was
often outwitted by Eddie Clamp, who certainly put himself about with some ferocious
tackling. He wasn't called 'Chopper' for nothing!

The nearest England came to scoring was when Kevan headed over from a
wonderful cross by Douglas and Bobby Robson fired wide from 12 yards when in
a good position. This was a solid all-round performance, and the point gained was
certainly well deserved.

15 June 1958   Austria 2 England 2
Boras, Ryavallen   Attendance 15,872

England Team: C. McDonald, D. Howe, T. Banks, E. Clamp, W. Wright, W. Slater,
B. Douglas, R. Robson, D. Kevan, J. Haynes, A. A'Court.
England had to beat the already eliminated Austria to qualify automatically for the
knockout stage, but unfortunately their tendency to make life hard by conceding early
goals was again in evidence – much to the annoyance of manager Winterbottom and
the travelling supporters. One down after just fifteen minutes to a booming right-footed
shot from outside the penalty area by Karl Koller, they were forced to chase the game.
They had at least three good opportunities to draw level before finally doing so – Johnny
Haynes tapping home in the fifty-sixth minute after Alan A'Court's cross and been headed
on by Kevan and fumbled by the Austrian goalkeeper Rudolf Szanwald. However, despite
England seemingly being in control, they fell behind again after another long-range effort
from Koller, which whizzed past 'keeper Colin McDonald's dive and went in off his right-
hand post in the seventy-first minute. England came back once more when workhorse
Kevan equalised three minutes later with a low drive from Haynes' reverse pass. Soon
afterwards, Bobby Robson thought he had scored the winner but his effort was ruled out
for handball when, in fact, it struck him in the stomach – poor refereeing, this, on the part
of Axel Asmussen.

17 June 1958   England 0 USSR 1
Gothenburg   Attendance 23,182

England Team: C. McDonald, D. Howe, T. Banks, R. Clayton, W. Wright, W. Slater, P. Brabrook, P. Broadbent, D. Kevan, J. Haynes, A. A'Court.
After playing out three draws, England had to face the USSR for a second time, with the winners to go through to the final eight. Manager Winterbottom decided to choose a brand-new right-wing pairing, giving debuts to two Peters; Brabrook of Chelsea and Broadbent of Wolves. Haynes turned out despite severe blistering on both feet.

Neither team played well in a rather dull first-half, chances being few and far between, with England's two debutants having the best openings. Things did improve a little after the break: Brabrook was unlucky with two efforts that struck the woodwork, and goalkeeper Lev Yashin pulled off two terrific saves to deny Derek Kevan and Johnny Haynes. England were certainly the better team, having most of the ball, and over-running the Russians at times, but they simply couldn't find a way past Yashin – he was brilliant.

Then, as so often happens in football, England fell to a suckerpunch, delivered by Anatoli Illyin twenty minutes from time. From goalkeeper Colin McDonald's poor clearance, the ball was quickly pumped back into England's half and, with defenders all at sea, Illyin pounced to sweep the ball home, in off a post. England rallied and Yashin saved two more goal-bound efforts, but this was a match Winterbottom's men were destined to lose and, without any cause for embarrassment, slipped out of the World Cup.

1958 World Cup Fact File

- Countries taking part: 16 (divided into four groups of 4).
- Final: Brazil 5, Sweden 2.
- Final venue: Råsunda Stadium, Solna, Stockholm (attendance: 51,800).
- Leading scorer: Just Fontaine (France), 13 goals including two hat-tricks.
- Pelé, aged 17 years, 239 days, became the youngest scorer in World Cup finals, netting against Wales. Five days later he became the youngest player to net a hat-trick and then he went on to become the youngest footballer to score in a World Cup final.

Back to the Drawing Board

After the failure in Sweden, another inquest was carried out, and it was thorough, as both Wales and Northern Ireland had gone further in the World Cup that year than England! Debates were heated as to why Bobby Charlton was omitted from the squad and why the Blackburn Rovers duo of Bryan Douglas and Ronnie Clayton were chosen. But the game had to continue. Winterbottom remained in charge and England had to go out and 'do better on the field', said the hierarchy.

England's first international after the 1958 World Cup was the Home Championship game against Northern Ireland at Windsor Park on 4 October. Manchester United's wing-half Wilf McGuinness was handed his first cap and the aforementioned Charlton, who last played in the 5-0 defeat in Yugoslavia five months earlier, returned to lead the attack. He had a fine game, scoring twice in a 3-3 draw. Later in the month, England walloped the USSR 5-0 at Wembley. Why couldn't they have done this in Sweden, one asked? Johnny Haynes bagged a hat-trick in this match – the first treble scored by an Englishman against an Eastern European country. This was also Tom Finney's final appearance for his country. He bowed out with seventy-six caps and thirty goals to his name. A month later, Nat Lofthouse left the international scene after playing in a 2-2 draw with Wales at Villa Park. He also netted thirty goals for his country in thirty-three outings. Top man.

In the final match of the 1958/59 season, against Scotland at Wembley, Billy Wright won his 100th cap, and was carried from the pitch shoulder-high after England's 1-0 win. The Wolves defender bowed out six weeks and five matches later as England concluded their summer tour of America and surrounding countries with a resounding 8-1 victory over the USA. They played four friendlies in all: losing 2-0 to World Champions Brazil in front of 160,000 spectators in Rio, succumbing 4-1 in Peru and losing 2-1 in Mexico before seeing off the Yanks in Los Angeles when Charlton (3) and Ron Flowers (with two 30-yard rockets) led the goal rush.

Initially, the Birmingham City centre-half Trevor Smith was chosen to replace Wright in England's defence. He played in a 1-1 draw with Wales and a 3-2 defeat against Sweden before West Ham's Ken Brown appeared in the 2-1 win over Northern Ireland. Left-back Tony Allen (Stoke City), winger John Connelly (Burnley) and the Middlesbrough duo of outside-left Eddie Holliday and centre-forward Brian Clough also made their senior international debuts against the Welsh. Goalkeeper Ron Springett (Sheffield Wednesday) and forwards Joe Baker from Hibernian and Bolton's Ray Parry won their first caps against the Irish – the latter both scored to celebrate the occasion.

Winterbottom, however, wasn't happy with his defence, bringing back Bill Slater and selecting Ray Wilson (Huddersfield Town) for the 1-1 Home International draw with Scotland at Hampden Park. He then handed a debut to centre-half Peter Swan (Sheffield Wednesday) in a 3-3 encounter with Yugoslavia.

Goals Galore

England completed three further games before their first 1962 World Cup qualifier against Luxembourg. They lost 3-0 in Spain, 2-0 in Hungary (when Dennis Viollet made his debut) and beat Northern Ireland 5-2 in Belfast, when Mick McNeil (Middlesbrough) stepped in at left-back. Luxembourg were slaughtered 9-0 and, over the next eighteen months or so before the 1962 World Cup finals in Chile, England contested three more qualifying matches, played seven friendlies and five Home International Championship games. Of these fifteen fixtures, ten resulted in victories, including Spain 4-2, Wales 5-1, Scotland 9-3, Mexico 8-0, Austria 3-1 and Switzerland 3-1, all at Wembley. Luxembourg were beaten again (4-1) in the return game, while England also took on Portugal twice; drawing 1-1 in Lisbon and winning 2-0 at Wembley to qualify for Chile.

Ten more players were given their baptism on the international stage, and they were: Aston Villa striker Gerry Hitchens (who scored against the Mexicans), the Burnley trio of John Angus, Brian Miller and Ray Pointer, Johnny Fantham from Sheffield Wednesday, Crystal Palace forward Johnny Byrne, the Ipswich Town No. 9 Ray Crawford, wing-half Stan Anderson from Sunderland, West Ham's Bobby Moore (against Peru) and the rugged Tottenham Hotspur centre-half Maurice Norman. Most of these had done well at the under-23 level.

The 1962 World Cup Qualifying Matches

19 October 1960   Luxembourg 0 England 9
Municipal Stadium   Attendance 5,486

England Team: R. Springett (Sheffield Wednesday), J. Armfield (Blackpool), M. McNeil (Middlesbrough), R. Robson, P. Swan (Sheffield Wednesday), R. Flowers (Wolverhampton Wanderers), B. Douglas, J. Greaves (Chelsea), R. Smith (Tottenham Hotspur), J. Haynes, R. Charlton (Manchester United).

Having struck twice in the 5-2 win over Northern Ireland, Jimmy Greaves made it five goals in two internationals at the start of the 1960/61 season with a well-taken hat-trick in this very comfortable and one-sided victory in Luxembourg. Bobby Charlton also scored three times and the Spurs striker Bobby Smith twice as England dominated from the first whistle to the last. The best goal of the game, however, came from skipper Johnny Haynes, who crashed home in a superb drive to make the score 6-0 just past the hour mark.

With Luxembourg at sixes and sevens, England raced into a four-goal lead inside the first quarter of the game, with strikes from Charlton on three and seven minutes, Greaves on sixteen and Smith on twenty-two. In effect, they should have been at least six, even eight goals ahead by half-time, so much were they on top. All credit to overworked Luxembourg goalkeeper Gaston Bauer, who pulled off some fine saves. England bagged a fifth goal right at the start of the second period through Smith. A brilliant rocket from Haynes, Charlton on sixty-six minutes and Greaves on eighty-three and eighty-five rounded things off. England's only previous game against Luxembourg was back in May 1927, when Dixie Dean scored a hat-trick in a 5-2 friendly win in Jeunnesse.

21 May 1961   Portugal 1 England 1
Lisbon   Attendance 64,890

England Team: R. Springett, J. Armfield, M. McNeil, R. Robson, P. Swan, R. Flowers, B. Douglas, J. Greaves, R. Smith, J. Haynes, R. Charlton.

A fifty-ninth-minute mix-up between goalkeeper Ron Springett and right-half Bobby Robson allowed Portugal striker José Águas the opening goal of this qualifier in Lisbon, where the temperature inside the stadium was 90 degrees Fahrenheit. Thankfully, Ron Flowers smashed home a free-kick eight minutes from time to earn England a draw; this after star of the show Johnny Haynes had been fouled on the edge of the penalty area. Portugal fielded several players from Benfica, including magnificent goalkeeper Costa Pereira, who pulled off at least six superb saves. But they were outplayed for most of the game as Haynes and Robson dictated play in centre-field. This was a game England certainly should have won.

28 September 1961   England 4 Luxembourg 1
Highbury   Attendance 33,409

England Team: R. Springett, J. Armfield, M. McNeil, R. Robson, P. Swan, R. Flowers, B. Douglas, J. Fantham (Sheffield Wednesday), R. Pointer (Burnley), D. Viollet (Manchester United), R. Charlton.
With Jimmy Greaves and Gerry Hitchens otherwise engaged in Italy, and Johnny Haynes sidelined through injury, John Fantham and Ray Pointer were handed their full international debuts, teaming up alongside Dennis Viollet in a much-changed attack. Unfortunately, all three struggled up front, especially Pointer and Viollet, who were well marshalled by rugged defenders. In fact, the Highbury crowd booed, jeered and slow clapped England during a lacklustre first half, despite smartly taken goals by Pointer (thirty-five minutes), Viollet (thirty-seven) and Bobby Charlton's right-foot rocket (forty-five).

After skipper Camille Dimmer had reduced the deficit – totally against the run of play on sixty-nine minutes – another long-range goal by Charlton in the seventy-sixth minute – this time with his other foot – sewed up an unusually hard-earned win for Winterbottom's side, who found visiting 'keeper François Konter in exceptionally fine form during the second half. Amazingly, the following month, Luxembourg caused one of the big upsets in World Cup football by beating Portugal 4-2. Things happen when least expected in this great game of football.

25 October 1961   England 2 Portugal 0
Wembley   Attendance 99,923

England Team: R. Springett, J. Armfield, R. Wilson (Huddersfield Town), R. Robson, P. Swan, R. Flowers, J. Connelly (Burnley), R. Pointer, J. Haynes, R. Charlton, B. Douglas.
The Burnley duo of John Connelly and Ray Pointer scored early goals, which booked England a place in the 1962 World Cup finals in Chile. In the fifth minute, winger Connelly was in the right place to collect his clubmate's knock-on from Ray Wilson's long free-kick and, four minutes later, Pointer himself raced onto a well-timed through ball before smashing home a right-foot shot from the edge of the penalty area.

Having gone down to 'little' Luxembourg in their previous game, Portugal needed to win to finish top of the group and, in front of a full-house at Wembley, they made a fight of it, Eusébio twice rattling the woodwork.

England, two-up inside the first ten minutes, played well below par. There was no real spark up front and there is no doubt that Jimmy Greaves, who was having a miserable time with AC Milan in Serie 'A', was sorely missed. The near-100,000 crowd realised record gate receipts at the time of £52,500.

Chile Awaits

Before flying out to Chile for the World Cup finals, England already knew they would be playing against Argentina, Bulgaria and Hungary in Group 4. It wouldn't be easy, by any means, and manager Winterbottom, along with his co-selectors, sat down to select twenty-one players. Johnny Haynes was named as captain, while Burnley's Jimmy Adamson was appointed as player-coach and assistant-manager.

This was Winterbottom's twenty-one-man squad for Chile:

Goalkeepers: Alan Hodgkinson (Sheffield United), Ron Springett (Sheffield Wednesday). Full-backs: Jimmy Armfield (Blackpool), Don Howe (West Bromwich Albion), Ray Wilson (Huddersfield Town). Half-backs: Stan Anderson (Sunderland), Ron Flowers (Wolves), Bobby Moore (West Ham United), Maurice Norman (Tottenham Hotspur), Peter Swan (Sheffield Wednesday), Jimmy Adamson* (Burnley), Bobby Robson (West Bromwich Albion). Forwards: Bobby Charlton (Manchester United), John Connelly (Burnley), Bryan Douglas (Blackburn Rovers), George Eastham* (Arsenal), Jimmy Greaves (Tottenham Hotspur), Johnny Haynes (Fulham), Gerry Hitchens (Inter Milan), Roger Hunt (Liverpool), Alan Peacock* (Middlesbrough).

NB: Named as reserves for Chile were full-back Graham Shaw (Sheffield United), centre-half Brian Labone (Everton) and centre-forward Ray Crawford (Ipswich Town).

* Uncapped players.

The 1962 World Cup
in Chile

31 May 1962	England 1 Hungary 2
Rancagua	Attendance 7,938

England Team: R. Springett, J. Armfield, R. Wilson, R. Moore, M. Norman, R. Flowers, B. Douglas, J. Greaves, G. Hitchens, J. Haynes, R. Charlton.
For their opening game, England were without defender Peter Swan, who had not recovered from an injury suffered in the pre-tournament win over Switzerland. The Spurs' centre-half Maurice Norman came into the back division alongside Bobby Moore, each of whom had only one full cap to their name.

On a wet, slippery pitch, England came under pressure from the start. And it must be known that generally they failed to get to grips with the lively Magyars. In the twentieth minute, goalkeeper Ron Springett was deceived by the flight of a strong 15-yard shot from Lajos Tichy as Hungary went in front. And although Ron Flowers equalised with a well-struck penalty fifteen minutes into the second half (after Jimmy Greaves' effort was handled on the line), the Wolves player was then reluctantly responsible for Hungary's winning goal soon afterwards. He slipped on the saturated turf, leaving Flórián Albert free to race away. The Honvéd player cut inside right-back Jimmy Armfield and found the net with a low, crisp shot. England's form had certainly nosedived since they scored seventeen goals in successive games against Scotland and Mexico in May/June 1961.

2 June 1962	England 3 Argentina 1
Rancagua	Attendance 9,794

England Team: R. Springett, J. Armfield, R. Wilson, R. Moore, M. Norman, R. Flowers, B. Douglas, J. Greaves, A. Peacock, J. Haynes, R. Charlton.
In the seventeenth minute, Alan Peacock, evading a brutal challenge by Argentine skipper Rubén Navarro, thought he had scored on his international debut when he headed Bobby Charlton's cross towards the goal, only to see Navarro chase back and keep the ball out with his hand. However, ice-cool Ron Flowers stepped up to net from the spot for the

third time in successive matches. After some interesting play by both teams, Charlton then smashed home one of his specials in the forty-second minute, before Jimmy Greaves netted a third halfway through the second half, after Argentina's goalkeeper Antonio Roma had failed to hold a low drive from Bryan Douglas. A defensive mix-up allowed José Sanfilippo in for an eighty-first-minute consolation goal. This was a much-improved England display. Suddenly, the confidence was back, after the squad had been posted to a remote training camp in the middle of nowhere.

7 June 1962	Bulgaria 0 England 0
Rancagua	Attendance 5,679

England Team: R. Springett, J. Armfield, R. Wilson, R. Moore, M. Norman, R. Flowers, B. Douglas, J. Greaves, A. Peacock, J. Haynes, R. Charlton.
This was, without a shadow of a doubt, the most boring, sterile and basically awful match England had been involved in since the Second World War, perhaps longer. Walter Winterbottom's men were dreadful, and Bulgaria not much better – they were like a string of dead fish, said one spectator. In fact, needing only a draw to qualify for the quarter-finals, England managed only three worthwhile shots in ninety minutes, the Bulgarians none at all. Indeed, the ball hardly left the midfield region. It was dreadful fare for the hardy spectators who attended this non-event. *Daily Mirror* reporter Frank Wilson summed up this dire encounter by saying, tongue in cheek, 'I had six cups of coffee during the match, but that didn't keep me awake.' The reigning World Champions were next up for poor England.

10 June 1962	Brazil 3 England 1
Viña del Mar	Attendance 17,736

England Team: R. Springett, J. Armfield, R. Wilson, R. Moore, M. Norman, R. Flowers, B. Douglas, J. Greaves, G. Hitchens, J. Haynes, R. Charlton.
Any hope England had of winning the World Cup, or even making progress, was snuffed out by a Brazilian team minus Pelé, but with the 'Little Bird' Manuel Francisco Dos Santos (Garrincha to his fans) at his brilliant best. After a fairly even half-hour, the ball-juggling 5-foot 7-inch winger put Brazil ahead fourteen minutes before the interval, when he climbed above Maurice Norman (6 inches taller than himself) to nod home Mário Zagallo's precise corner. England hit back quickly when, eight minutes later, Gerry Hitchens swept the ball home after Jimmy Greaves had headed against the woodwork from a sweetly struck Haynes' free-kick.

England were well in the game at this stage, before Garrincha turned on his magic in the second-half. His powerful free-kick in the fifty-third minute bounced straight off goalkeeper Ron Springett's chesty, allowing the onrushing Vavá to steer home a short-range header. Six minutes later, Garrincha – described in the press as 'the man with two feet as good as each other' – whipped in a viciously swerving 25-yard shot high past the groping Springett. There is no doubt that England played with pride and passion – captain Johnny Haynes being outstanding yet again – but in the end they were, in truth, outclassed by a team of all talents. 'For a time we chased shadows,' recalled Greaves, while skipper Johnny Haynes said, 'Throughout, Brazil played with confidence, skill and panache, we simply couldn't get hold of the ball, and when we did, for perhaps a minute or so, our passing let us down big time.'

1962 World Cup Fact File

- Countries taking part: 16 (divided into four groups of 4).
- Final: Brazil 3, Czechoslovakia 1.
- Final venue: Estádio Nacional, Santiago (attendance: 68,679).
- Leading scorers: Flórián Albert (Hungary), Garrincha (Brazil), Valentine Ivanov (USSR), Dražan Jerković (Yugoslavia), Leonel Sánchez (Chile), Vavá (Brazil), all with 4 goals.
- English referee Ken Aston was in charge of the Chile *v.* Italy Group 2 game, which was dubbed the 'Battle of Santiago'. Italian defender Giorgio Ferrini was sent off after just seven minutes, and shortly before half-time his teammate Mario David followed him down the tunnel. His dismissal came after Leonel Sánchez (Chile) had broken the nose of Humberto Maschio with a left hook, an incident missed by Aston, but seen by virtually everyone else. David took revenge and kicked Sánchez, but the Italian wouldn't leave the pitch. This led to scuffles, flailing fists and spitting, involving players, officials, supporters and reporters. Play was held up for eight minutes. Besides the two send-offs, eight other players were booked.
- Enrique Sívori and José Altafini played for Italy, having previously won caps for Argentina and Brazil respectively, while José Santamaría (ex-Uruguay) and Ferenc Puskás (ex-Hungary) appeared for Spain.

All Change As Ramsey Moves In

So, what happened in Chile? England, highly rated, were expected to do well, as they had been ahead of the two previous World Cups in 1954 and 1958. But they failed to produce the goods, much to the annoyance of their loyal fans and, more so, the press. Certain players were out of form, others simply didn't gel, and although the commitment was there in most cases, the loss through injury of centre-half Peter Swan, Bobby Robson and centre-forward Bobby Smith certainly weakened the team. Swan had been in wonderful form leading up to the tournament, Robson had been working so well in tandem with Johnny Haynes in midfield, while Smith was seen to be the perfect foil for his Spurs striker partner Jimmy Greaves.

Unfortunately, Greaves, who prior to going to Chile sincerely believed England had a team that was good enough to win the World Cup in 1962, was not at his best. He struggled at times and was certainly nothing like the player he had been twelve months previous, before he chose to go and play in Italy. As a result, the forward line looked rather disjointed. All credit to fellow strikers Gerry Hitchens and Alan Peacock (far removed from the bullish Smith), who both did well, but Greaves was the one player expected to score the goals. He notched just one in four starts.

Subsequently, failure in Chile resulted in the 21 November 1962 departure of manager Walter Winterbottom, who had been in office for sixteen years. He had done a good job overall but was probably asked to do too much. His personal manner was exemplary, he accepted criticism to the full, and was always willing to talk to the press. But, in the end, it was obvious a new face was required. At the time of his sacking, Winterbottom was earning £2,000 per year, a modest professional figure back in 1962. Adamson, who had been Winterbottom's assistant, was a strong candidate for the job, but in the end the FA chose the former Southampton, Tottenham Hotspur and England right-back Alf Ramsey, who had just guided Ipswich Town to the Division One championship. Ramsey, in fact, saw out his contract at Portman Road, officially taking over as England chief in late November 1962, just twenty-four hours after a 4-0 home win over Wales. This was effectively Winterbottom's last game in charge, although the team that evening was chosen by a committee, with Chelsea's Bobby Tambling being the last player selected by such means.

No Qualifying Matches

With the 1966 World Cup finals taking place in England, there was no qualifying programme for Alf Ramsey to worry about, and therefore he had a great opportunity to formulate new plans, introduce new players and assemble a squad strong enough to win the biggest prize in international football.

From 27 February 1963, when Ramsey took charge of his first game – a 5-2 defeat by France in a European Nations Cup qualifier in Paris when goalkeeper Ron Springett had a nightmare – right through to 5 July 1966, just six days before the start of the 1966 World Cup, England played a total of thirty-eight matches, winning twenty-four, drawing eight and losing six; scoring ninety-five goals in the process, and conceding forty-nine. There were some big wins, among them Switzerland 8-1, Northern Ireland 8-3, the USA 10-0, Norway 6-1 (with a four-timer from Jimmy Greaves) and Wales 4-0. England also drew 1-1 with the 1962 World Champions Brazil at Wembley, beat the Rest of the World 2-1 in the FA's Centenary match, defeated West Germany 1-0, eclipsed Spain 2-0, overcame Czechoslovakia 4-2 and edged past East Germany 1-0. However, they crashed to a heavy defeat in a return match with Brazil, going down 5-1 in Rio. They also suffered two losses (2-1 and 1-0) at the hands of their arch-rivals Scotland. In fact, the Scots made it three wins on the bounce against England for the first time in almost eighty years, having triumphed 2-0 in Glasgow ten months before Ramsey took charge. There were plenty of good, solid performances, a few mediocre displays and only a handful of real disappointments. The signs were there ... could Ramsey get his plan working?

In 1963, Ramsey confidently stated, publicly, that England would win the World Cup. 'We have the ability, strength and character, and players with the right temperament to lift the trophy in three years' time,' he said with a grin on his face. Ramsey, always willing and eager to check out several uncapped players, awarded senior debuts to almost forty in his first three and a half years in charge: among them were three goalkeepers – Gordon Banks, Peter Bonetti and Tony Waiters; six full-backs including George Cohen and Keith Newton; two rock-solid hard men in central defender Jack Charlton and his Leeds United teammate Norman 'bite yer legs' Hunter; ten midfielders with Alan Ball, George Eastham, Terry Venables, Alan Mullery, Nobby Stiles and Martin Peters among them; some useful goalscoring forwards such as Geoff Hurst, Frank Wignall, Mick Jones and Barry Bridges; four talented wingers – Ian Callaghan, Peter Thompson, Terry Paine and Derek Temple; and a handful of utility players. Messrs Ball, Banks, Charlton, Cohen, Hurst, Peters and Stiles, of course, would all go on to become 'Stars of '66'.

England, unbeaten in ten internationals prior to competing in the 1966 World Cup, were among the favourites when the draw was made to determine the four groups, each containing four teams. There were placed in Group 1, along with France, Mexico and Uruguay. Title holders Brazil were in Group 3 with Bulgaria, Hungary and Portugal, while West Germany was paired with Argentina, Spain and Switzerland. England used the wonderful facilities at Lilleshall ahead of the World Cup, and in charge of a strict training schedule was Ramsey's efficient and highly respected right-hand man Les Cocker, then head trainer at Elland Road. He took the players out from 9 a.m. until 9 p.m. most days. It was intense but well worth it in the end. There were a few spats between players but this pleased Ramsey to a certain extent, prompting him to say, 'I love to see a bit of fire in the bellies of my squad.'

After all the hard pre-tournament work had been completed, it was now up to the players to do the nitty-gritty, to get out there and try to win the coveted Jules Rimet Trophy on home soil. The whole nation was behind Ramsey's men, with the official tournament mascot 'World Cup Willie' leading the way.

This was Ramsey's selected squad for the 1966 World Cup:

Goalkeepers: Gordon Banks (Leicester City), Peter Bonetti (Chelsea), Ron Springett (Sheffield Wednesday). Full-backs: Jimmy Armfield (Blackpool), Gerry Byrne (Liverpool), George Cohen (Fulham), Ray Wilson (Huddersfield Town). Half-backs: Jack Charlton (Leeds United), Ron Flowers (Wolverhampton Wanderers), Norman Hunter (Leeds United), Bobby Moore (West Ham United), Nobby Stiles (Manchester United). Forwards: Alan Ball (Blackpool), Ian Callaghan (Liverpool), Bobby Charlton (Manchester United), John Connelly (Manchester United), George Eastham (Arsenal), Jimmy Greaves (Tottenham Hotspur), Roger Hunt (Liverpool), Geoff Hurst (West Ham United), Terry Paine (Southampton), Martin Peters (West Ham United).

NB: *Placed on reserve were full-back Keith Newton (Blackburn Rovers), wing-half Gordon Milne (Liverpool), centre-half Brian Labone (Everton), winger Peter Thompson (Liverpool), forwards Johnny Byrne (West Ham United), Fred Pickering (Everton) and Bobby Tambling (Chelsea).*

9

The 1966 World Cup in England

11 July 1966   England 0 Uruguay 0
Wembley   Attendance 87,148

England Team: G. Banks, G. Cohen, R. Wilson, N. Stiles, J. Charlton, R. Moore, A. Ball, J. Greaves, R. Charlton, R. Hunt, J. Connelly.

This, the opening game of the 1966 World Cup competition, was almost called off by Hungarian referee Istvan Zsolt when he discovered that seven England players had left their identity cards at the team hotel. A police dispatch rider had to be sent to retrieve them. Can you believe that?

Unfortunately, the game against the South Americans was as a flat as a pancake! Basically it was a dull and uninspiring contest that left the neutrals – inside the ground and watching live on television – wondering, even contemplating, what manager Alf Ramsey had based his confidence on that England would win the tournament!

Uruguay, with eight outfield players, plus their goalkeeper, behind the ball most of the match, defied England's attack time and again. It was a boring tactic that was not amusing to watch. There was no one in the England team with the wit, craft or imagination to breach the tightly packed defence. They simply couldn't break down a brick barrier, although some fine handling by one of the world's best goalkeepers at that time, Ladislao Mazurkiewicz, helped see to that. So, for the first time in twelve internationals, Ramsey's side had failed to score. It was not a pretty sight and, in fact, the Uruguay players celebrated at the final whistle as if they had won! Goalkeeper Banks did not have a serious shot to save and England's winger, Connelly, never had a look in. Thankfully, things would change dramatically in due course.

16 July 1966   England 2 Mexico 0
Wembley   Attendance 92,570

England Team: G. Banks, G. Cohen, R. Wilson, N. Stiles, J. Charlton, R. Moore, T. Paine, J. Greaves, R. Charlton, R. Hunt, M. Peters.

Alf Ramsey confirmed before the start of England's second game against Mexico that he had not, as yet, completely abandoned the idea of playing an out-and-out winger, naming Southampton outside-right Terry Paine in place of Connelly, while the more attack-minded Martin Peters came into midfield in place of Alan Ball.

England played a lot better against the Mexicans, who tried to copy the Uruguayan approach by erecting a blanket defence in the hope of smothering all forms of attack by their opponents. Although it was pedestrian at times, there's no doubt that England's display was decidedly better overall. There seemed a lot more mobility in midfield and up front, while the back four looked solid enough in front of goalkeeper Banks. After twice going close, and seeing goalkeeper Ignacio Calderón pull two fine saves, Bobby Charlton set England on their way with a magnificent right-footed 25-yard thunderbolt in the thirty-eighth minute. Picking the ball up some 40 yards from goal, he headed towards the Mexican penalty area, veered right before launching his 'rocket' into the top of Calderon's net.

England had several chances to increase their lead, but all went begging. Then, after having a 'goal' disallowed, Liverpool's Roger Hunt sealed victory by tucking away number two in the seventy-fifth minute, after Calderon could only palm Jimmy Greaves' low cross into his path. This hard-earned victory convinced a lot of people that England could live with the best, if they buckled down to business from the off. Banks once again was hardly troubled, so well did Bobby Moore and his fellow defensive colleagues perform. Stiles, as always, worked his socks off in the engine room, putting in some bone-shaking tackles, while Peters was always a threat at set pieces. Ramsey's England's team was up and running.

20 July 1966   **England 2 France 0**
Wembley   **Attendance 98,270**

England Team: G. Banks, G. Cohen, R. Wilson, N. Stiles, J. Charlton, R. Moore, I. Callaghan, J. Greaves, R. Charlton, R. Hunt, M. Peters.
Two goals by Roger Hunt gave England a confidence boost as they booked their place in the quarter-finals. Ian Callaghan replaced Paine to become the third winger used by Alf Ramsey so far in the tournament, and he had his moments, albeit only a few. Unfortunately Jimmy Greaves finished the match nursing a severe gash on his shin, which required six stitches. From his point of view, he would miss the rest of the World Cup.

Tough guy Nobby Stiles was booked for yet another crunching tackle late in the game on elusive French striker Jacques Simon. He was fortunate not to have been sent off and, after the game, manager Ramsey ignored calls from FA officials that he should drop the Manchester United player because of his over-eager 'competitiveness'. 'If Stiles goes, so do I,' said Ramsey, and he was not feigning. He knew how vital Nobby's ball performances would be to the team in an era when fierce-tackling midfield players were a necessary evil. Both stayed put.

Hunt's goals against the resilient French came in the thirty-ninth minute – a tap-in after Jack Charlton had struck a post and a downward header from Callaghan's right-wing cross a quarter of an hour from time. Bobby Charlton and Greaves both had goals ruled out for offside while France's most creative player, Robert Herbin, suffered an early match-ending injury.

Next up, for a place in the semi-finals, it was Argentina, regarded by some as potential finalists. The Argentinians last visited Wembley in May 1951, some fifteen years previously when they lost 2-1 in a friendly.

23 July 1966	**England 1 Argentina 0**
Wembley	**Attendance 90,584**

England Team: G. Banks, G. Cohen, R. Wilson, N. Stiles, J. Charlton, R. Moore, A. Ball, G. Hurst, R. Charlton, R. Hunt, M. Peters.

Argentina's manager Juan Carlos Lorenzo told his players to shelve their superior ball skills and instead resort to what seemed a premeditated policy of rough and ready tactics. They did just that, committing a spate of petty, niggling fouls in an attempt to disrupt England's game. Their arrogant captain Antonio Rattín complained about every decision made by the referee against his team; indeed, he continuously waved his arms in the air like a policeman on traffic duty. In the end, German official Rudolf Kreitlein could take no more and ordered the Argentinian off in the thirty-fifth minute. It was almost comical seeing the relatively small referee staring up at the giant Rattín with his finger pointing to the bench. It took almost ten minutes of arguing before the irate Argentinian finally left the pitch.

This was the first match England had played under manager Alf Ramsey without a winger. Geoff Hurst came in for the injured Greaves, while Alan Ball returned in place of Callaghan, taking up a wide position on the right side of midfield. From here he was being asked to trek back as often as possible, as well as holding a touchline position, to stretch the Argentinian defence to its limits.

It was a good match, although stoppages disrupted play virtually every two minutes. The all-important goal was scored by Hurst in the seventy-eighth minute and it had 'West Ham' written all over it. Left-back Ray Wilson fed the impressive 'Hammer' Martin Peters, who crossed perfectly for his clubmate Hurst to head home from 8 yards. Gordon Banks, who created a record by keeping a clean sheet for the seventh consecutive game, made two crucial saves as England held on to reach the semi-finals. Yet it must be said that Argentina, who played with ten men for virtually an hour with added time, looked dangerous on the break and Nobby Stiles twice had to intervene on the edge of his own penalty area, while George Cohen, one of England's fastest players, was outpaced by Oscar Más, who only just failed to make an angle for a shot. Stiles, after the game, said, 'They are the best team we've played so far.'

NB: *Regarding Rattín's dismissal, Ken Aston, the English supervisor of referees, entered the field to try to persuade the Argentinian captain to leave the field quietly, but he only exacerbated the situation as the Latin American teams had already suspected that the English and Germans were collaborating to eliminate them from the competition. After his sending-off, Rattín finally sat down on the red carpet, reserved for HRH the Queen. What cheek.*

After the match, England manager Alf Ramsey refused to allow his players to swap shirts with their counterparts (as is traditional after the conclusion of a football match) and later described the Argentinians as 'animals' in the press. Back in Buenos Aires, the Argentine press and public were outraged, and one newspaper published a picture of the tournament's official mascot, World Cup Willie, dressed in pirate regalia, to demonstrate their opinion of the England's team.

Portugal, with goal-machine Eusébio in form, won through to play England in the semi-final. They beat Brazil 3-1 in their group, yet had to fight every inch of the way to knock out North Korea 5-3 in the quarter-finals. They were quietly confident of putting on a good display against Alf Ramsey's men, who after four games had yet to concede a goal, whereas the Portuguese had already let in five.

26 July 1966	England 2 Portugal 1
Wembley	Attendance 94,493

England Team: G. Banks, G. Cohen, R. Wilson, N. Stiles, J. Charlton, R. Moore, A. Ball, G. Hurst, R. Charlton, R. Hunt, M. Peters.

This, without doubt, was one of the best of all the 1966 World Cup matches. It lacked the high drama of the final itself, but the football produced by both teams had rarely been bettered, certainly at Wembley. Perhaps Portugal's thrilling end-to-end eight-goal quarter-final encounter North Korea all but matched it.

This semi-final victory over the Portuguese, under the Wembley floodlights, belonged to Bobby Charlton more than anybody. One reporter wrote, 'He had the grace of a Nureyev on grass and the power of a panther.' His reward for a super performance was two magnificent goals. His first in the thirtieth minute was a well-drilled, hard, low shot into the bottom corner of the net when he followed up a rebound after Roger Hunt's effort had been saved. His second, in the seventy-eighth minute, was a real beauty, fired high into the net from 20 yards after Geoff Hurst had pulled the ball back from the byline.

Seven minutes from time, England conceded a goal – their first in the World Cup and the first to go into Gordon Banks' net since Scotland scored past the Leicester 'keeper three months earlier. It was a penalty, put away by Eusébio after Jack Charlton had handled a header by giant centre-forward José Torres on the line. Nobby Stiles did a fine job in containing Eusébio, who was fresh from scoring a four-timer against the Koreans. In fact, the Portuguese star left the pitch in tears as the two teams received a standing ovation from the crowd at the end of a pulsating match.

This was the first time at the 1966 World Cup that an England performance was praised universally. The derisive voices that were keen on wingers disappeared without trace!

10

The 1966 World Cup Final

30 July 1966   England 4 West Germany 2 (after extra time)
Wembley   Attendance 96,924

England Team: G. Banks, G. Cohen, R. Wilson, N. Stiles, J. Charlton, R. Moore, A. Ball,
G. Hurst, R. Charlton, R. Hunt, M. Peters.
Alf Ramsey named an unchanged team for the final – England's biggest match *ever* –
against a strong and workmanlike West German outfit that had conceded only two goals
in five matches covering 450 minutes, belting Switzerland 5-0 and Uruguay 4-0 in the
process. And as every solitary England supporter knows, the eleven players who took the
field at Wembley back in 1966 were all destined to become national heroes.

In their book, *The Essential History of England* (Headline Publishing, 2002), authors
Andrew Mourant and Jack Rollin stated in their match report of the England *v.* West
Germany final, 'On a day drenched in patriotism and tension, in an epic match of
shifting fortunes too pitted with errors, too grinding, ultimately, to merit description
as a classic, England won the World Cup. As drama it was stupendous, rendered all
the more so through the imperfections and controversies that chafed against its fitful,
glinting brilliance.'

Ramsey's players performed out of their skin. They produced an excellent display in
front of a fervent crowd of supporters, coming back from a goal down and then having
to raise their game again following a last-ditch equaliser that resulted in extra time.
Germany went in front in the twelfth minute when Helmut Haller netted with a crisp,
low strike, after a rather feeble header by Wilson. England responded well, and within six
minutes drew level. Moore, quick in thought, delivered a terrific long free-kick towards
his West Ham colleague Hurst, who found the net with a smart flicked header past Hans
Tilkowski.

For the next twenty-five minutes or so, the football played by the two teams was
outstanding, full of flair and subtlety, passion and commitment. There was excitement
at both ends of the field, with both goalkeepers producing fine saves. For a concentrated
period after half-time, the game lost impetus and this is when Messrs Stiles and Ball came
into their own. England gradually took control and, with thirteen minutes remaining,

gained a corner on the right thanks to Ball's eagerness. Ball floated over the flag-kick, and Hurst's shot bounced into the air off Wolfgang Weber, allowing Peters to swoop with great efficiency, the ball flying low into the German net.

Germany drove forward in numbers in search of an equaliser; England simply had to remain calm, cool and collected. Barely a minute remained on the watch of Swiss referee Gottfried Dienst when Jack Charlton was penalised when jumping for a high ball with Sigfried Held. Lothar Emmerich drove the free-kick towards a packed penalty area, and somehow it was diverted out, into the path of Weber, who belted it home.

All eleven England players and their fans were stunned, the Germans ecstatic. Ramsey, though, gave a boosting peptalk at the final whistle, saying bluntly, among other things, 'You've beaten them once. Now go out and bloody beat them again.' Moore's team stormed out of the traps at the start of the extra time, with 'Mr Perpetual Motion' Alan Ball leading the way.

In the 101st minute, he chased a long ball down the right before crossing to Hurst, who turned and let rip a vicious shot that crashed against the underside of the bar. 'Goal' shouted the crowd, and the England players. The Germans said the ball hadn't crossed the line, but thankfully, after consulting his Russian linesman, Tofiq Bakhramov, referee Dienst awarded the goal and England were back in front.

Germany frantically went in pursuit of a second equaliser. England held firm with Moore outstanding, and it was fitting that the England skipper should set up the clinching goal for Hurst with just seconds remaining. His long pass was picked up by his Upton Park teammate, who drove forward before smashing a left-foot shot high into the net to become the first player in history to score a World Cup final hat-trick ... and his third goal *won* the World Cup for England.

Everyone who listened to the BBC commentator Kenneth Wolstenholme on TV will never forget this statement as Hurst's third goal went in, 'Some people are on the pitch, they think it's all over, it is now.'

After the triumph, workaholic Ball said this about the England Team: 'We had built up a perfect understanding with each other. I could find Hurst with a pass in the dark. We had worked our moves so often together. Ramsey knew exactly what we were capable of doing.'

The celebrations went on for days – weeks in some places. England were World Champions! Will we ever say this again?

England's successful winning team each received a £1,000 bonus and £60 appearance money (less tax). Manager Alf Ramsey was given a £6,000 bonus by the FA.

1966 World Cup Fact File

- Countries taking part: 16 (divided into four groups of 4).
- Final: England 4 West Germany 2 (after extra time).
- Final venue: Wembley Stadium, London (attendance: 96,984).
- Leading scorer: Eusebio (Portugal), 9 goals including a record 4 penalties.

- England's Geoff Hurst became the first player to score a hat-trick in a World Cup final.
- Mexican goalkeeper Antonio Carbajal played in the last of his five World Cup tournaments.

Four-Year Wait for the Champions

As holders of the Jules Rimet Trophy, England did not have to go through the agonising qualifying routine for the 1970 World Cup in Germany, but four years was an awful long while to wait before the next tournament in Mexico.

England's first game as World Champions was a Home International/European Nations Cup qualifier against Northern Ireland in Belfast. Manager Ramsey sent out the same eleven players who had been victorious against West Germany and, in front of 48,600 spectators, they produced the goods once more, winning 2-0 with goals from Roger Hunt and Martin Peters.

A friendly 0-0 draw with Czechoslovakia followed before Wales were slammed 5-1 in another Home International/European Nations Cup qualifier at Wembley – Hurst (2), brothers Bobby and Jack Charlton and a Terry Hennessey own-goal doing the damage. England, unchanged for the sixth successive game, played exceptionally well as Bobby Moore collected his fiftieth cap.

A third Home International/European Nations Cup qualifier was next on the agenda when Scotland visited Wembley in mid-April 1967. It is reckoned that 40,000 of the 99,063 spectators inside the stadium were Scots, and they indulged in wild celebrations after seeing (and cheering) their team to a 3-2 victory. At the final whistle, hundreds ran onto the pitch, ripping up pieces of turf as souvenirs after the great battle had been won.

With Jimmy Greaves back in the forward line in place of Roger Hunt, England came under pressure as early as the fifteenth minute when Jack Charlton broke a toe and Greaves took a nasty knock on the leg. The team didn't play at all badly despite carrying two passengers. Indeed, it was 1-0 to the Scots right up until the seventy-eighth minute before four goals were scored prior to the final whistle. England's nineteen-match unbeaten run was over.

Six weeks later, when England met Spain, manager Ramsey brought in goalkeeper Peter Bonetti, full-back Keith Newton, wing-half Alan Mullery, centre-back Brian Labone and midfielder John Hollins, while also recalling Roger Hunt. A solid 2-0 victory was achieved as another good run got underway. Over the next eight months, up to February 1968, England beat Austria 1-0, defeated Wales 3-0 and Northern Ireland 2-0, and drew 1-1 with Scotland in three more Home International/European Nations Cup qualifiers, also drawing 2-2 with the USSR.

Ramsey didn't make too many changes to his team. He brought back Norman Hunter against Austria and Peter Thompson against Northern Ireland, also giving David Sadler his first cap against the Irish. Cyril Knowles was introduced against the USSR and Mike Summerbee for the Scots game at Hampden Park, when the turnout was 134,000.

Bronze Medallists

Having duly qualified for the 1968 European Nations Cup, England ousted Spain in the quarter-final, winning 1-0 at Wembley and 2-1 in Madrid, but unfortunately they succumbed to Yugoslavia in the semi-final, going down 1-0 in Florence, and Alan Mullery became the first England player to be sent off in a full international. They then beat the USSR in the third-place play-off match to collect a bronze medal.

In between times, England beat Sweden 3-1 but lost 1-0 to West Germany in friendlies. Before the end of the year, further non-competitive matches against Romania and Bulgaria both ended in draws. Ramsey had, by now, given several more players the opportunity to perform at senior international level – among them goalkeepers Alex Stepney and Gordon West, full-backs Tommy Wright, Bob McNab and Paul Reaney, midfielder Colin 'Nijinsky' Bell and his clubmate forward Francis Lee. Four of them – Stepney, Bell, Lee and Wright – would go on to play in the next World Cup.

During the year 1969, England fulfilled ten internationals, three on tour to South America. They won seven and lost just one of those matches, recording their best victories at Wembley; 5-0 against France, when Geoff Hurst netted a hat-trick, and 4-1 over Scotland when Gordon Banks won his fiftieth cap. On tour, 105,000 fans saw England draw 0-0 with Mexico in the capital, which was more than 7,000 feet above sea level; over 54,000 saw them beat Uruguay 2-1 in Montevideo and 135,000 spectators packed into the Estádio do Maracanã in Rio de Janeiro to see Brazil win 3-1.

Manager Alf Ramsey was as keen as ever to try out new players, giving debuts to Terry Cooper (a converted winger), Emlyn Hughes and the West Brom striker Jeff Astle, and all would make it into his World Cup squad.

In the five months leading up to the 1970 World Cup, England remained unbeaten in seven more well-contested friendlies. They were certainly given stern tests by The Netherlands and Scotland, who both earned creditable 0-0 draws, and by Wales (1-1). They defeated Northern Ireland 3-1 in the Home International Championship (when Bobby Charlton scored to celebrate the winning of his 100th cap) and Belgium by the same score in Brussels. While acclimatising again in Latin America, they ran up good wins over Colombia 4-0 in Bogotá and Ecuador 2-0 in Quito. The heat, humidity and playing at altitude was tough, but the players coped exceptionally well. The ground in Bogota was 8,500 feet above sea level, and the one in Quito as high as 9,000 feet above sea level. Three more players – Peter Osgood, Ralph Coates and Brian Kidd – were all handed their senior international baptisms on this trip.

So, with the spadework done, Ramsey and his squad of players duly set off to Mexico, confident of retaining the World Cup, but unfortunately things didn't start too well in their base of Guadalajara. A noisy band played throughout the night within yards of their hotel, the world press tended to follow the players everywhere they went – even into their dressing room before training sessions – and there was generally a lack of security. This annoyed Ramsey and he wasn't at all happy with what followed next.

The Bobby Moore Saga

Skipper Bobby Moore was alleged to have stolen a bracelet from a shopping centre near the Tequendama Hotel where England were staying. Moore was taken to a police station, questioned at length and detained for four days. The newspaper headlines revelled in this incident. After diplomatic intervention, Moore was released, composed and with his dignity intact. 'It was a set up, a farce, an absolute farce,' said his manager.

England were drawn in Group 3 of the 1970 World Cup, along with favourites Brazil, Czechoslovakia and Romania. Despite being accommodated in unwelcoming territory with all the local and indeed national newspapers harshly and wrongly branding the players as thieves and drunkards, manager Ramsey said, 'This is a tough group but we'll get on with the job in hand. The players are confident, very confident. We'll get through this; I'm just annoyed with what has gone on. What has England's football team done wrong ... nothing, as far as I know.'

Alf Ramsey selected this twenty-two-man squad for Mexico:

Goalkeepers: Gordon Banks (Stoke City), Peter Bonetti (Chelsea), Alex Stepney (Manchester United). Full-backs: Terry Cooper (Leeds United), Keith Newton (Everton), Tommy Wright (Everton). Half-backs: Jack Charlton (Leeds United), Emlyn Hughes (Liverpool), Norman Hunter (Leeds United), Brian Labone (Everton), Bobby Moore (West Ham United), Alan Mullery (Tottenham Hotspur), Nobby Stiles (Manchester United). Forwards: Jeff Astle (West Bromwich Albion), Alan Ball (Everton), Colin Bell (Manchester City), Bobby Charlton (Manchester United), Allan Clarke* (Leeds United), Geoff Hurst (West Ham United), Francis Lee (Manchester City), Peter Osgood (Chelsea), Martin Peters (Tottenham Hotspur).

NB: Named as reserves for the 1970 World Cup were defenders John Kaye (West Bromwich Albion) and David Sadler (Manchester United), winger Ralph Coates (Tottenham Hotspur) and forward Tony Brown (West Bromwich Albion).

* Uncapped player.

11

The 1970 World Cup in Mexico

2 June 1970	England 1 Romania 0
Guadalajara	Attendance 50,560

England Team: G. Banks, K. Newton, T. Cooper, A. Mullery, B. Labone, B. Moore, F. Lee, A. Ball, R. Charlton, G. Hurst, M. Peters. Substitutes: T. Wright for Newton, P. Osgood for Lee.

Six players who won the World Cup four years earlier started the game against Romania: Alan Ball, Gordon Banks, Bobby Charlton, Geoff Hurst, captain Bobby Moore and his former West Ham United teammate Martin Peters, who was now playing for Tottenham, having become the game's first £200,000 footballer when he moved to White Hart Lane three months earlier. And it was England's 1966 hat-trick hero Hurst who emerged, once again, as his country's goalscoring hero.

In the sixty-fifth minute, he controlled Franny Lee's aerial flick from Ball's tempting pass, delivered from 15 yards inside the Romanian half, and nipped round right-back Alexandru Sătmăreanu before smashing a low, left-footed drive through the legs of the Romanian goalkeeper Sterica Adamache to earn a narrow, but deserved victory. Playing against tough-tackling opponents who, in effect, relied on mass defending in the hope of scraping a draw, several England players were clattered unceremoniously at times, with rugged Romanian defender Mihai Mocanu the main culprit. He wasn't even lectured by Belgium referee Vital Loraux.

In a fiercely contested match – and it was fierce at times – England had the majority of the ball but created little. Hurst and Bobby Charlton had the best efforts in a scrappy first half, while Hurst (after his goal) and Peters came close during the last twenty minutes. Right-back Keith Newton (crunched twice by Mocanu) and wing-forward Lee were both badly injured and replaced by substitutes Tommy Wright (fifty-one minutes) and Peter Osgood (seventy-seven) respectively. Wright, in fact, was the first 'sub' used by England in World Cup finals. On the opposite flank, the adventurous Terry Cooper was outstanding at left-back, attacking at every opportunity. 'He played like winger,' said one reporter.

7 June 1970   Brazil 1 England 0
Guadalajara   Attendance 70,950

England Team: G. Banks, T. Wright, T. Cooper, A. Mullery, B. Labone, B. Moore, F. Lee, A. Ball, R. Charlton, G. Hurst, M. Peters. Substitutes: J. Astle for Lee, C. Bell for Charlton.
England's only change from their opening game saw Tommy Wright taking over at right-back from the injured Keith Newton. Brazil, fresh from a 4-1 victory over Czechoslovakia, had all their superstars on view, namely Pelé, Rivelino, Jairzinho, Tostão, Carlos Alberto and Everaldo, among others.

As it was, England should not have lost the game. They had their chances – more than Brazil in effect – the best being fluffed by the usually accurate West Bromwich Albion striker Jeff Astle, who fired wide from close range just minutes after coming on as a substitute for the tiring Bobby Charlton.

Played on a Sunday, with the midday sun beating down, England struggled at times in the heat, but they matched the Brazilians kick for kick. The all-important and match-winning goal was scored on the hour by Jairzinho. Hard-working midfielder Tostão arrowed a brilliant pass through the England defence to Pelé who, in turn, deftly set up Jairzinho who had moved inside left-back Terry Cooper. Banks had no chance of saving the Brazilian's precise and well-executed ground shot.

As early as the eleventh minute, Banks had pulled off one of the greatest saves ever seen in World Cup football, perhaps anywhere in any country. Carlos Alberto, Brazil's right-back and captain, pushed a beautiful ball down the flank to Jairzinho. He accelerated past Cooper like a panther before delivering a superb high cross into the heart of the England penalty area. There, waiting to pounce (or rather jump) was Pelé. He got to the ball and speared a downward header towards the bottom right-hand corner of Banks' goal, but the England No. 1, showing astounding athleticism, dived down and somehow got his hand to the ball, flicked it up and over the bar. Pelé himself admitted afterwards that he shouted 'goal' and actually stopped dead in mid-celebration to mourn what had somehow become a missed chance. It was an astonishing save, quite brilliant. It was stunning and one that millions of football fans worldwide will never forget.

Bobby Moore was outstanding at the heart of England's defence and at the end he and Pelé hugged each other, exchanged shirts, and reflected on a fine game between two evenly matched teams. It was a pity one had to lose.

It was revealed afterwards that at least five England players lost up to ten pounds in weight after running round inside the Jalisco Stadium in temperatures touching almost 39°C.

11 June 1970   Czechoslovakia 0 England 1
Guadalajara   Attendance 49,292

England Team: G. Banks, K. Newton, T. Cooper, A. Mullery, J. Charlton, B. Moore, C. Bell, R. Charlton, J. Astle, A. Clarke, M. Peters. Substitutes: A. Ball for Charlton, P. Osgood for Astle.

With Geoff Hurst ruled out, the Leeds United striker Allan Clarke came into the attack, alongside Jeff Astle for his England debut against the Czechs. He celebrated his call-up by scoring the game's only goal, a disputed penalty in the forty-ninth minute. With both Franny Lee and Hurst absent, the Midland-born striker volunteered to take the spot-kick and he delivered safely, sending the ball into the net with aplomb.

England, stuttering along occasionally (showing signs perhaps of fatigue after the arduous game with Brazil) dominated play for long periods, and the closest the Czechs came to scoring was when a speculative 25-yard shot by right-back Karol Dobiaš swerved in midair, causing Gordon Banks to react superbly as he tipped the ball over the bar at full stretch. Banks, in fact, had to avoid a continuous bombardment of flying objects, including coins, which were thrown into the penalty area from behind his goal by Mexican persecutors.

It was now off to Leon for Ramsey's men where they would once more face their 1966 opponents, West Germany, this time for a place in the final.

11 June was the birthday of Clarke's wife, the anniversary of their wedding and also the anniversary of his transfer from Fulham to Leicester City. It turned out to be a great day all round.

14 June 1970   England 2 West Germany 3 (after extra time)
Leon   Attendance 23,357

England Team: P. Bonetti, K. Newton, T. Cooper, A. Mullery, B. Labone, B. Moore, F. Lee, A. Ball, R. Charlton, G. Hurst, M. Peters. Substitutes: N. Hunter for Peters, C. Bell for Charlton.

With Gordon Banks ruled out with a stomach upset, manager Alf Ramsey brought in Chelsea's Peter Bonetti to try and stop the Germans. Unfortunately, 'The Cat' didn't have the greatest of games.

Brian Labone was recalled at centre-half while Franny Lee, Alan Ball and Geoff Hurst were also back in action, and England played very well for over an hour. Their passing was fluid and precise, the forward play was decisive and penetrative and the normally attack-minded Franz Beckenbauer struggled to contain Bobby Charlton who covered acres of ground. Alan Mullery deservedly fired England ahead from 8 yards, from Keith Newton's low pass, in the thirty-second minute. And that lead should have been doubled before half-time, but erratic shooting let the Germans off the hook.

Continuing to dominate proceedings, England eventually scored again in the fiftieth minute when Martin Peters ghosted in at the far post to convert another excellent cross by Newton. But then it all fell apart. German legend Beckenbauer quickly pulled a goal back, beating Peter Bonetti to his right from long range in the sixty-eighth minute, after taking Wolfgang Overath's pass in his stride.

At this juncture, and seemingly confident of victory, England boss Alf Ramsey removed Bobby Charlton to rest him for the semi-final. It was a catastrophic mistake, and it also brought to an end the Manchester United player's international career. He left the scene with 106 caps and 49 goals to his credit, achieved over a thirteen-year period, 1957–70.

Charlton's removal galvanised Germany, and they drew level in the seventy-eighth minute. Brian Labone's poor clearance was picked up by left-back Karl-Heinz Schnellinger, whose long ball found Uwe Seeler, and Seeler's looping back-header dropped over the head of the stranded Bonetti.

England couldn't get out of their own half but they somehow held on and took the game into extra time. But it was Germany who proved strongest and, in the 108th minute, following a dashing run by the dangerous Jürgen Grabowski, who at this time was giving left-back Terry Cooper a real roasting, he crossed for Hannes Löhr to set up Gerd Müller for the winning goal.

If Banks had played, and Ramsey had not made a pig's ear of his substitutions, taking off Charlton and then Martin Peters (eighty-one minutes), replacing them with Colin Bell and defender Norman Hunter, things might have been different. We shall never know, of course. England's crown had been taken – they were no longer World Champions.

NB: English Prime Minister Harold Wilson blamed his election defeat a few days later on this result against the Germans, and England's so-called 'World Cup Curse' began.

1970 World Cup Fact File

- Countries taking part 16 (divided into four groups of 4).
- Final: Brazil 4, Italy 1.
- Final venue: Estadio Azteca, Mexico City (attendance 107,412).
- Leading scorer: Gerd Müller (West Germany), 10 goals including two hat-tricks.
- The Jules Rimet Trophy became property of Brazil after their third victory in twelve years.
- Pelé collected his third World Cup winner's medal.
- Yellow and red cards were shown to players for the first time in Mexico.

Twelve Years of Toil Ahead

Unfortunately, England did not take part in the 1974 and 1978 World Cup finals, being eliminated in both qualifying campaigns. Manager Alf Ramsey acknowledged that he was solely responsible for England's defeat at the hands of West Germany in Mexico: 'I made some bad mistakes and I hold my hands up to that.' Unfortunately, he never got on with the press – that's common knowledge. His view of the press was simple: 'They know nothing about football, so why should I talk to them.'

The international careers of the Charlton brothers ended in Mexico. Jack bailed out with thirty-five caps to his credit, Bobby with 106 – one more than Billy Wright's previous record.

Some five months elapsed before England played its next international – a friendly against East Germany at Wembley in late November, when 93,000 spectators saw England win 3-1. The team consisted of Peter Shilton (collecting the first of what would be a record 125 caps), Emlyn Hughes, Terry Cooper, Alan Mullery, David Sadler, Bobby Moore, Francis Lee, Alan Ball, Geoff Hurst, Allan Clarke and Martin Peters.

Competitive football commenced in the shape of the European Championship qualifiers in February 1971. England squeezed out a disappointing 1-0 win over Malta in Valletta, and Ramsey handed debuts to Derby County defender Roy McFarland, Spurs striker Martin Chivers and the Everton duo of midfielder Colin Harvey and goalscorer Joe Royle. Ten weeks later, England beat Greece in their second EC qualifier, when Arsenal's Peter Storey won his first cap at right-back. Halfway through May they saw off Malta, winning 5-0 at Wembley. Liverpool's Chris Lawler scored on his debut and goalkeeper Gordon Banks only touched the ball four times in ninety minutes. Three Home International Championship matches came next and it is fair to say that Alf Ramsey's players did okay, winning the title with hard-earned victories over Northern Ireland (1-0) and Scotland (3-1). They drew with Wales (0-0) when four Liverpool players lined up in front of goalkeeper Shilton, namely Chris Lawler, Tommy Smith, Larry Lloyd and Emlyn Hughes. Smith and Lloyd and West Bromwich Albion's attacking midfielder Tony Brown made their senior debuts against the Welsh, while Alan Ball collected his fiftieth full cap against the Irish.

Then it was back to the business of qualifying for the European Championships, and England once again achieved their aim, beating Switzerland in Basel 3-2 and then drawing 1-1 against them at home before defeating Greece 2-0 in Piraeus. Rodney Marsh made his international bow against the Swiss at Wembley. But it was the foe from West Germany who put paid to any hopes of Ramsey's team winning that tournament when they knocked England out in the quarter-finals, winning 3-1 at Wembley and drawing 0-0 in Berlin.

After three more Home Internationals – a 3-0 victory over Wales (when the Newcastle United striker Malcolm Macdonald made his debut), a 1-0 defeat in Ireland (first caps for the versatile Derby County star Colin Todd and the Sheffield United midfielder Tony Currie) and a single-goal win over Scotland at Hampden Park – England drew 1-1 in a friendly with Yugoslavia at Wembley before playing their first qualifying game for the 1974 World Cup. They took on and beat Wales 1-0 at Ninian Park just a few weeks after Gordon Banks was involved in a serious car crash, which resulted in him losing an eye and brought about the end of his career. Surprisingly, England were then held by the Welsh at Wembley in the return fixture, and effectively this result would prove disastrous.

Following a resounding 5-0 friendly win over Scotland at Hampden Park, which saw Bobby Moore collect his 100th cap, England won all three of their Home International matches against Northern Ireland (2-1), Wales (3-0) and the Scots again (1-0). Wolves' marksman John Richards made his senior bow against the Irish. Another friendly resulted in a 1-1 draw with Czechoslovakia before England crashed 2-0 in Poland in their third 1974 World Cup qualifier. This was an awful result and, to make things worse, Alan Ball was sent off.

Before taking on the Poles at Wembley, England fulfilled three more friendlies. They beat USSR 2-1 in Moscow, lost 2-0 in Turin to Italy and walloped hapless Austria 7-0 at Wembley. Then came the crunch match – Poland at home. Victory would see England safely through to the World Cup finals but, alas, the game ended 1-1 and sadly there would be no trip to Germany for Ramsey & Co.

It was hard to take; several players were in tears, and so were thousands of supporters. Six months and two matches later, following a 1-0 defeat in Italy – when Bobby Moore made his 108th and last appearance for his country – and a goalless draw in Portugal, when no fewer than six players made their debuts, including centre-half Dave Watson of Sunderland, Stan Bowles of Queens Park Rangers and West Ham's Trevor Brooking, the unfortunate Ramsey was sacked as manager in April 1974, after being summoned to the FA headquarters at Lancaster Gate.

12

The 1974 World Cup Qualifying Matches

15 November 1972	Wales 0 England 1
Ninian Park	Attendance 36,384

England Team: R. Clemence (Liverpool), P. Storey (Arsenal), E. Hughes (Liverpool), N. Hunter, R. McFarland (Derby County), R. Moore, K. Keegan (Liverpool), M. Chivers (Tottenham Hotspur), R. Marsh (Manchester City), C. Bell, A. Ball.
Liverpool colleagues Ray Clemence and Kevin Keegan, both former Scunthorpe United players, made their international debuts in this, Sir Alf Ramsey's 100th game in charge.

   With Arsenal's Peter Storey snuffing out the threat of Leighton James, England always looked the better side, but only managed one goal for their efforts. This was a smart finish in the thirty-sixth minute by Colin Bell after some good approach work by Alan Ball. Keegan, with his bubble-perm hair, missed a relatively simple chance late on.

24 January 1973	England 1 Wales 1
Wembley	Attendance 62,273

England Team: R. Clemence, P. Storey, E. Hughes, N. Hunter, R. McFarland, R. Moore, K. Keegan, C. Bell, M. Chivers, R. Marsh, A. Ball.
A long-range shot three minutes before the interval by Leeds United defender Norman Hunter, which speared beyond his Elland Road clubmate Gary Sprake in the Welsh goal, salvaged a point for England after John Toshack had given the visitors a deserved lead halfway through the first-half. Peter Rodrigues and Mike England were outstanding in defence for Wales while England's forwards floundered, hardly creating a worthwhile opening during the second period.

6 June 1973   Poland 2 England 0
Chorzów   Attendance 73,714

England Team: P. Shilton (Leicester City), P. Madeley (Leeds United), E. Hughes,
P. Storey, R. McFarland, R. Moore, A. Ball, C. Bell, M. Chivers, A. Clarke, M. Peters.
This was a disastrous defeat for England. They were a goal down after just nine minutes
to Robert Gadocha, whose shot deflected off Bobby Moore and the arm of 'keeper Peter
Shilton. They were the better side throughout and could have easily won by a bigger score.
An uncharacteristic mistake by Moore led to the Poles' second goal, scored again by 'Man
of the Match' Lubanski early in the second half. It screamed out for Ramsey to send on
attacking players when Poland went two up, but he stuck to his rigid formation of packing
midfield, and it didn't work. To compound England's misery, Alan Ball became the second
England player to be sent off in a major international – rightly dismissed for grabbing
opposing defender Leslaw Ćmikiewicz around the neck twelve minutes from time.

17 October 1973   England 1 Poland 1
Wembley   Attendance 99,886

England Team: P. Shilton, P. Madeley, E. Hughes, C. Bell, R. McFarland, N. Hunter,
A. Currie (Sheffield United), M. Channon (Southampton), M. Chivers, A. Clarke,
M. Peters. Substitute: K. Hector (Derby County) for Chivers
England had to win this game to qualify for the 1974 World Cup final in West Germany.
There is no doubt they played pretty well, having 75 per cent of the play and putting
in no less than thirty-five attempts at goal, compared to just two by the Poles, one of
the which found the net! This was in the fifty-fifth minute when, in a rare breakaway,
Norman Hunter missed a tackle near the halfway line. The ball was switched inside to
Jan Domarksi, who fired low and hard under the diving Peter Shilton. Although Allan
Clarke equalised with a penalty halfway through the second half, there was no way past
'Man of the Match' Jan Tomaszewski in the Polish goal after that. Earlier labelled 'a
clown' by Brian Clough, he was quite superb under the Wembley lights, pulling off at
least five superb saves, two of them being described as 'out of this world'. Substitute
Kevin Hector (Derby County) was sent on ahead of Keegan for his senior debut and
should have scored with a last-minute header. Unfortunately, his miss meant that England
were out of the World Cup – although it wasn't all about that. One newspaper headline
the following day said it all: 'Pole Axed'.

1974 World Cup Fact File

- Countries taking part: 16 (divided into four groups of 4).
- Final: West Germany 2, The Netherlands 1.
- Final venue: Olympiastadion, Munich (attendance: 77,833).

- Leading scorer: Grzegorz Lato (Poland), 7 goals.
- Johan Neeskens (The Netherlands) netted the fastest-ever World Cup final goal, a penalty after just ninety seconds, awarded by English referee Jack Taylor.

Ramsey Departs

At the time of Alf Ramsey's dismissal, some honestly thought that it was 'brutal and short-sighted', and Alan Ball said, 'I was shocked when I heard the news. He was a true knight ... always a hero in my eyes.' Alan Mullery commented, 'Alf Ramsey was without any football weakness. He was very clever tactically ... a brilliant manager.' And Bobby Moore stated, 'He was like a God to the players, a great manager.'

Ramsey's record as England's manager (February 1963 to April 1974) was to all intents and purposes pretty good: 113 games played; 69 wins, 27 draws and 17 defeats. The former Everton and Arsenal international wing-half Joe Mercer, aged fifty-nine, who had already managed Sheffield United, Manchester City, Aston Villa and Coventry City, was temporarily placed in charge. He was at the helm for just five weeks (11 May to 5 June 1974) and seven matches – two Home International victories over Wales 2-0 and Northern Ireland 1-0 (when Leicester City's centre-forward Frank Worthington was introduced), plus a 2-0 defeat by Scotland at Hampden Park, a 2-2 home draw with Argentina, a 1-1 scoreline in Leipzig against East Germany, a 1-0 victory in Sofia over Bulgaria and a 2-2 draw in Belgrade with Yugoslavia.

In Comes Revie

In July 1974, the FA appointed Don Revie to follow in the footsteps of 'Gentleman Joe' Mercer. Given a five-year contract, he had done wonders as boss of Leeds United and one of his first acts was to invite no less than eighty-one present, potential and future players to gather at a bonding meeting in Manchester. He negotiated a handful of new deals and introduced the hymn 'Land of Hope and Glory' as the team's anthem before home matches.

Revie's first two games in charge were European Championship qualifiers, both at Wembley, against Czechoslovakia (won 3-0) and Portugal (0-0). Then came a quite superb morale-boosting 2-0 victory over West Germany, where Stoke City midfielder Alan Hudson was outstanding. England won two more EC qualifiers against Cyprus, 5-0 at home, with Malcolm Macdonald scoring all five goals to equal the record set by Willie Hall in 1938 for most goals by an Englishman in a full international, and 1-0 in Limassol. For the record, Mick Channon set up all of SuperMac's goals against the Cypriots.

Two draws – against Northern Ireland 0-0 and Wales 2-2 – plus an emphatic 5-1 win over Scotland in the Home International Championship were next, followed by a 2-1 friendly win over Switzerland. Then things started to go slightly wrong. Czechoslovakia won a crucial EC qualifier by 2-1 in Bratislava, and Portugal claimed a 1-1 draw in Lisbon. This meant that England failed to qualify for the finals.

In March 1976, for the friendly with Wales at Wrexham, Revie introduced as many as *eight* new players to senior international football, awarding first caps to Trevor Cherry (Leeds United), Neil Clement (Queens Park Rangers), the Liverpool duo of Phil Neal and Phil Thompson, Mick Doyle (Manchester City), Peter Taylor (Crystal Palace), Phil Boyer (Norwich City) and Ray Kennedy (also of Liverpool). England won 2-1 with Taylor and Kennedy on target.

Two wins – against Wales 1-0 and Northern Ireland 4-0 – along with a 2-1 defeat by Scotland in the Home International Championship, preceded a 1-0 defeat against Brazil and a 3-2 victory over Italy in the US Bicentennial Tournament, when the team turned out in an all-yellow strip. England then set out trying to qualify for the 1978 World Cup finals in Argentina.

They started well, doubling up over Finland with 4-1 and 2-1 victories, on a bumpy pitch in Helsinki and on a lush surface at Wembley respectively. In between, they played out an interesting 1-1 draw with the Republic of Ireland, the first time the two countries had met since 1964. However, there was a setback when Italy won a qualifier 2-0 in Rome. England had it all to do, even at this early stage in the proceedings.

Revie stayed on for eight more matches, of which only two were won. England were well beaten – outplayed in fact – when losing 2-0 at home to a magnificent Dutch team, with Messrs Cruyff, Neeskens, Rep and van de Kerkhof in stupendous form. As expected, they managed to gain a comfortable 5-0 victory over Luxembourg in a World Cup qualifier and just got the better of Northern Ireland 2-1, but lost to both Wales (1-0) and Scotland (2-1) at home in Home International Championship matches. It would be another thirty-six years before England would suffer successive defeats at Wembley, doing so against Chile and Germany in 2013.

In June 1977, Revie's last mission was to take England on an end-of-season tour to South America, where they drew all three games – against Brazil (0-0), Argentina (1-1) and Uruguay (0-0). A month or so after returning to the UK, Revie had his contract officially cancelled by the FA on 12 July 1977.

It had been universally reported that he had been approached to become head coach of the United Arab Emirates and, in fact, had actually flown out to Dubai, direct from England's South American tour base, to meet UAE officials before transferring to Helsinki to watch Finland play Italy in a World Cup qualifier. Convinced he was going to get the sack, Revie had initially asked for his and trainer Les Cocker's contracts to be paid up while they were in Buenos Aires. Chairman of the FA committee Dick Wragg was shocked, as were Ted Croker and other officials. 'It was laughable,' said Croker. Indeed, the FA asked Revie to 'see the job through'. They even asked him to sign an extended contract. At the time he was noncommittal, but soon everything came out in the wash. He was gone, on his way to pastures new and a place in the UAE sun, with a huge salary, estimated to be around £340,000 spread over a four-year period. 'Nearly everyone in the country [England] seems to want me out. So I'm giving them what they want,' said Revie, as he publicly announced his departure. His defection to the UAE was a massive scoop for *Daily Mail* reporter Jeff Powell, who had flown out to the Middle East with Revie. The newspaper carried banner headlines on its front page, confirming the manager's wish to go and try his luck in the Far East. The FA weren't too pleased, as the news broke before Revie had handed in his notice of resignation. Small wonder, after all this furore, that he was portrayed as a soccer mercenary.

There followed a rather messy legal tussle, with Revie being accused of bringing the game into disrepute on no less than four counts. After the first hearing in December 1978, the FA commission banned Revie from any involvement whatsoever in English football for ten years. Twelve months later, after an eighteen-day-long High Court hearing, Revie got the ban overturned. However, the damage had been done and his reputation was tarnished forever.

Revie had been in office for just over three years, during which time England played twenty-nine matches, of which fourteen were won, eight drawn and seven lost. During his time in charge, he awarded more than thirty players their first cap, among them Trevor Francis (Birmingham City), Paul Mariner (Ipswich Town) and Ray 'Butch' Wilkins (Chelsea), plus two players mentioned earlier, Neal and Thompson, who would all go to Spain for the 1982 World Cup.

Greenwood Takes Charge

Revie was replaced as England chief by the former West Ham United manager Ron Greenwood, then aged fifty-five, who took over the reins, initially on a caretaker basis, on 17 August 1977. He was upgraded to full-time manager a month later. A vastly experienced and knowledgeable campaigner, having previously coached the youth and under-23 teams, he had been lined up to succeed Walter Winterbottom before Alf Ramsey was appointed.

Greenwood's first game in charge ended goalless against Switzerland, and only 42,000 fans turned up at Wembley. He selected seven players from Liverpool's European Cup-winning team against the Swiss: Ray Clemence, Phil Neal, Terry McDermott, Emlyn 'Crazy Horse' Hughes, Ray Kennedy, Kevin Keegan (then of Hamburger SV) and Ian Callaghan, whose last cap had been gained eleven years earlier. Greenwood's second and third games were against Luxembourg (away) and Italy (home) in World Cup qualifiers. Both resulted in 2-0 victories but, disappointingly, England missed out on a trip to Argentina, simply on the total of goals scored: fifteen to Italy's eighteen.

So, like Ramsey in 1973, Greenwood failed to get England to the World Cup finals. He probably came in far too late, but he knew, deep down, that the players available to him were all top-class professionals and experienced campaigners, and he sincerely believed that World Cup glory could be achieved once more in the not too distant future.

The 1978 World Cup Qualifying Matches

13 June 1976	Finland 1 England 4
Helsinki	Attendance 24,336

England Team: R. Clemence, C. Todd (Derby County), M. Mills (Ipswich Town), P. Thompson (Liverpool), P. Madeley, T. Cherry (Leeds United), K. Keegan, M. Channon, S. Pearson (Manchester United), T. Brooking (West Ham United), G. Francis (Queens Park Rangers).

Kevin Keegan was outstanding at the Olympic Stadium in Helsinki when England got their 1978 World Cup qualifying campaign off to a flying start. He laid on a fourteenth-minute opener for Stuart 'Pancho' Pearson, who then returned the compliment on the half-hour mark after the Finns had surprisingly grabbed an equaliser through Mixu Paatelainen in the twenty-seventh minute. Mick Channon found space to make it 3-1 twelve minutes into the second half before Keegan put the icing on the cake with a fourth goal on the hour, netting with a splendidly executed lob. After that, several chances went begging against the team officials, rated as the 'whipping boys' in the group. Gerry Francis captained England and he had a fine game, Finland's goalkeeper Göran Enckleman denying a goal.

13 October 1976	England 2 Finland 1
Wembley	Attendance 91,912

England Team: R. Clemence, C. Todd, K. Beattie (Ipswich Town), P. Thompson, B. Greenhoff (Manchester United), R. Wilkins (Chelsea), K. Keegan, M. Channon, J. Royle (Manchester City), T. Brooking, D. Tueart (Manchester City). Substitutes: M. Mills for Brooking, G. Hill (Manchester United) for Tueart.

England took the lead inside three minutes when Dennis Tueart found the net just minutes before Joe Royle's header had been saved on the line following a Trevor Brooking floated left-wing corner. But, after that, the overall performance produced by Don Revie's team was poor – very poor – and at the final whistle, the chants of 'rubbish, rubbish' echoed round Wembley. England were expected to overpower the Finns. They failed miserably and, after conceding an equaliser early in the second-half, scored by the lively Jyrki Nieminen, it was down to Manchester City striker Royle to win the match in the fifty-second minute with a well-taken, close-range header from Mick Channon's inviting cross.

Those close to the England camp knew that all was not well between Revie and a faction of the Football Association, some having quietly questioned his methods of management and his commercial interests, but the boss knew what he was doing and the game went on.

17 November 1976	Italy 2 England 0
Rome	Attendance 70,718

England Team: R. Clemence, N. Clement (Queens Park Rangers), M. Mills, B. Greenhoff, R. McFarland, E. Hughes, K. Keegan, M. Channon, S. Bowles (Queens Park Rangers), T. Cherry, T. Brooking. Substitute: K. Beattie for Clement.
Italy, fielding six Juventus players, proved to be a class above England, who were second best from virtually the word go inside Rome's Stadio Olimpico. Giancarlo Antognoni scored the first goal in the thirty-sixth minute, and Roberto Bettega struck the second with thirteen minutes remaining. Only some smart saves by Ray Clemence and some resolute defending by Roy McFarland and Emlyn Hughes kept the score down.

Manager Revie had made six changes to the team that struggled to beat Finland, but those who came in were no better than those he left out. After this bad defeat, the first signs of 'Revie Out' started to appear as newspaper headlines. Argentina 1978 looked an awful long way away!

30 March 1977	England 5 Luxembourg 0
Wembley	Attendance 81,718

England Team: R. Clemence, J. Gidman (Aston Villa), T. Cherry, R. Kennedy (Liverpool), D. Watson (Manchester City), E. Hughes, K. Keegan, M. Channon, J. Royle, T. Francis (Birmingham City), G. Hill. Substitute: P. Mariner, (Ipswich Town) for Royle.
Four goals in the last half hour just about kept England's faint hopes of qualifying alive for the 1978 World Cup finals. Kevin Keegan scored as early as the tenth minute, and at that point it was a question of how many England could or would score. Unfortunately, their play became far too anxious against the part-timers, who battled for every ball. Tiredness eventually crept in to the visitors' play. Trevor Francis tucked in a second on fifty-eight minutes, Ray Kennedy added a third five minutes later, and then Mick Channon scored twice – the first from debutant right-back John Gidman's cross on sixty-nine minutes and the second from the penalty spot with nine minutes remaining.

Late on in the game, hard-tackling Luxembourg defender Gilbert Dresch was sent off for a foul on Channon – only the second player to have been dismissed at Wembley up to that time. The first was Argentinian captain Antonio Rattín in the 1966 World Cup quarter-final against England.

12 October 1977   Luxembourg 0 England 2
Luxembourg   Attendance 10,621

England Team: R. Clemence, T. Cherry, E. Hughes, T. McDermott, D. Watson (Manchester City), R. Kennedy, I. Callaghan (Liverpool), R. Wilkins, T. Francis, P. Mariner, G. Hill. Substitutes: K. Beattie for Watson, T. Whymark (Ipswich Town) for McDermott.
England needed a goal avalanche (something like four or five) to breathe life into fading hopes of qualifying for Argentina, but they failed to capitalise on some slack defending by the home side and missed a hatful of chances. It wasn't a good performance by any means. A thirtieth-minute opener by Ray Kennedy and an injury-time goal from Paul Mariner earned sluggish England their first win in seven matches, but it was too little, too late. Debutant Trevor Whymark came on as a substitute for Terry McDermott in a bid to add more life into a floundering attack. But generally speaking, England never looked like scoring more than twice. Bitterly disappointed, manager Ron Greenwood said after the game, 'Anxiety got the better of us.' He could say that again.

16 November 1977   England 2 Italy 0
Wembley   Attendance 91,886

England Team: R. Clemence, P. Neal, T. Cherry, R. Wilkins, D. Watson, E. Hughes, S. Coppell (Manchester United), K. Keegan, R. Latchford (Everton), T. Brooking, P. Barnes (Manchester City). Substitutes: T. Francis for Keegan, S. Pearson for Latchford.
Kevin Keegan was outstanding in this excellent win over Italy. The Liverpool star headed home Trevor Brooking's cross in the eleventh minute and the same combination linked up again for Keegan's second goal nine minutes from time. They collected a wonderful through ball before coolly rounding the impressive figure of Dino Zoff to score with consummate ease. For once, England played well, with wide man Peter Barnes showing some great skill down the left. This left Italy, who were sitting proudly on top of the group, needing a single-goal win against Luxembourg to clinch their place in the finals in Argentina. They comfortably won by 3-0 and, as a result, England, for the second time running, failed to qualify for the World Cup.

1978 World Cup Fact File

- Countries taking part: 16 (divided into four groups of 4).
- Final: Argentina 3, The Netherlands 1 (after extra time).
- Final venue: Estadio Monumental, Buenos Aires (attendance: 76,985).
- Leading scorer: Mario Kempes (Argentina), 6 goals.
- Rob Rensenbrink (The Netherlands) equalled Eusébio's 1966 record by scoring four penalties in World Cup finals matches.

Third Time Lucky for England?

Ron Greenwood's first two games as full-time manager were against two of the world's best teams: West Germany on 22 February 1978, and Brazil three months later. England lost to the Germans 2-1 in Munich but held Brazil to a 1-1 draw at Wembley. There followed three wins in the Home International Championship: 3-1 against Wales and 1-0 against both Northern Ireland and Scotland. Tony Woodcock was introduced against the Irish but left out against the Scots. Eight goals were then scored in the next two matches. Hungary were defeated 4-1 in a friendly, and Denmark got slaughtered 4-0 in a European Championship decider. A month later, England shared the points (1-1) with the Republic of Ireland in a second EC qualifier in Dublin.

England continued their run with a 1-0 friendly win over Czechoslovakia, and followed up with successive victories over Northern Ireland: 4-0 in another EC qualifier and 2-0 in the Home International Championship. Wales forced a 0-0 draw and Scotland were defeated 3-1, both at Wembley. The first 100,000 crowd for four years watched the latter.

England took care of Bulgaria 3-0 in their next EC qualifier in Sofia and, after a 0-0 friendly draw with Sweden in Stockholm, the team's fourteen-match unbeaten run was ended when Austria won a seven-goal thriller by 4-3 in Vienna in June 1979.

First Black Player

During that impressive run, which spanned fourteen months, Greenwood gave full international debuts to only four players: the aforementioned Woodcock, full-backs Kenny Sansom and Viv Anderson – who became the first black player to appear in a full international match for England – and Laurie Cunningham, the West Bromwich Albion utility forward. Cunningham, in fact, was the first black player to wear an England shirt in a senior game, lining up against Scotland in an under-21 international at Bramall Lane in 1977. Anderson would go on to win thirty caps while Sansom collected eighty-six, a record for an England left-back until Ashley Cole surpassed it a few years ago.

Greenwood stuck with several of the old guard, but he did chop and change his team quite a bit, trying different formations, different styles and generally doing a good job – so most of the fans thought anyway.

Four more EC qualifiers were next on the agenda, and England won them all: Denmark 1-0, Northern Ireland 5-1 (in Belfast), Bulgaria 2-0, and the Republic of Ireland 2-0, inspired by future 'Captain Marvel' Bryan Robson, who made his senior debut. With these victories, England readily booked their place in the 1980 finals, which would be staged in Italy in June/July. Before that, however, and prior to the Home Internationals in May, England registered a fine 2-0 win over Spain in Barcelona. They beat Argentina 3-1 at Wembley, this being only the third meeting between the countries since the 1966 World Cup.

In the then traditional Home International Championship, England didn't play at all well. They suffered their heaviest defeat at the hands of Wales since 1882, losing 4-1 at

Wrexham. This was also England's biggest defeat (in terms of goal difference) since May 1964 when they lost 5-1 to Brazil in Rio, 160 matches ago. Held 1-1 by Northern Ireland in front of just 33,676 fans – the lowest Wembley crowd since November 1962 when 27,498 saw Wales beaten 4-0 – England managed to get to grips with things in their final game, defeating the Scotland 2-0 at Hampden Park.

Ahead of the European Championships, Greenwood took his players to Australia for a warm-up friendly in Sydney. They beat the Aussies (just) by 2-1 when fourteen players were used – all hoping to gain a place in the squad for Italy! Two of those who appeared Down Under were Alan Sunderland (Arsenal) and substitute Peter Ward (Brighton), for whom it would be their only senior outing for England. The Ipswich Town defensive duo of Terry Butcher and Russell Osman, along with David Armstrong (Middlesbrough), also made their debuts against the Aussies.

Placed in Group B, England unfortunately failed to deliver. They were held 1-1 by Belgium in Turin, lost to the host nation 1-0 at the same venue, and beat Spain 2-1 in Naples. Three points, however, were simply not enough; England finished third in the group and were therefore eliminated. It was a disappointing show all round. It was not a great tournament, Greenwood wasn't happy; neither were the travelling supporters, again. So, back at base, Greenwood and his coaching staff – with his players – did some serious talking before knuckling down to three vital World Cup qualifying matches over a three-month period: September–November 1980.

And England started off well, beating Norway 4-0 in their first game when midfielders Graham Rix and Eric Gates made their senior debuts and Terry McDermott scored twice. However, a 2-1 defeat by Romania in Bucharest put a spanner in the works before Switzerland were eclipsed 2-1 at Wembley. A friendly defeat by Spain in March 1981 was followed by a 0-0 draw with Romania in the home World Cup qualifier. Before the next batch of qualifiers, England lost 1-0 in a home to Brazil, drew 0-0 and lost 1-0 to Scotland in the Home Internationals. Goals, all of a sudden, were seemingly hard to come by – only four in seven games. This was not good. Greenwood tried to inject some life into his attack by selecting the Aston Villa striker Peter Withe, but his inclusion wasn't a success.

It must be said that England went into their four-match World Cup programme on a low and their poor form continued in Basel when Switzerland won 2-1. A victory over Hungary (3-1) eased the pain somewhat, but another loss, this time against Norway in Oslo (2-1), didn't go down too well with the press.

Thankfully, with almost 92,000 expectant fans inside Wembley, England – needing just a point as it transpired – performed with passion and willpower to beat Hungary in the return fixture. They booked their place in Spain and, of course, reached the World Cup finals for the first time in twelve years. Paul Mariner's scrappy goal separated the teams, although England were far superior on the night against a country that had already qualified.

14

The 1982 World Cup Qualifying Matches

10 September 1980	England 4 Norway 0
Wembley	Attendance 48,200

England Team: P. Shilton (Nottingham Forest), V. Anderson (Nottingham Forest), K. Sansom (Arsenal), T. McDermott, D. Watson (Southampton), P. Thompson, B. Robson (West Bromwich Albion), G. Rix (Arsenal), A. Woodcock (FC Cologne), P. Mariner, E. Gates (Ipswich Town).

Without five key players – Kevin Keegan, Ray Wilkins, Trevor Brooking, Steve Coppell and Trevor Francis – a new-look England midfield/attack took a long time to get into its stride in this opening qualifying encounter for the 1982 World Cup finals. After long, laborious periods of inactivity, England eventually scored four goals. Terry McDermott's strike on thirty-five minutes calmed the nerves somewhat, but it wasn't until the last third of the game that Norway caved in completely. Tony Woodcock (sixty-six minutes), McDermott's penalty (on seventy-five) and a superb individual effort by Paul Mariner (eighty-five) completed the scoring. Bryan Robson was the stand-out player, again performing excellently in midfield, while both Eric Gates and Graham Rix made satisfactory debuts alongside the West Brom workhorse.

15 October 1980	Romania 2 England 1
Bucharest	Attendance 74,886

England Team: P. Shilton, P. Neal, K. Sansom, T. McDermott, D. Watson, P. Thompson, B. Robson, G. Rix, A. Woodcock (FC Cologne), G. Birtles (Nottingham Forest), E. Gates. Substitutes: L. Cunningham (West Bromwich Albion) for Birtles, S. Coppell for Gates.

A controversial seventy-fifth-minute penalty decided this tight encounter and, as a result, England's hopes of qualifying for the 1982 World Cup finals were delivered a severe blow. Left-back Kenny Sansom angrily protested his innocence after his tackle on Anghel Iordănescu had been ruled a foul. The Romanian picked himself and scored from the spot. Afterwards, a distraught Sansom said, 'No way was that a penalty.' At the time of the decision, England were well on top after Tony Woodcock had netted an equaliser in the sixty-fourth minute, following a neat exchange of passes with Garry Birtles. Romania had the better of a scrappy first half and took the lead on thirty-five minutes through Marcel Răducanu. It was a hard-fought game but, in all honesty, England should never have lost.

19 November 1980   England 2 Switzerland 1
Wembley   Attendance 69,929

England Team: P. Shilton, P. Neal, K. Sansom, B. Robson, D. Watson, M. Mills, S. Coppell, T. McDermott, P. Mariner, T. Brooking, A. Woodcock. Substitute: G. Rix for Brooking.
England were comfortably in control at half-time, leading 2-0 after an own-goal by Markus Tanner, who deflected home Tony Woodcock's crisp shot on twenty minutes, and Paul Mariner on the half-hour. In fact, there had been no hint whatsoever that the pendulum would swing Switzerland's way during the second period. However, Trevor Brooking, outstanding throughout the first forty-five minutes, started to feel the effects of an old injury and, when his input dropped, England began to struggle in midfield. From the seventieth minute onwards, the lively Swiss team took over, pressed hard and reduced the deficit when Hans-Jörg Pfister drilled a stunning shot past Peter Shilton with a quarter of an hour remaining. Thankfully, England clung on, just, to record a much-needed victory and so keep alive their World Cup hopes.

30 May 1981   Switzerland 2 England 1
Basel   Attendance 39,859

England Team: R. Clemence, M. Mills, K. Sansom, R. Wilkins, D. Watson, R. Osman (Ipswich Town), S. Coppell, B. Robson, K. Keegan, P. Mariner, T. Francis. Substitutes: P. Barnes for Watson, T. McDermott for Francis.
For nearly half an hour England completely outplayed the Swiss, but then it all went wrong. The home team broke away and, on twenty-eight minutes, Alfred Scheiwiler gave them the lead. Two minutes later, Claudio Sulser struck to make it 2-0. Manager Ron Greenwood attempted to salvage the operation by sending on Terry McDermott (for Trevor Francis) and pushing Kevin Keegan up front. And it was McDermott who brought the scores closer with a fine shot from Steve Coppell's pass in the fifty-fifth minute. In fact, this was England's first goal in almost eight hours of football. As much as they tried, an equaliser was not forthcoming. This meant that victory was imperative in their next qualifying game against Hungary in Budapest, or England could possibly say goodbye to their World Cup dreams for 1982. Unfortunately, to add to England's despair, the hooligan element among their supporters caused more sickening problems on the terraces inside the St Jakob Park stadium in Basel, and after the game there were whispers that the powers-that-be at FIFA were considering a ban on England fans travelling abroad. Thankfully, this never materialised.

6 June 1981   Hungary 1 England 3
Budapest   Attendance 67,905

*England Team: R. Clemence, P. Neal, M. Mills, P. Thompson, D. Watson, B. Robson,
S. Coppell, T. McDermott, P. Mariner, T. Brooking, K. Keegan. Substitutes: R. Wilkins for
Brooking.*
England dug deep, very deep, in Budapest, to come up with one of their finest performances
under manager Ron Greenwood. Against all the odds, they beat Hungary, and beat them
well, to breathe life back into their World Cup campaign. A fully fit Trevor Brooking
gave England an eighteenth-minute lead, which was cancelled out sixty seconds before
half-time when Imre Garaba scored from close range. In the second half, though, England
produced some quality football, turning on the pressure to secure the points in style.

   In the fifty-ninth minute, Brooking thumped home his second goal with a rising shot,
so powerful and strong that the ball lodged between the net and the stanchion. And the
industrious Kevin Keegan then sewed up victory with a penalty in the seventy-second
minute after he had been brought down by a desperate, clumsy tackle. There is no
doubt that Brooking and Keegan, accompanied by the powerful Bryan Robson, were all
outstanding, while goalkeeper Ray Clemence also played exceptionally well, pulling off
three superb saves.

9 September 1981   Norway 2 England 1
Oslo   Attendance 28,446

*England Team: R. Clemence, P. Neal, M. Mills, P. Thompson, R. Osman, B. Robson,
K. Keegan, T. McDermott, P. Mariner, T. Francis, G. Hoddle (Tottenham Hotspur).
Substitutes: P. Withe (Aston Villa) for Mariner, P. Barnes (Leeds United) for Hoddle.*
After hitting the heights in Hungary three months earlier, England slumped to an all-time
low when they succumbed to a team of part-timers in Oslo. It was a wretched performance
and one that upset a lot of travelling supporters and, of course, the millions watching on
television. Bryan Robson scored as early as the fifteenth minute, and a comfortable victory
looked on the cards – that is, until the Norwegians started to play. In the thirty-fourth
minute they drew level through Roger Albertsen and, six minutes later, Halvar Thorensen
took advantage of some schoolboy-like dithering from England defenders Phil Thompson
and Russell Osman, to force the ball home for what proved to be the match-winning goal.

   This humiliating defeat ranked in the same category as England's 1-0 loss against the
USA in the 1950 World Cup finals, and straightaway the knives, fully sharpened, were
out for Ron Greenwood. This qualifying game lives on through the delirious words of
Norwegian commentator Bjørge Lillelien, who switched to English as the final whistle
sounded, telling the world, 'Lord Nelson! Lord Beaverbrook! Sir Winston Churchill! Sir
Anthony Eden! Clement Atlee! Henry Cooper! Lady Diana! Maggie Thatcher – can you
hear me, Maggie Thatcher? Your boys took one hell of a beating. Your boys took one hell
of a beating!'

18 November 1981　　　　　　　　　　　　　　　England 1 Hungary 0
Wembley　　　　　　　　　　　　　　　　　　Attendance 91,797

England Team: P. Shilton, P. Neal, M. Mills, P. Thompson, A. Martin (West Ham United), D. Watson, B. Robson, S. Coppell, K. Keegan, P. Mariner, T. Brooking. Substitute: A. Morley (Aston Villa) for Coppell.

It had been confirmed earlier that England required only a point from their return fixture with Hungary to reach the 1982 World Cup finals. In effect, they went one better by registering a nervously constructed, hard-earned 1-0 victory over the Group 4 winners. The door to Spain had reopened when Romania made a mess of their last qualifying game (drawing 0-0 in Switzerland), meaning that England only needed to avoid defeat against the Magyars to book their tickets. And it was Paul Mariner who netted the all-important goal in the sixteenth minute, scrambling the ball over the line after a miscued shot from Trevor Brooking confused the Hungarian defenders. Debutant winger Tony Morley, from Aston Villa, almost added a second after the break but his shot was brilliantly saved by 'keeper Ferenc Mészáros. One reporter wrote after the game, 'The death of English football was greatly exaggerated.'

Looking Ahead to Sunny Spain

After all the hype, tension and uncertainty of the World Cup qualifiers, it was back to the bread and butter of Home International football for England, with three friendlies thrown in for good measure before the end of the 1981/82 season.

England won their three games against the home nations. They beat Northern Ireland 4-0 when the Brighton defender Steve Foster and West Bromwich Albion's in-form striker Cyrille Regis made their debuts. Wales were beaten by a single Trevor Francis goal and Scotland were also beaten 1-0, in the 100th meeting between the two countries – the gate receipts topped £500,000, compared with the £103 that was taken at the first meeting back in 1872. There were also friendly wins over The Netherlands (2-0) and Finland (4-1), and a draw with Iceland (1-1) – substitute Paul Goddard of West Ham scoring in Reykjavik on his first and only appearance at senior level. England were drawn in Group 4 of the World Cup, along with France, Czechoslovakia and Kuwait.

Manager Ron Greenwood named this squad for sunny Spain:

Goalkeepers: Ray Clemence (Tottenham Hotspur), Joe Corrigan (Manchester City), Peter Shilton (Nottingham Forest). Full-backs: Viv Anderson (Nottingham Forest), Mick Mills (Ipswich Town), Phil Neal (Liverpool), Kenny Sansom (Arsenal). Defenders: Terry Butcher (Ipswich Town), Steve Foster (Brighton & Hove Albion), Phil Thompson (Liverpool). Midfielders: Trevor Brooking (West Ham United), Glenn Hoddle (Tottenham Hotspur), Terry McDermott (Liverpool), Graham Rix (Arsenal), Bryan Robson (Manchester United), Ray Wilkins (Manchester United). Forwards: Steve Coppell (Manchester United), Trevor Francis (Manchester City), Kevin Keegan (Southampton), Paul Mariner (Ipswich Town), Peter Withe (Aston Villa), Tony Woodcock (Arsenal).

NB: Four players named in reserve were defender Dave Watson (Stoke City), winger Tony Morley (Aston Villa), midfielder Alan Devonshire (West Ham United) and striker Cyrille Regis (West Bromwich Albion).

Based in Bilbao in Northern Spain, England were strong favourites, in some quarters, to win their group. With Mick Mills skippering the side, they began superbly, beating France 3-1 in their opening match before recording a solid 2-0 win over Czechoslovakia, followed by a narrow 1-0 victory over Kuwait. They topped Group 4 with maximum points, and they didn't even concede a goal. In the second phase (Group B), England had to play Spain and West Germany. It wasn't going to be easy, and so it proved.

England could only manage two goalless draws and therefore, despite not losing a single game and Peter Shilton keeping a clean sheet for more than 450 minutes, they were eliminated with the competition still to gain momentum.

15

The 1982 World Cup in Spain

16 June 1982   England 3 France 1
Bilbao   Attendance 44,172

England Team: P. Shilton, M. Mills, K. Sansom, P. Thompson, T. Butcher, B. Robson, S. Coppell, R. Wilkins, P. Mariner, T. Francis, G. Rix. Substitute: P. Neal for Sansom.
As mentioned earlier, England made a dream start in Spain when Bryan Robson scored what was, at the time, the fastest goal in World Cup finals history. He found the net with a vicious left-footer after just twenty-seven seconds, following Terry Butcher's headed flick from Steve Coppell's throw-in from the right. The French recovered well from that early setback to equalise in the twenty-fifth minute through Gérard Soler, but England, despite the scorching heat, and without the injured Kevin Keegan, sidelined with a back injury, regrouped and came again after the interval. Graham Rix (replacing the injured Trevor Brooking) was given a free role in midfield, and it turned out to be a tactical masterstroke by manager Ron Greenwood. Robson burst forward to head his second goal in the sixty-seventh minute from Trevor Francis' right-wing cross. Paul Mariner underlined England's supremacy with a third in the eighty-third minute, following a mix-up in the French defence. This was the fifth successive international in which Mariner had scored. Could it last?

20 June 1982   Czechoslovakia 0 England 2
Bilbao   Attendance 41,123

England Team: P. Shilton, M. Mills, K. Sansom, P. Thompson, T. Butcher, B. Robson, S. Coppell, R. Wilkins, P. Mariner, T. Francis, G. Rix. Substitute: G. Hoddle for Robson.
Two fortunate goals in quick succession midway through the second half booked England a place in the second phase. After a fairly even contest, Trevor Francis broke the deadlock in the sixty-second minute, smashing the ball home after Czech goalkeeper Stanislav Semen had dropped a Ray Wilkins corner. Four minutes later, Jozef Barmoš diverted the ball into his own net as Francis closed in on Mariner's ground pass. There was, however,

another blow for England when another key player, Bryan Robson, joined Keegan and Brooking on the injury list. Future Aston Villa manager Jozef Vengloš was in charge of the Czech team.

25 June 1982   England 1 Kuwait 0
Bilbao   Attendance 39,687

England Team: P. Shilton, P. Neal, M. Mills, R. Wilkins, P. Thompson, S. Foster (Brighton & Hove Albion), S. Coppell, G. Hoddle, P. Mariner, T. Francis, G. Rix.
A gem of a goal by Trevor Francis was one of very few highlights as England battled every inch of the way to record their third win of the finals. Plucky Kuwait battled bravely throughout and displayed some eye-catching skill, but thankfully they lacked firepower. Francis' exquisite goal came in the twenty-seventh minute when Paul Mariner back-heeled a long clearance by Peter Shilton into his path. The striker then set off a 30-yard run that ended with him sliding the ball low past the oncoming Kuwait 'keeper Ahmed Al-Tarabulsi. After the game, it was announced that Kevin Keegan had flown over to Germany to consult a back specialist.

29 June 1982   England 0 West Germany 0
Madrid   Attendance 74,776

England Team: P. Shilton, M. Mills, K. Sansom, R. Wilkins, P. Thompson, T. Butcher, S. Coppell, B. Robson, P. Mariner, T. Francis, G. Rix. Substitute: A. Woodcock for Francis.
Over the years there have been some classic encounters between England and Germany, but this was not one of them. The German coach elected to play a 'suffocating game', with extra men behind the ball and, as a result, the match deteriorated into a crowded midfield muddle. Bryan Robson came closest to scoring for England with a first-half header, which Harald Schumacher tipped over the bar at full stretch. A half-fit Karl-Heinz Rummenigge threatened occasionally for Germany and, indeed, he rattled Peter Shilton's crossbar with a 25-yard piledriver in the closing minutes. After this 'best forgotten' game, England needed to beat the hosts, Spain, by two goals in their final game to reach the semi-finals. It was a tall order.

5 July 1982   England 0 Spain 0
Madrid   Attendance 74,919

England Team: P. Shilton, M. Mills, K. Sansom, R. Wilkins, P. Thompson, T. Butcher, S. Coppell, B. Robson, P. Mariner, T. Francis, A. Woodcock, G. Rix. Substitute: K. Keegan for Woodcock.
Ron Greenwood's final game as England's manager ended in a frustrating draw, resulting in a sad exit from the World Cup. Again, he chose to leave his best two players – Trevor

Brooking and Kevin Keegan – on the substitute's bench, and that was a big mistake. Despite producing some enterprising football and creating several chances, England unfortunately failed to get the ball past agile goalkeeper Luis Arconada. Substitute Keegan, introduced with twenty-seven minutes remaining, missed the best chance of the game, sending a late header wide. Brooking, who entered the fray at the same time as Keegan, also came close when his rasping shot was saved by Arconada. There is no doubt that England played well, but it was not enough. Later, Keegan wrote in his autobiography, 'Leaving myself and Trevor on the bench was Ron Greenwood's biggest mistake. We were his best two players, we were very influential.'

1982 World Cup Fact File

- Countries taking part: 24 (divided in six groups of 4).
- Final: Italy 3, West Germany 1.
- Final venue: Estadio Santiago Bernabéu, Madrid (attendance 89,774).
- Leading scorer: Paolo Rossi (Italy), 6 goals.
- László Kiss (Hungary) scored a seven-minute hat-trick in his country's 10-1 group win over El Salvador – the first double-figure victory in World Cup finals.
- Northern Ireland forward Norman Whiteside, aged 17 years, 41 days, became the youngest player in World Cup history (*v.* Yugoslavia on 17 June).
- Italian Dino Zoff was forty years of age when he kept goal in the final.
- Another Italian, Giampiero Marini, earned the quickest booking in World Cup finals – shown the yellow card after just fifty-six seconds *v.* Poland.

The Robson Era

Greenwood's reign as England manager covered fifty-five matches, of which thirty-three resulted in victories, twelve draws and ten defeats. Enter former international player Bobby Robson, who won twenty caps for his country between 1957 and 1962. The FA had, in fact, already named him as the next boss during the World Cup. Reporter Brian Glanville's verdict on Greenwood's managerial exploits was 'simply not bright or good enough', and he wasn't too pleased either by the 'careful negativity' displayed by senior coach Don Howe.

There's no doubt that Bobby Robson's achievements as boss of Ipswich Town got him the England job, although he did turn down an offer of a ten-year contract extension and increased salary from the Portman Road club's director Patrick Cobbold. On 7 July 1982, just forty-eight hours after England had been knocked out of the World Cup, he took charge, keeping his former West Bromwich Albion teammate Don Howe as his chief coach.

For his first game in charge, Robson caused controversy by dropping Kevin Keegan (sixty-three caps to his credit) for the European Championship qualifier against Denmark in Copenhagen. The game ended 2-2. This was followed by a 2-1 friendly defeat by West Germany at Wembley before important victories were registered in two more EC qualifiers: firstly 2-0 against Greece, followed by a 9-0 drubbing of Luxembourg when England's first black goalscorer, Luther Blissett, starting as a full international for the first time, netted a hat-trick. Unfortunately, there were only 35,000 fans there to see England record their biggest-ever win at Wembley.

Between late February and mid-November 1983, England played eleven matches. In the Home International Championships they beat Wales 2-1, Scotland 2-0 and drew with Northern Ireland 0-0. They also drew 0-0 with Greece, defeated Hungary twice (2-0 at home and 3-0 away), and Luxembourg 4-0, but lost 1-0 to Denmark in European Championship qualifiers (Robson's only loss in twenty-eight qualifiers, which ultimately led to England failing to make for the finals). They met Australia three times Down Under on a summer tour, winning 1-0 in Brisbane and drawing in Sydney 0-0 and Melbourne 1-1.

In 1983, Robson handed debuts to twelve players including John Barnes, who would go on to win a total of seventy-nine full caps over the next thirteen years. Following that defeat by the Danes, he actually offered to resign in favour of Brian Clough. The resignation was rejected by the FA chairman, Bert Millichip, primarily because neither he nor the rest of the FA committee liked Clough. Robson remained in office and went on to lead the England into the 1986 World Cup finals in Mexico.

By coincidence, England fulfilled another eleven fixtures in 1984. Three came in the Home International Championship, when they recorded a 1-0 win over Northern Ireland, lost 1-0 to Wales and drew 1-1 with Scotland. The goals flew in thick and fast in the next two World Cup qualifiers against Finland and Turkey. The hapless Finns were thrashed 5-0, with left-back Kenny Sansom scoring his only senior goal for his country in what would be eighty-six appearances, while the Turks were slaughtered 8-0 in Istanbul when Bryan Robson bagged a hat-trick.

The other six matches were all friendlies. Three ended in 2-0 defeats against France in Paris; the USSR at Wembley, and Uruguay in Montevideo. Brazil and East Germany were beaten 2-0 and 1-0 in Rio and at Wembley respectively, while Chile forced a 0-0 draw in Santiago. Robson shuffled his team around continuously, trying to get the right ingredients into his cake, and among the ten new faces to appear at senior level were centre-half Mark Wright and striker Gary Lineker, who won his first cap against Scotland at Hampden Park at the end of May. Of the twelve internationals that were completed the following year, when Robson once again rang the changes, six were World Cup qualifiers.

England beat Northern Ireland 1-0 in Belfast, and Turkey in the return fixture 5-0, but drew twice with Romania 0-0 (away) and 1-1 (home), and also shared the spoils with Finland 1-1 (in Helsinki) and Northern Ireland 0-0 (at Wembley). Although beaten 1-0 by Scotland in the Rous Cup, England defeated the Republic of Ireland 2-1 in a friendly and whipped the USA 5-0 in Los Angeles. On their Mexican tour they lost 2-1 to Italy, and went down 1-0 to the host nation, yet surprised many by getting the better of West Germany 3-0 – all three games were staged in Mexico City.

Nine new faces appeared in the team during this period, Chris Waddle and Peter Reid being two of them, while Peter Shilton became England's most capped goalkeeper when he played in his seventy-fourth international against Turkey in mid-October.

16

The 1986 World Cup Qualifying Matches

17 October 1984   England 5 Finland 0
Wembley   Attendance 47,234

England Team: P. Shilton, M. Duxbury (Manchester United), K. Sansom, S. Williams (Southampton), M. Wright (Southampton), T. Butcher, B. Robson, R. Wilkins (AC Milan), M. Hateley (AC Milan), A. Woodcock, J. Barnes (Watford). Substitutes: G. Stevens (Tottenham Hotspur) for Duxbury, T. Francis (Sampdoria) for Woodcock.

While the Finland players were warming up before the kick-off, the floodlights failed, leaving them in the dark … and it stayed that way for the visitors. England began their 1984 World Cup qualifying programme with a fairly comfortable and predictable win over a rather weak opposition. In fact, the final score could and should have been in double figures, so much were England on top. Mark Hateley was the star of the show with his old-fashioned style of centre-forward play. He powered his way through a rather moderate defence several times, had five attempts on goal and scored twice, in the twenty-ninth and fiftieth minutes. Tony Woodcock made it 2-0 four minutes before half-time and, as England eased up, Bryan Robson (seventy minutes) and Kenny Sansom (eighty-eight) added the last two goals. This was Sansom's only goal in eighty-six full internationals for his country. Gary Stevens (Tottenham) made his debut as a second-half substitute for Mike Duxbury.

14 November 1984   Turkey 0 England 8
Istanbul   Attendance 26,494

England Team: P. Shilton, V. Anderson, K. Sansom, S. Williams, M. Wright, T. Butcher, B. Robson, R. Wilkins, P. Withe, A. Woodcock, J. Barnes. Substitutes: G. Stevens for Williams, T. Francis for Withe.

This qualifying romp over Turkey saw Bryan Robson become the first England captain since Vivian Woodward in 1909 to score a hat-trick in a full international. England stormed to victory in style, recording their biggest overseas victory since the 10-0 walloping of hapless USA in May 1964. Robson opened the scoring in the thirteenth minute. Four minutes later, Tony Woodcock added a second and the same player made it 3-0 shortly before the interval. Winger John Barnes then fired in goals number four and five in the first eight minutes of the second half before Robson, with strong finishes in the fifty-ninth and sixty-first minutes, and Viv Anderson (eighty-six minutes) completed the rout.

27 February 1985	Northern Ireland 0 England 1
Belfast	Attendance 28,442

England Team: P. Shilton, V. Anderson, K. Sansom, R. Wilkins, A. Martin, T. Butcher, T. Steven (Everton), G. Stevens, M. Hateley, A. Woodcock, J. Barnes. Substitute: T. Francis for Woodcock.

England took a giant step to qualifying for the 1986 finals with a narrow but deserved 1-0 victory over the Irish at Windsor Park. Jimmy Quinn headed against Peter Shilton's crossbar, Terry Butcher cleared Norman Whiteside's shot off the line, and Gerry Armstrong closed for the hosts, as did England's duo of Tony Woodcock and Trevor Steven – who was winning his first cap. Mark Hateley settled the issue with a fine finish in the seventy-seventh minute. Butcher acted swiftly by booting Pat Jennings' clearance back downfield into the path of Hateley, who moved forward to finish with aplomb.

1 May 1985	Romania 0 England 0
Bucharest	Attendance 61,770

England Team: P. Shilton, V. Anderson, K. Sansom, T. Steven, M. Wright, T. Butcher, B. Robson, R. Wilkins, P. Mariner, T. Francis, J. Barnes. Substitute: C. Waddle (Newcastle United) for Barnes.

England retained top spot in their qualifying group with a well-earned draw in Bucharest's Stadionul. It might easily have been a victory had Bryan Robson's fine header from John Barnes' free-kick not hit a post, and Paul Mariner had time to steady himself before missing the best chance of the game. Goalkeeper Peter Shilton and full-backs Viv Anderson and Kenny Sansom (winning his fiftieth cap) were all outstanding in defence.

22 May 1985	Finland 1 England 1
Helsinki	Attendance 30,311

England Team: P. Shilton, V. Anderson, K. Sansom, T. Steven, T. Butcher, T. Fenwick (Queens Park Rangers), B. Robson, R. Wilkins, M. Hateley, T. Francis, J. Barnes. Substitute: C. Waddle for Steven.

Finland stunned England with an early goal, Jari Rantanen shooting past Peter Shilton in the fifth minute. And it could have been 2-0 soon afterwards but for Terry Butcher, who was well positioned to clear the ball off the line with Shilton beaten. England settled down, got to grips with the situation and drew level through Mark Hateley five minutes into the second half. The Finns fought bravely after that and thoroughly deserved to draw. At this juncture, England required just three points from three home group games to reach the finals, which had been switched from financially strapped Colombia to Mexico.

11 September 1985	England 1 Romania 1
Wembley	Attendance 59,486

England Team: P. Shilton, G. Stevens, K. Sansom, P. Reid (Everton), M. Wright, T. Fenwick, B. Robson, G. Hoddle, M. Hateley, G. Lineker (Everton), C. Waddle (Tottenham Hotspur). Substitutes: J. Barnes for Waddle, T. Woodcock for Lineker.

Romania's talented forward Gheorghe Hagi, who would go on to play for Real Madrid and Barcelona, hit England's woodwork twice before Glenn Hoddle settled the nerves with a wonderfully constructed twenty-fifth-minute goal after collecting a smart free-kick by Kenny Sansom. Romania hit back and equalised through Rodion Cămătaru on the hour after England's defenders seemed to stop, anticipating a whistle for handball. It was two points required now, with two home games remaining. Mexico here we come.

16 October 1985	England 5 Turkey 0
Wembley	Attendance 52,506

England Team: P. Shilton, G. Stevens, K. Sansom, G. Hoddle, M. Wright, T. Fenwick, B. Robson, R. Wilkins, M. Hateley, G. Lineker, C. Waddle. Substitutes: G. Steven for Robson, A. Woodcock for Hateley.

Earlier in the day, Northern Ireland beat Romania, and in doing so confirmed, barring freak results, that England would play in the 1986 World Cup finals in Mexico. To celebrate the occasion – for the first hour at least, until Bryan Robson went off injured – Bobby Robson's team played with bite and pace, and an enormous amount of confidence, completely outplaying the Turks, again. Chris Waddle (fifteen minutes), Gary Lineker (eighteen and forty-three) and Robson (thirty-five) scored in the first half, and Lineker duly completed his hat-trick nine minutes after the resumption. But manager Robson wasn't completely happy, saying, 'Knowing we had already qualified, took the edge off things and we lacked the killer instinct. We must learn to be positive at all times. We should have scored at least another four goals, but I suppose five was enough!' Peter Shilton gained his seventy-fourth cap in this game, becoming England's most decorated goalkeeper.

13 November 1985   England 0 Northern Ireland 0
Wembley   Attendance 70,524

England Team: P. Shilton, G. Stevens, K. Sansom, R. Wilkins, M. Wright, T. Fenwick, P. Bracewell (Everton), G. Lineker, K. Dixon (Chelsea), G. Hoddle, C. Waddle (Tottenham Hotspur).

Northern Ireland confirmed their place in the World Cup finals with a gutsy performance at Wembley. Goalkeeper Pat Jennings celebrated his world-record 113th cap with sensational saves to deny England's trio of Glenn Hoddle, Kerry Dixon and Gary Lineker, and received a standing ovation at the end of each half. England should have had a penalty when Alan McDonald handled during a goalmouth scramble, but a corner-kick was awarded instead.

Mixed Bag of Results

Moving into 1986, England began the year in style – sort of. They comfortably accounted for Egypt 4-0 in Cairo, beat Israel 2-1 in Tel Aviv, and won 1-0 in Tbilisi against the USSR. After gaining revenge over the Scots in the Rous Cup, winning 2-1 at Wembley, England visited Los Angeles where they played and beat Mexico 3-0. A week later, they defeated Canada 1-0 in Vancouver. Robson brought in three new players during this spate of 'friendlies' – forward Peter Beardsley, midfielder Steve Hodge and winger Danny Wallace – while the evergreen Peter Shilton, left-back Kenny Sansom and Ray Wilkins started every game, and Terry Butcher and Chris Waddle played in the last five. The manager was slowly but surely getting his squad assembled.

Robson formally drew up a shortlist of forty, from which he would subsequently choose his final twenty-two to board the plane for Mexico. And, as always, there were few surprises.

This was Robson's twenty-two-strong squad for the 1986 World Cup finals:

Goalkeepers: Gary Bailey (Manchester United), Peter Shilton (Southampton), Chris Woods (Norwich City). Full-backs: Viv Anderson (Arsenal), Gary Stevens (Everton), Kenny Sansom (Arsenal). Defenders: Terry Butcher (Ipswich Town), Terry Fenwick (Queens Park Rangers), Alvin Martin (West Ham United), Gary Stevens (Tottenham Hotspur). Midfielders: Glenn Hoddle (Tottenham Hotspur), Steve Hodge (Aston Villa), Peter Reid (Everton), Bryan Robson (Manchester United), Trevor Steven (Everton), Chris Waddle (Tottenham Hotspur), Ray Wilkins (AC Milan). Forwards: John Barnes (Watford), Peter Beardsley (Newcastle United), Kerry Dixon (Chelsea), Mark Hateley (AC Milan), Gary Lineker (Everton).

NB: In reserve for the trip to Mexico were defenders Dave Watson (Norwich City) and Mark Wright (Southampton), midfielder Gordon Cowans (Bari) and forward Trevor Francis (Sampdoria).

England 'Handed' No Favours in Mexico

Drawn with Morocco, Poland and Portugal in Group F, it is safe to say that England began the 1986 World Cup tournament poorly, losing 1-0 to the Portuguese, and drawing 0-0 with ten men against the Moroccans (after Ray Wilkins had been sent off) in their opening two matches. Captain Bryan Robson, clearly suffering with a recurring dislocated shoulder, was substituted in both games, meaning that manager Robson had to change his, and the team's, tactics for the final encounter with Poland, selecting Peter Beardsley ahead of Mark Hateley as a striking partner for Gary Lineker.

England performed very well against the Poles, winning 3-0, with Gary Lineker netting a hat-trick. Paraguay were next up in the last sixteen, and were duly dispatched, once again by 3-0. In the quarter-finals, England were defeated by Argentina with a brace from Diego Maradona – the infamous 'Hand of God' goal, followed five minutes later by the 'Goal of the Century'.

Disappointed to say the least, manager Robson was unimpressed by Maradona's claim of divine intervention, saying, 'It wasn't the hand of God. It was the hand of a rascal. God had nothing to do with it ... That day, Maradona was diminished in my eyes forever.'

17

The 1986 World Cup in Mexico

3 June 1986   England 0 Portugal 1
Monterey   Attendance 19,998

*England Team: P. Shilton, G. Stevens (Everton), K. Sansom, G. Hoddle, T. Fenwick,
T. Butcher, B. Robson, R. Wilkins, M. Hateley, G. Lineker, C. Waddle. Substitutes:
S. Hodge for Robson, P. Beardsley for Waddle.*
England started their World Cup campaign rather disappointingly. A rare defensive
blunder by the usually reliable Kenny Sansom let in Carlos Manuel for Portugal's winning
goal in the seventy-fifth minute. Gary Lineker played with a heavily strapped sprained
wrist, and Bryan Robson came off after seventy-nine minutes to protect an already
injured shoulder. England did not play well, yet they created enough chances to have won
comfortably. Grim-faced manager Bobby Robson wasn't a happy chap, saying, 'That was
a shocking start.'

6 June 1986   England 0 Morocco 0
Monterey   Attendance 20,198

*England Team: P. Shilton, G. Stevens (Everton), K. Sansom, G. Hoddle, T. Fenwick,
T. Butcher, B. Robson, R. Wilkins, M. Hateley, G. Lineker, C. Waddle. Substitutes:
S. Hodge for Robson, G. Stevens (Spurs) for Hateley.*
England's World Cup turned into a nightmare in the space of five minutes just before
half-time. First Bryan Robson was led from the field due to his shoulder injury, and then
acting captain Ray Wilkins was sent off for throwing the ball at the referee following
an offside decision. However, the ten men of England battled with enormous energy
and spirit throughout the second half and thoroughly deserved a point against decent
opposition. The temperature at pitch level soared to 39°C (100°F) and a handful of players
from both sides were reduced to walking pace. Terry Butcher was a colossus at the heart
of England's defence, stifling out the threat of the Moroccan front men, Mustafa Merry
and Abdelkarim Krimau.

11 June 1986   England 3 Poland 0
Mexico City   Attendance 22,690

England Team: P. Shilton, G. Stevens, K. Sansom, T. Steven, T. Fenwick, T. Butcher, G. Hoddle, P. Reid, S. Hodge, P. Beardsley, G. Lineker. Substitutions: C. Waddle for Beardsley, K. Dixon for Lineker.
This result was enough for England to finish runners-up in their group and so progress into the second round. Gary Lineker was star of the show, netting a first-half hat-trick. He opened his account on eight minutes (from Gary Stevens' pass). His second followed five minutes later with assistance from Steve Hodge, and he bagged his third in the thirty-sixth minute from Trevor Steven's delivery. Manager Bobby Robson was forced to make changes against the Poles, fielding a 4-2-4 formation. It worked wonderfully well with Hodge and Peter Reid running their socks off in centre-field. Robson said afterwards, 'This was a phenomenal performance, given the pressure my players were under. Phenomenal!'

18 June 1986   England 3 Paraguay 0
Mexico City   Attendance 98,728

England Team: P. Shilton, G. Stevens, K. Sansom, G. Hoddle, A. Martin, T. Butcher, T. Steven, P. Reid, S. Hodge, G. Lineker, P. Beardsley. Substitutions: G. Stevens (Spurs) for Reid, M. Hateley for Beardsley.
After surviving some early scares, when Peter Shilton had to pull off two smart saves, England took control with a first-half goal by Gary Lineker after thirty-two minutes. Chances were begging after that – at both ends of the field. Paraguayan 'keeper Roberto Fernández kept England at bay with some terrific interventions before Peter Beardsley made it 2-0 eleven minutes into the second-half – Lineker was off the pitch receiving treatment after being struck in the throat by an elbow! The Everton striker then returned to the action and, in the seventy-third minute, tucked away a third goal from a pass by his Goodison Park colleague Gary Stevens to clinch an excellent victory. Awaiting England in the quarter-finals were Argentina and a certain Diego Maradona.

22 June 1986   Argentina 2 England 1
Mexico City   Attendance 114,580

England Team: P. Shilton, G. Stevens, K. Sansom, G. Hoddle, T. Fenwick, T. Butcher, T. Steven, P. Reid, S. Hodge, G. Lineker, P. Beardsley. Substitutions: C. Waddle for Reid, J. Barnes for Steven.
Diego Maradona – with his 'Hand of God' – effectively knocked England out of the competition. The Estadio Azteca was packed for this encounter against Argentina, which is now listed as one of the most eventful games in World Cup history. Heavy with tension

because of the overspill of feeling between the two countries following the Falklands War, squads of military police brandishing white batons patrolled the ground. But apart from a few isolated incidents, the two sets of fans gave all their attention to the action out on the pitch, electric with action and atmosphere. All eyes were focused on Maradona, who at the time was in the best form of his life. He was the shortest player on the field at just 5 foot 4 inches, but the chunky, wide-shouldered forward paraded across the pitch with the assured air of a giant among pygmies. England's defenders shuddered when he was in possession of the ball, and he certainly saw plenty of that, demanding it all the time, from short or deep positions, from both flanks and even racing back to collect it from his goalkeeper.

England's Terry Fenwick, out of the retaliate-first school of football, chose to play a physical game in an attempt to keep Maradona quiet. It didn't work. He hardly got near him, and when he did he was either penalised or brushed aside – he was yellow-carded for one clumsy tackle. England may have fared better in a goalless first half if they had been more adventurous, but after the break it was a one-man show, with Maradona the star performer, in more ways than one.

In the fifty-first minute came one of the most controversial incidents ever seen in international football. Jorge Valdano's cross was deflected high into the air off Steve Hodge, just inside the England penalty area. Maradona went for it, along with Peter Shilton. The goalkeeper stretched out his arms ready to catch or even punch the ball clear. Maradona jumped alongside him and, to everyone's amazement, used his left hand to send the ball into the net. Shilton led a posse of protesting players in trying to persuade referee Ali Bin Nassur to disallow the goal for deliberate handball. The referee indicated that Maradona had 'headed' the ball and not used his hands, and continued pointing to the centre circle as Maradona danced in celebration. Four minutes later it was all over, really, when this time Maradona scored a quite stunning individual goal – one of the best ever seen in World Cup football. The stocky Argentinean ran with the ball close to his feet from the halfway line, tricking his way past Peter Beardsley, Peter Reid, Terry Butcher, Fenwick, Butcher (again), and finally goalkeeper Peter Shilton. In 2002, this brilliant effort was voted 'Goal of the Century' in a poll carried out by FIFA.com.

England, to their credit, battled on, and substitute John Barnes laid on a goal for the razor-sharp Gary Lineker with ten minutes remaining. But despite attacking in numbers, an equaliser never arrived and it was 'lucky' Argentina who went on to beat Belgium in the semi-final and then West Germany in the final. Lineker won the coveted 'Golden Boot' award for his six goals. Crestfallen England manager Bobby Robson said, 'There's no room in football for cheating. He [Maradona] should be thoroughly ashamed of himself.'

1986 World Cup Fact File

- Countries taking part: 24 (6 groups of 4).
- Final: Argentina 3, West Germany 2.
- Final venue: Estadio Azteca, Mexico City (attendance 114,580).
- Leading scorer: Gary Lineker (England), 6 goals.

• Uruguayan José Batista was sent off in his team's group game against Scotland after just fifty-six seconds – a World Cup record.

Let's Start Again

It was back to the drawing board after the disappointment of Mexico. England's first game of the 1986/87 season ended in a 2-1 defeat by Sweden in Stockholm. Thankfully, England recovered to register two important victories in the 1988 European Championship qualifiers at Wembley; beating Northern Ireland and Yugoslavia 3-0 and 2-0 respectively. After that they registered an excellent 4-2 friendly win over Spain in Madrid, where Gary Lineker netted all four goals and Tony Adams made his debut. He was the first player to appear for England at senior level who was born after the World Cup triumph in 1966. He was born on 10 October of that year. Two more European Championship qualifiers followed soon afterwards, but after easing past Northern Ireland 2-0, out-of-sorts England could only scramble a point from a disappointing 0-0 draw in İzmir against Turkey, the country they had put thirteen goals past in their two previous meetings. England rounded off the season by drawing their two Rous Cup matches: 1-1 with Brazil and 0-0 with Scotland.

A 3-1 defeat to West Germany in Düsseldorf started the 1987/88 campaign, before England recorded two more big European Championship qualifying victories: thrashing hapless Turkey 8-0 at Wembley (with another Lineker treble) and licking Yugoslavia 4-1 in Belgrade. Prior to competing in the 1988 Championships in Germany, England – who dropped only one point in qualifying by the way – played six non-competitive matches and remained unbeaten. They drew with Israel (0-0), The Netherlands (2-2 at Wembley), Hungary (0-0) and Colombia (0-0), and beat Scotland in the Rous Cup (1-0 at home) and Switzerland (1-0).

Over the next two years, after returning from the 1986 World Cup up to May 1988, manager Bobby Robson, always keen to introduce fresh blood, fielded seven new players: namely the aforementioned Adams, Tony Cottee, Mick Harford, Steve McMahon, Gary Pallister, Stuart Pearce and Neil Webb, who was the 1,000th player to gain a full England cap, debuting against West Germany in September 1987. Adams and Pearce would go on to amass almost 150 senior international appearances between them.

Everyone expected England to perform well in Germany, but alas they failed miserably, finishing bottom of Group 2 after succumbing to defeats against the Republic of Ireland 1-0, The Netherlands 3-1 (when Peter Shilton won his 100th cap) and the USSR, also 3-1. Robson was vilified by the British press, and after a draw in a friendly with Saudi Arabia, one newspaper demanded, 'In the name of Allah, go.' Once again, Robson submitted his resignation, and once again it was rejected by FA chairman Bert Millichip. And again, Brian Clough was cited (by some) as the main reason. Things had to change for the better, surely? And all credit to Robson and his players, they did.

With the next World Cup tournament scheduled to take place in Italy during June and July 1990, the England players – and manager Robson in particular – knew they had ample time in which to get things sorted out.

Twenty-Five Years of Underachieving

The nation had witnessed twenty-five years of underachieving – nothing had really happened in all fairness since the Jules Rimet Trophy was lifted by Bobby Moore in 1966. So, out came the drawing board. Tactical talks were interesting, many training sessions took place and there was a lot of debate, both internally and externally, regarding England's future. It transpired that Robson led England through the six-match qualification campaign for the 1990 World Cup without conceding a goal. They finished second in the group, a point behind the Swedes, after beating Albania 2-0 (away) and 5-0 (home), drawing twice with Sweden (0-0 both times) and defeating Poland 3-0 at Wembley and drawing 0-0 in Chorzów in the final game.

England somehow survived a Polish onslaught in the game in Chorzów to scrape the point, which effectively clinched their place in Italy as the best second-place finisher in the smaller groups. Indeed, only Peter Shilton's magnificence in goal and the crossbar's deflection of a last-minute 30-yard shot prevented elimination – had that late Poland effort been a few inches lower, then Robson's men would have been out.

The 'qualifying' team comprised (4-2-4 formation): Shilton, Gary Stevens, Butcher, Des Walker, Pearce, Waddle, Robson, Webb, Barnes, Beardsley, Lineker. David Rocastle, Paul Gascoigne (often used as a substitute) and McMahon also figured.

18

The 1990 World Cup Qualifying Matches

19 October 1988   England 0 Sweden 0
Wembley   Attendance 65,628

England Team: P. Shilton, G. Stevens, S. Pearce (Nottingham Forest), N. Webb (Nottingham Forest), T. Butcher, T. Adams (Arsenal), B. Robson, P. Beardsley, C. Waddle, G. Lineker, J. Barnes. Substitutes: D. Walker (Nottingham Forest) for Adams, T. Cottee (West Ham United) for Barnes.

England made a tame start to their 1990 World Cup qualifying campaign when they were held to a goalless draw by Sweden, whose main objective was not to lose. It is a fact that England's front men were well below par and, in truth, only Bryan Robson put in a real manful performance. Once again, the press carried various headlines as the snipers got cracking with regards to the manager being sacked. One said, 'In the name of God, go!' – using the famous historical quote made by Oliver Cromwell. There was no need to panic, and Robson stayed on.

8 March 1989   Albania 0 England 2
Tirana   Attendance 25,872

England Team: P. Shilton, G. Stevens, S. Pearce, D. Rocastle (Arsenal), T. Butcher, D. Walker, B. Robson, N. Webb, G. Lineker, C. Waddle, J. Barnes. Substitutes: A. Smith (Arsenal) for Lineker, P. Beardsley for Waddle.

In a game strangely lacking in atmosphere, a toothless Albanian team failed to fire a single worthwhile shot at Peter Shilton's goal as England eased to a comfortable 2-0 victory. John Barnes (sixteen minutes) and Bryan Robson (sixty-three) found the net. But it was Gary Lineker's seventh outing without a goal. 'Man of the Match' Robson, making his fiftieth appearance for his country, covered virtually every square foot of the pitch, once again.

26 April 1989   England 5 Albania 0
Wembley   Attendance 60,602

England Team: P. Shilton, G. Stevens, S. Pearce, N. Webb, T. Butcher, D. Walker, B. Robson, D. Rocastle, P. Beardsley, G. Lineker, C. Waddle. Substitute: P. Gascoigne (Newcastle United) for Rocastle.

Finally, Gary Lineker ended his goal famine, which had lasted nearly a year, when he headed past Albania's rookie seventeen-year-old 'keeper Blendi Nallbani as early as the fifth minute. After that it was all England, who won comfortably without breaking into a sweat. Impressive throughout, Lineker laid on two goals for Peter Beardsley in the twelfth and sixty-fourth minutes, Chris Waddle bagged number four in the seventy-second minute and Paul Gascoigne rounded things off with a fifth, two minutes from time.

3 June 1989   England 3 Poland 0
Wembley   Attendance 69,203

England Team: P. Shilton, G. Stevens, S. Pearce, N. Webb, T. Butcher, D. Walker, B. Robson, C. Waddle, P. Beardsley, G. Lineker, J. Barnes. Substitutes: D. Rocastle for Waddle, A. Smith for Beardsley.

Gary Lineker was back to his irresistible best against the Poles. He scored the first goal in the twenty-fourth minute and helped set up the other two for John Barnes and Neil Webb, who netted in the sixty-ninth and eighty-second minutes respectively. Peter Shilton equalled Bobby Moore's total haul of 108 caps in this, his 1,200th competitive game of football. The Poles were second-best throughout and could well have suffered a five- or even six-goal drubbing.

6 September 1989   Sweden 0 England 0
Stockholm   Attendance 38,588

England Team: P. Shilton, G. Stevens, S. Pearce, S. McMahon (Liverpool), T. Butcher, D. Walker, C. Waddle, N. Webb, P. Beardsley, G. Lineker, J. Barnes. Substitutes: D. Rocastle for Barnes, P. Gascoigne for Webb.

England played out their second successive 0-0 draw with Sweden to virtually clinch a place in the 1990 World Cup finals. Defender Terry Butcher, with his head swathed in bandages, was England's 'bloody hero'. The Ipswich star, who was introduced to League football by manager Bobby Robson, insisted on playing despite having ten stitches inserted in a deep gash on his forehead. Scorer Neil Webb limped off with an Achilles tendon injury, which would keep him out of international football for five months.

11 October 1989
Chorzów

Poland 0 England 0
Attendance 32,423

England Team: P. Shilton, G. Stevens, S. Pearce, S. McMahon, T. Butcher, D. Walker, B. Robson, D. Rocastle, P. Beardsley, G. Lineker, C. Waddle.

While the task was eased by the fact that only a point was required from their last group game to qualify for the finals in Italy, Bobby Robson's side were, nevertheless, playing away in the cauldron of Chorzów, where anything could happen. This time it was England's turn to remain steadfast in defence and withstand the pressures of Poland's skilful forward line. They did just that – just.

The two centre-backs, Des Walker and Terry Butcher, were quite superb, blocking, kicking, heading and tackling with confidence and resilience throughout the entire game. Peter Shilton, aged forty, was absolutely brilliant between the posts, stopping everything that came his way until the dying seconds; that is, until Ryszard Tarasiewicz's thumping 30-yard screamer slammed against his crossbar. Had that effort gone in there would have been no World Cup semi-final, no David Platt volley against Belgium, no semi-final tears for Gazza and, worst of all, England would have been out.

Peter Beardsley and Gary Lineker came closest to breaking the deadlock for a well-below-par England side. But in the end, it all worked out for the best. There were, for sure, plenty of short, chewed fingernails ready to be treated by manicurists the following day. And the annoying press reporters were off manager Bobby Robson's back, again.

Before heading for Germany, England featured in thirteen 'other' matches, losing only one of them: 2-1 at home to Uruguay. They beat Brazil 1-0, courtesy of a smartly taken goal by Lineker, defeated Czechoslovakia 4-2 at Wembley, accounted for Denmark twice, 1-0 (home) and 2-1 (away), and drew 1-1 with the Danes in Copenhagen. Greece were edged out 2-1 in Athens and Yugoslavia were eclipsed 2-1, with Bryan Robson scoring the fastest-ever England goal at Wembley, just thirty-eight seconds into the match. This win was also England's 100th at the Empire Stadium (1923–89). Competing in the Rous Cup, England drew 0-0 with Chile in front of the lowest-ever international crowd at Wembley – just 15,628 – and got the better of Scotland 2-0 when Steve Bull from Wolves scored on his debut. They also shared the spoils with Saudi Arabia, drawing 1-1 in the heat of Riyadh, claimed a deserved 0-0 draw with Italy and finished level at 1-1 with Tunisia, both at Wembley.

The Italian Job

One of six seeded teams in the 1990 World Cup, England were placed in the same group (F) as The Netherlands and the Republic of Ireland, with Egypt the fourth side. As in the 1986 finals, Robson was denied the service of his captain, Bryan Robson, who suffered an Achilles tendon injury that prevented him playing in the latter stages of the tournament. England topped their qualifying group, accumulating four points from their three games. However, their progress was not without controversy.

After a scrappy opening 1-1 draw with the Republic of Ireland, Robson changed his expected formation from a traditional 4-4-2 line-up for the second game against the Dutch to incorporate a sweeper. Some sources suggested that this was due to player revolt. Robson denied the claim, saying, 'I made the switch, not them. I had no intention of allowing van Basten and Gullit to rip holes in us.' England held the Dutch to a goalless draw (this was a good display), England went on to comfortably beat Egypt 4-0, and followed up with victories over Belgium 1-0 (with a late David Platt goal), and Cameroon 3-2 (courtesy of two Lineker spot-kicks) in the knock-out stages, to set up a semi-final clash with West Germany. England battled hard and long against their arch-rivals, but agonisingly lost the match on a penalty shoot-out, after drawing 1-1 in regulation time. Robson said afterwards that 'not a day goes by when [he] does not think about the semi-final and other choices [he] might have made'. He remains only the second coach after Alf Ramsey to take England to a World Cup semi-final, and the only coach to do so on foreign soil.

After all the anxious moments, paper-talk, many ifs and buts and general controversy, England, it seemed, were well prepared for the 1990 World Cup, confident of doing well, especially after learning they had been drawn in Group F, along with Egypt, The Netherlands and the Republic of Ireland. Robson had so many options to choose from regarding the players available for selection, having introduced a handful more possibilities during the 1989/90 season, including goalkeeper Dave Beasant, three full-backs, namely Lee Dixon, Australian-born Tony Dorigo and Nigel Winterburn, and two midfielders, Mike Phelan and David Platt.

This was manager Bobby Robson's final twenty-two-man squad for Italy in 1990:

Goalkeepers: Dave Beasant (Chelsea), Peter Shilton (Derby County), Chris Woods (Glasgow Rangers). Full-backs: Tony Dorigo (Chelsea), Paul Parker (Queens Park Rangers), Stuart Pearce (Nottingham Forest), Gary Stevens (Rangers). Defenders: Terry Butcher (Rangers), Des Walker (Nottingham Forest), Mark Wright (Derby County). Midfielders: Paul Gascoigne (Tottenham Hotspur), Steve Hodge (Nottingham Forest), David Platt (Aston Villa), Steve McMahon (Liverpool), Bryan Robson (Manchester United), Trevor Steven (Rangers), Chris Waddle (Marseille), Neil Webb (Manchester United). Forwards/ strikers: John Barnes (Liverpool), Peter Beardsley (Liverpool), Steve Bull (Wolverhampton Wanderers), Gary Lineker (Tottenham Hotspur).

NB: *Initially, Arsenal's David Seaman was chosen as the third goalkeeper, but he pulled out at the last minute, FIFA giving Robson permission to name a replacement. Three other Arsenal players were named as reserves: full-back Lee Dixon, central defender Tony Adams and wide midfielder David Rocastle.*

19

The 1990 World Cup in Italy

11 June 1990
Cagliari

England 1 Republic of Ireland 1
Attendance 35,238

England Team: P. Shilton, G. Stevens, S. Pearce, P. Gascoigne, T. Butcher, D. Walker, B. Robson, P. Beardsley, C. Waddle, G. Lineker, J. Barnes. Substitutes: S. Bull for Lineker, S. McMahon for Beardsley.

England could not have got off to a better start for their 1990 World Cup campaign when Gary Lineker chested down a Chris Waddle pass to force the ball home in the eighth minute. But it was the Irish who grew in stature and confidence, and their long ball tactics, ugly though they were, started to cause problems in England's defence. Thankfully, Peter Shilton, who equalled Pat Jennings' world record of 119 international appearances, pulled off some fine saves before conceding an equaliser in the seventy-second minute. Substitute Steve McMahon, with his first touch of the ball, lost possession to his fellow Merseyside midfielder from Everton, Kevin Sheedy, who instantly drove a left-foot shot into the net. No one could dispute that Ireland deserved to draw level, but generally the game itself was a poor advertisement for British football.

16 June 1990
Cagliari

England 0 The Netherlands 0
Attendance 35,267

England Team: P. Shilton, P. Parker, S. Pearce, M. Wright, T. Butcher, D. Walker, B. Robson, P. Gascoigne, C. Waddle, G. Lineker, J. Barnes. Substitutes: S. Bull for Waddle, D. Platt for Robson.

England played well, very well in fact, to earn a creditable draw with The Netherlands. Manager Bobby Robson used a sweeper system, with Mark Wright prominent at the back, and his team matched the Dutch kick for kick, pass for pass. They even had poor efforts on goal. Paul Gascoigne came of age as an international footballer, while substitute David Platt (replacing the injured Bryan Robson) also proved himself on the world stage. There was dramatic late action when Stuart Pearce – known affectionately as 'Psycho'

– drove a late free-kick past a defensive wall and into the net, but England's celebrations were cut short when the referee disallowed the goal, indicating that he had awarded an indirect free-kick. The ball could only have missed the fingertips of goalkeeper Hans van Breukelen by inches. England had come mighty close to claiming a richly deserved victory. In this game, Peter Shilton set a new world record for a goalkeeper by winning his 120th full cap.

21 June 1990   England 1 Egypt 0
Cagliari   Attendance 34,959

England Team: P. Shilton, P. Parker, S. Pearce, S. McMahon, M. Wright, D Walker, C. Waddle, P. Gasgoigne, S. Bull, G. Lineker, J. Barnes. Substitutes: D. Platt for Robson, P. Beardsley for Bull.

Mark Wright's first goal at senior level catapulted England into the second phase of the 1990 World Cup. Egypt came with just one ambition – to stop Bobby Robson's team from scoring. They almost succeeded, too, by trying to strangle the life out of the game with aggravating, time-wasting tactics and deliberate, petty fouls. In the end, they lost – and rightly so – when, in the fifty-ninth minute, England won a free-kick near the left touchline midway in the Egyptian half. Paul Gascoigne floated the ball deep into the packed penalty area. It hung tantalisingly in the air and, as goalkeeper Ahmed Shobeir came off his line to collect, he was beaten to it by Wright, whose glancing header found the net off defender Hesham Yakan. This was a big win.

26 June 1990   Belgium 0 England 1 (after extra time)
Bologna   Attendance 34,520

England Team: P. Shilton, P. Parker, S. Pearce, M. Wright, T. Butcher, D. Walker, S. McMahon, P. Gascoigne, C. Waddle, G. Lineker, J. Barnes. Substitutes: S. Bull for Barnes, D. Platt for McMahon.

David Platt stepped into this full-blooded filler as a substitute and, with a penalty shoot-out just seconds away, he drifted in, unnoticed, to volley home his first international goal and lift England into the quarter-finals. Although Paul Gascoigne, Steve McMahon and Chris Waddle all competed well, it was Belgium's Enzo Scifo who bossed the game in midfield, striking Peter Shilton's right post, as did Jan Ceulemans, while England's John Barnes had what looked like a good fortieth-minute goal disallowed for offside. Thankfully, Platt stole the show with just one minute of extra time remaining when he got on the end of Gazza's free-kick to smack the ball wide of the Belgian goalkeeper Michel Preud'homme, and so register what some say is 'one of the greatest goals ever scored for England'.

1 July 1990
Naples

Cameroon 2 England 3 (after extra time)
Attendance 55,205

England Team: P. Shilton, P. Parker, S. Pearce, M. Wright, T. Butcher, D. Walker, D. Platt, P. Gascoigne, C. Waddle, G. Lineker, J. Barnes. Substitutes: P. Beardsley for Barnes, T. Steven for Butcher.

Gary Lineker netted twice from the penalty spot, not only to put England into the World Cup semi-finals but to save them from one of the most humiliating defeats in their history. The harsh truth is that Cameroon played England off the park for eighty minutes. They were superb, but in the end fatigue set in and they were beaten in extra time. Cameroon's thirty-eight-year-old Roger Milla wrote himself into World Cup folklore. With his silken skills, he entered the fray at the start of the second half when his team were a goal down, David Platt having netted in the twenty-fifth minute. Milla had an immediate impact. He was bundled over by Paul Gascoigne inside the box in the sixty-first minute, allowing Emmanuel Kundé to equalise from the spot. Four minutes later he drew defenders towards him before threading an inch-perfect pass through to Eugéne Ekéké, who sprinted clear before flicking the ball nonchalantly over Peter Shilton's head to put Cameroon in front. England were stunned, but they recovered, pressed forward and, with six minutes of normal time remaining, Lineker spun inside the penalty area and was brought down by Thomas Libiih. Lineker netted from the spot and England were back in the game. Mark Wright suffered a nasty head wound (after clashing with Milla) but battled on through extra time, pulling off two last ditch tackles as Cameroon threatened to cause a major upset. In the fourteenth minute of extra time, Gascoigne fed an inch-perfect pass through to Lineker, who moved forward, only to be upended by goalkeeper Thomas N'Kono. Penalty. Up stepped Lineker. Goal! England had won a memorable match – just – and they were one step away from their second World Cup final.

4 July 1990
Turin

England 1 West Germany 1 (after extra time)
(3-4 on penalties)
Attendance 62,628

England Team: P. Shilton, P. Parker, S. Pearce, M. Wright, T. Butcher, D. Walker, D. Platt, P. Gascoigne, P. Beardsley, G. Lineker, C. Waddle. Substitute: T. Steven for Butcher.

There's no doubt whatsoever that England saved their best performance of the 1990 World Cup for this epic semi-final against arch-rivals West Germany. Unfortunately, they finished up with empty hands and broken hearts, as the Germans conquered them in a torturous penalty shoot-out. The 1-1 draw after extra time was a fair indication of what had been seen in this masterpiece of a match. There was just one irritating incident when Thomas Berthold made a meal of a tackle by Paul Gascoigne in extra time. This resulted in a second yellow card of the tournament for Gazza, who was close to tears, knowing that he would miss the final if England qualified.

England matched Germany kick for kick for almost an hour. Indeed, they might have scored in the very first minute when Gascoigne and Beardsley set up Gary Lineker, whose shot was saved by goalkeeper Bodo Illgner. Peter Shilton was desperately unlucky to concede the first goal in the fifty-ninth minute when Andreas Brehme's hopeful shot deflected off Paul Parker's heel and ballooned freakishly upwards before looping over the 'keeper's head and into the net.

After some good pressure, England deservedly equalised in the eightieth minute. For once, right-back Parker moved towards the halfway line, from where he chose to pump a hopeful ball upfield towards Gary Lineker, who looked heavily outnumbered inside the German penalty area. The ball was allowed to bounce and when Jürgen Kohler went for it, he actually helped it on to the England striker. One clever touch away from two defenders gave Lineker the half a yard he needed and, as Kohler desperately tried to recover, the Spurs striker smashed a left-footed drive back across Illgner and into the bottom corner.

Chris Waddle and Guido Buchwald both hit the woodwork in a thrilling finale before the nail-biting penalty shoot-out decided the contest. Lineker took the first spot-kick and scored. Brehme made it all square; Peter Beardsley put England 2-1 in front, only for Lothar Matthäus to level things up again at 2-2. David Platt stepped forward to edge England back in front at 3-2, only for Karl-Heinze Riedle to make it 3-3 with the game's sixth successful spot-kick. Sitting in the centre circle, Gascoigne's eyes began to fill with tears as Stuart Pearce fired his well-struck penalty at the legs of the diving Bodo Illgner. The first miss… When Olaf Thon netted Germany's fourth penalty, his team was now firmly in the driving seat at 4-3. Next to step up for England was a seemingly nervous Chris Waddle, who had never before taken a penalty in a competitive match. Unfortunately, he blazed his 12-yard kick high and wide. England were out, but they had played their part in a wonderful game that was a credit to the World Cup and to football in general. 'I was so proud of the lads – we didn't deserve to lose,' said England boss Bobby Robson.

7 July 1990	England 1 Italy 2
Bari	Attendance 51,426

England Team: P. Shilton, P. Parker, A. Dorigo, P. Parker, M. Wright, D. Walker, D. Platt, S. McMahon, P. Beardsley, G. Lineker, T. Steven. Substitutes: N. Webb for McMahon, C. Waddle for Steven.

This match, played to decide the third and fourth places in the 1990 World Cup, was to be Bobby Robson's last in charge of England, and it was also Peter Shilton's farewell appearance after 125 games between the posts. Unfortunately, the goalkeeper, who had been one of the most reliable players in the history of English football, made a calamitous mistake in the seventy-first minute. After collecting a long ball, he looked around for a colleague to give it to, but didn't spot the loitering Roberto Baggio alongside him. As he dropped the ball to the ground, the Italian nipped in, took possession, exchanged passes with Salvatore Schillaci and dribbled across the face of the goal for an easy tap-in. England drew level in the eighty-first minute when Australian-born left-back Tony Dorigo delivered the perfect cross for David Platt to net one of the best headed goals of the tournament. However, five minutes later, Paul Parker was judged to have fouled Schillaci inside the box. The Italian picked himself and duly drilled home his sixth goal of the finals to give his country a narrow victory and a bronze medal.

NB: *Peter Shilton's full international career spanned twenty years and he won eighty-three of his record 125 caps under manager Bobby Robson.*

1990 World Cup Fact File

- Countries taking part: 24 (divided into six groups of 4).
- Final: West Germany 1, Argentina 0.
- Final venue: Stadio Olimpico, Rome (attendance 73,603).
- Leading scorer: Salvatore Schillaci (Italy), 6 goals.
- Andreas Brehme's controversial eighty-sixth-minute penalty decided the final.

Robson Out, Taylor In, World Cup Woe

The former Lincoln City, Watford and Aston Villa manager Graham Taylor was the man the FA chose to take over as England's new boss, and outgoing chief Bobby Robson said, 'I wish him all the luck in the world, and for Graham's sake, I just hope the press reporters are kinder to him than they were to me.' Robson had been in charge for almost eight years, during which time England had played ninety-five matches, of which forty-seven had been won, thirty drawn and only eighteen lost.

When Taylor was appointed, critics in the media complained that he had never won a major trophy – although he had guided teams to second place in the League twice and an FA Cup final once. It was also pointed out Taylor had never himself played in the top flight or indeed at international level, and that gaining the respect of the players might be somewhat difficult. His critics also noted that although he had recently ditched the long-ball game when in charge of Aston Villa, there were still tactical worries about his intentions, given that English clubs were looking to dispense with using the traditional 'route one' policy in favour of a more 'picturesque route to goal'. Despite the unease at his appointment, England lost just once in Taylor's first twenty-three matches, going down 1-0 to Germany at Wembley in September 1991. In friendlies, they twice beat Hungary 1-0, accounted for Cameroon and France both 2-0, defeated Finland 2-1 in Helsinki, registered victories over Australia 1-0, New Zealand 1-0 and 4-0, and Malaysia 4-2 in tour matches, won 3-1 against the USSR and a drew 2-2 with Argentina in England Challenge Cup encounters, while also sharing the spoils with Brazil 1-1, Czechoslovakia 2-2 and the Commonwealth Independent States (CIS) 2-2.

However, England struggled to qualify for Euro '92. In a group containing Turkey, the Republic of Ireland and Poland, Taylor's men were held to 1-1 twice by the Irish and managed narrow 1-0 home and away wins over Turkey. And it was only a last-ditch goal from Gary Lineker against Poland that saw England qualify at the expense of the Irish in the final group game in Poznań, clinching a place in the finals in Sweden.

The number of players that Taylor was using in the run up to the championship was also questioned. The press and public viewed this as evidence that Taylor did not know his best team. He used fifty-nine players in total as he struggled to find a 'new spine' after the retirement of the legendary and long-standing goalkeeper Peter Shilton, centre-half Terry Butcher and 'Captain Marvel' Bryan Robson. He also faced accusations he could not cope with 'stars' after he dropped Paul Gascoigne for Gordon Cowans for a qualifying game against Ireland, fearing the midfielder might 'lose his head' in what would be a 'bruising' encounter. Matters were not helped by Taylor's reluctance to use creative players who did not have high work-rates, such as Chris Waddle and Peter Beardsley. He also suffered several injuries, notably to full-backs Gary Stevens and Lee Dixon, winger John Barnes and Gascoigne, leaving the squad in a makeshift mode going into the finals. The loss, also, of defender Mark Wright led to Taylor trying to call up Tony Adams, but UEFA refused, saying that 'it was too late.'

With players having their name on the backs of their shirts for the first time ever, England had to face France, Denmark and the host nation Sweden in Group 1 of the group stage. In their opening match against Denmark, they started brightly, but missed several chances to take a healthy lead, Platt being guilty of particularly glaring miss. Thereafter, the Danes began to dominate the match, and nearly won the game with minutes left when Arsenal's John Jensen struck a post. The game ended 0-0. The game against France finished goalless, Platt almost netting with a diving header and Stuart Pearce hitting the bar with a free-kick.

This left England needing to beat Sweden to advance to the semi-finals. Gary Lineker crossed for Platt to open the scoring with a volley on four minutes. However, after several chances went begging, they went in at half-time leading by a single goal. After the interval, the Swedes changed their team and formation, and dominated the second half, scoring twice to win 2-1 and so put paid to England's hope of success.

In the sixtieth minute of their final Pool game, with the score at 1-1, Taylor took off Lineker and, in doing so, prevented the striker from having the chance of equalling, or possibly even breaking, Bobby Charlton's record of forty-nine goals for England. Many were dismayed to see the substitution of England's top striker when his side needed a goal. This led to the media's vilification of Taylor, including the 'turnip' campaign by *The Sun* newspaper, which began the morning after the game under the headline, 'Swedes 2 Turnips 1'. During that campaign, the newspaper's back page featured an image of Taylor's face superimposed onto a turnip.

Stuttering Start to 1994 Qualification

Manager Taylor's relationship with the press was partially restored when he admitted his mistakes a few weeks after the Euro '92 finals. However, this did not last long. England's first game after returning from Sweden ended in a 1-0 defeat to Spain in a friendly. This time *The Sun* depicted Taylor as a 'Spanish onion'. England were drawn in Group 2 of the 1994 World Cup qualifiers, along with Norway, Turkey, The Netherlands, San Marino and Poland. And everyone realistically expected England to qualify along with the Dutch. Unfortunately, Taylor's men began with a disappointing 1-1 draw with Norway, who, as it transpired, became the early pacesetters with three victories.

Despite dominating the game, England could muster only half-chances. Platt gave them the lead in the fifty-fifth minute. Norway rarely threatened, but they equalised with thirteen minutes remaining. The draw flattered the Norwegians, but put them clear in the group. Such is football.

The campaign seemed to get back on track with two wins against Turkey (4-0 at home and 2-0 away) and a 6-0 home drubbing of San Marino, before England faced The Netherlands at Wembley. After shooting into a 2-0 lead inside twenty-five minutes, Taylor's luck took a turn for the worse when Gascoigne was elbowed off by Jan Wouters. Dennis Bergkamp reduced the deficit, albeit against the run of play. With just four minutes remaining, England on course for a win that would have ended Dutch hopes of qualification. But Peter Van Vossen netted a penalty to make it 2-2, and suddenly there was danger looming.

England's next chance of reviving their flagging fortunes came within the space of three days, in late May/early June 1993. Requiring at least four points from away games in Poland and Norway, England were poor against the Poles but salvaged a point when Ian Wright equalised on eighty-five minutes. Taylor was vilified again for his team's poor performance, and even more so after the next one against the Norwegians, who had arrived from obscurity to take the group by storm.

Taylor made wholesale changes, which again drew criticism, his actions considered risky in what was now a crucial game. Lee Sharpe and Lee Dixon were introduced as wing-backs, Carlton Palmer and Platt occupied midfield berths, Gascoigne supported Teddy Sheringham and Les Ferdinand up front, while Des Walker, Tony Adams and Gary Pallister formed a back three. England, with precious few attempts on goal, lost 2-0. Taylor said afterwards, 'We made a complete mess of it. I'm here to be shot at and take the rap. I have no defence for our performance.' His honesty did not spare him a roasting from the press, who were now calling for his head big time, with the newspaper headlines saying 'Norse Manure' and 'Oslo Rans'.

With their World Cup hopes hanging by a thread, England played in a four-team tournament in the USA Cup, which was expected to be a precursor to the following summer's tournament. Taylor stated before the game against their American hosts:

In football, you're only as good as your last game, and at the moment we're poor. You can always lose any game, to anyone. It's how you lose that matters. That was the thing that shocked us all in Norway. We would have been looking for a win here anyhow, but if we'd won last week it wouldn't have been considered essential. Now it is. Whether we like it or not, people expect us to beat America. There is definitely more intensity about this game because of our performance in the last one.

For Taylor, the USA Cup began with a humiliating 2-0 defeat in Boston, which prompted *The Sun* to carry this headline: 'Yanks 2 Planks 0.' Thankfully, some pride was restored with a credible 1-1 draw with Brazil and a narrow 2-1 defeat to Germany. However, Taylor was now living on borrowed time. The 1993/94 season began with a much-improved performance, which resulted in a 3-0 win over Poland, thus raising the nation's hopes prior to a crucial match against The Netherlands in Rotterdam. Unfortunately, poor refereeing denied England at least a point against the Dutch, who won 2-0.

England still had an outside chance to qualify for the World Cup in the States if they ran in a hatful of goals against San Marino, and The Netherlands lost their final group game in Poland. But it was not to be. In what was to be Taylor's last game in charge, England suffered the ultimate humiliation, conceding a goal after just 8.3 seconds of play, scored by David Gualtieri, a computer salesman, after an error from Stuart Pearce. England took another twenty minutes to find an equaliser and eventually won 7-1, but the Dutch won in Poland and it was all over.

Taylor officially resigned on 24 November 1993. He went 'with great sadness', saying, 'No one can gauge the depth of my personal disappointment at not qualifying for the World Cup.' There had been no question of him wanting to stay on, in any capacity. 'This is the appropriate course of action in the circumstances,' he said. 'If we didn't qualify, it was always my intention to offer my resignation.' He had been in charge for three years and two months, during which time England had played thirty-eight full internationals, winning eighteen, drawing thirteen and losing seven.

1. England's line-up from 1949. Back row, from left to right: A. Ramsay, N. Franklin, B. Streten, B. Williams, W. Watson, J. Aston, J. Milburn. Front row: T. Finney, S. Mortenson, J. Rowley, W. Wright (Capt.), S. Pearson, J. Froggatt.

2. England ahead of the 1962 World Cup in Chile. Back row, from left to right: J. Armfield, S. Anderson, P. Swan, R. Springett, R. Flowers, R. Wilson. Front row: B. Douglas, J. Greaves, R. Smith, J. Haynes, R. Charlton.

Above left: 3. Stanley Matthews in Stoke City kit.

Above right: 4. Gil Merrick (*centre*) keeping goal for Birmingham City *v.* Wolves in 1950.

Left: 5. Duncan Edwards (Manchester United). (*Courtesy of Iain McCartney*)

6. Roger Byrne, captain of Manchester United, in action. (*Courtesy of Iain McCartney*)

Above left: 7. The statue of Bobby Charlton at Old Trafford. (*Courtesy of Iain McCartney*)

Above right: 8. Tommy Taylor (Manchester United). (*Courtesy of Iain McCartney*)

9. England's skipper Bobby Moore, flanked by hat-trick hero Geoff Hurst and Ray Wilson, holds aloft the World Cup after West Germany were defeated 4-2 after extra-time in the 1966 final at Wembley. (© *PA*)

10. Argentina's Diego Maradona scores his infamous 'Hand of God' goal against England goalkeeper Peter Shilton in the 1986 World Cup. (© *PA*)

11. England's Bryan Robson heads a goal in the 1982 World Cup game *v*. France. (© *PA*)

12. England's David Beckham celebrates after scoring the winning goal in the 2002 game *v.* Argentina from a penalty kick. (© *PA*)

13. Joe Hart in action for Manchester City.

14. England's Wayne Rooney (third from right) scores the opening goal during the World Cup Group H qualifier between England and Poland at Wembley on 15 October 2013. (© *PA*)

Left: 15. Laurie Cunningham, one of the first black players to appear in a full international match for England.

Below: 16. The author (*right*) with Nobby Stiles (*left*).

The 1994 World Cup Qualifying Matches

14 October 1992   England 1 Norway 1
Wembley   Attendance 51,441

England Team: C. Woods (Sheffield Wednesday), L. Dixon (Arsenal), S. Pearce, D. Batty (Leeds United), T. Adams, D. Walker, D. Platt, P. Gascoigne, A. Shearer (Blackburn Rovers), I. Wright (Arsenal), P. Ince (Manchester United). Substitutes: C. Palmer (Sheffield Wednesday) for Dixon, P. Merson (Arsenal) for Wright.

David Platt maintained the goalscoring form that had been one of the few bonuses for manager Graham Taylor. But England had to fight hard to salvage a point against a vastly improved and workmanlike Norwegian side in a well-contested World Cup '96 qualifier at Wembley.

Paul Gascoigne stood on his return to international duty, his flair and imagination putting a smile back on the face of English football. Unfortunately, Ian Wright, despite his excellent club form, struggled up front, managing only two efforts on target. Paul Merson and even Alan Shearer also found it hard going against a well-organised defence. Tony Adams was England's best defender, while goalkeeper Chris Woods made two fine saves, and was only beaten by a well-struck, long-range shot on seventy-seven minutes by Kjetil Rekdal, which earned Norway a flattering draw. Platt had given England the lead in the fifty-fifth minute from Stuart Pearce's left-wing cross.

18 November 1992   England 4 Turkey 0
Wembley   Attendance 42,984

England Team: C. Woods, L. Dixon, S. Pearce, C. Palmer, T. Adams, D. Walker, D. Platt, P. Gascoigne, A. Shearer, I. Wright, P. Ince.

Brilliant Paul Gascoigne monopolised this World Cup qualifying encounter with a spectacular solo performance. He scored two goals and had a huge say in the third. The outplayed Turks were lucky not have suffered a far bigger defeat, so much were England in control. Gazza continually speared through defence-splitting passes, and if Alan Shearer and Ian Wright had been quicker and more sure-footed, then the final scoreline would surely have been eight, even nine or ten nil. England led 1-0 after sixteen minutes with a smart goal by Gascoigne, who then helped set up Shearer for a second on twenty-eight minutes. Pearce (sixty minutes) and Gascloigne (sixty-one) netted in a rather one-sided second half. Des Walker had a good game to celebrate the winning of his fiftieth cap.

17 February 1993	**England 6 San Marino 0**
Wembley	**Attendance 51,154**

England Team: C. Woods, L. Dixon, A. Dorigo, C. Palmer, T. Adams, D. Walker, D. Platt, P. Gascoigne, L. Ferdinand (Queens Park Rangers), D. Batty, J. Barnes.
Four goals by an in-form David Platt helped England to a satisfactory rather than stunning victory against mediocre opposition. San Marino, fielding a team of part-time professionals, came to Wembley intent on defending, but they failed miserably. In fact, Platt, acting as captain in place of Stuart Pearce, had a great chance to equal the individual scoring record of five goals in a full international by an Englishman, but saw his eighty-eighth-minute penalty was brilliantly saved by overworked goalkeeper Pierluigi Benedettini. The Arsenal attacking midfielder had given England a 2-0 half-time lead, with strikes in the thirteenth and twenty-fourth minutes. He completed his hat-trick in the sixty-seventh minute and grabbed his fourth on eighty-three. The lanky Carlton Palmer (seventy-eight minutes) and debutant Les Ferdinand (eighty-six) scored England's other two goals.

31 March 1993	**Turkey 0 England 2**
Izmir	**Attendance 59,276**

England Team: C. Woods, L. Dixon, A. Sinton (Queens Park Rangers), C. Palmer, T. Adams, D. Walker, D. Platt, P. Gascoigne, I. Wright, P. Ince, J. Barnes. Substitutes: N. Clough (Nottingham Forest) for Dixon, L. Sharpe (Manchester United) for Wright.
A well-executed, sixth-minute goal by David Platt, his tenth in ten internationals, put England on the road to a courage-carved victory in what was a real rough-and-tumble World Cup qualifier in front of a very hostile crowd in Izmir. England's players had to show tremendous character as the home supporters continually tossed coins, bottles and even fireworks at them from the terraces. It was atrocious behaviour. A looping header by Paul Gascoigne a minute before half-time gave England a comfortable lead, which they held onto despite coming under a lot of pressure. Arsenal's Lee Dixon was brutally 'kicked' out of the match; Paul Ince took over at right-back, allowing Nigel Clough to win his ninth cap. Tony Adams was a source of strength (again) at the back, while John Barnes regained his dignity with a solid display on the left.

28 April 1993　　　　　　　　　　　　　　England 2 The Netherlands 2
Wembley　　　　　　　　　　　　　　　　　Attendance 73,163

England Team: C. Woods, L. Dixon, M. Keown (Arsenal), C. Palmer, T. Adams, D. Walker, D. Platt, P. Gascoigne, L. Ferdinand, P. Ince, J. Barnes. Substitute: P. Merson for Gascoigne.
England somehow squandered a two-goal lead after controlling this World Cup qualifier with an impressive display, which matched anything previously produced under manager Graham Taylor. John Barnes smashed home a free-kick to give England the lead after ninety seconds, and David Platt popped in a second in the twenty-fourth minute as the Dutch struggled to get going. But then, out of the blue, Dennis Bergkamp netted with a quite brilliant volley in the thirty-fourth minute to inject some life into the visitors and, as England stood back, waves of orange shirts started to drive forward.

Gascoigne went off injured after being elbowed in the face by Jan Wouters, who was allowed to stay on the pitch thanks to poor refereeing. From this point on, The Netherlands took charge. They pressed and pressed and deservedly earned a draw when Des Walker clumsily conceded a penalty in the eighty-fifth minute by tugging the shirt of danger man Marc Overmars. Peter van Vossen gleefully tucked away the spot-kick to deny England victory, and suddenly put their World Cup stay in danger. 'I wasn't at all happy with our second-half performance,' said manager Taylor. 'We have an awful lot to do from now on in.'

29 May 1993　　　　　　　　　　　　　　　Poland 1 England 1
Katowice　　　　　　　　　　　　　　　　　Attendance 59,782

England Team: C. Woods, P. Bardsley (Queens Park Rangers), A. Dorigo, C. Palmer, T. Adams, D. Walker, D. Platt, P. Gascoigne, T. Sheringham, P. Ince, J. Barnes. Substitute: I. Wright for Palmer.
Following a mix-up between Des Walker and John Barnes, England fell behind to a thirty-fourth-minute goal by Dariusz Adamczuk. But with Teddy Sheringham making his presence felt on his debut, England fought back and, although leaving it late, Ian Wright netted with just six minutes remaining – his first international goal in nine appearances. There was a new subtlety in the England attack with the introduction of the gifted Sheringham, and at the end of the game, manager Graham Taylor admitted that 'our destiny is on our own hands, and if we play to our full potential there is no doubt at all that we can qualify for the finals'.

2 June 1993　　　　　　　　　　　　　　　　Norway 2 England 0
Oslo　　　　　　　　　　　　　　　　　　　Attendance 22,250

England Team: C. Woods, L. Dixon, L. Sharpe, G. Pallister (Manchester United), T. Adams, D. Walker, D. Platt, C. Palmer, L. Ferdinand, T. Sheringham, P. Gascoigne. Substitutes: N. Clough for Walker, I. Wright for Sheringham.

Graham Taylor gambled by fielding three central defenders – Gary Pallister, Tony Adams and Des Walker. None looked comfortable, and at times they were bemused as to what to do. Walker was perhaps at fault for both goals. In the forty-third minute he hesitated, thinking that Øyvind Leonhardsen was offside. He wasn't and the Norwegian darted through to give his side the lead. Eight minutes after half-time, Walker, easily one of the quickest defenders in world game, was outwitted and outpaced by Lars Bohinen, who went on to crack a fierce drive, hard and low past Chris Woods at his near post.

Taylor came in for some strong and savage criticism, particularly for introducing new, untried tactics in such a crucial game. As a result of this defeat, England knew they had to win all three of their remaining qualifying matches to stand even an outside chance of going to the USA for World Cup '94.

8 September 1993	England 3 Poland 0
Wembley	Attendance 71,220

England Team: D. Seaman (Arsenal), R. Jones (Liverpool), P. Ince, T. Adams, G. Pallister, D. Platt, P. Gascoigne, L. Ferdinand, I. Wright, L. Sharpe.
England, inspired by a fiery and fluent performance from Paul Gascoigne, were rarely stretched by a dispirited-looking Poland side. Starting off like a house on fire, England scored in the fifth minute when Les Ferdinand, taking David Platt's perfect pass in his stride, found the net with ease. This well-timed opener certainly settled the nerves of the players and lifted the tension in the crowd. England strove hard for a second, both Ian Wright and Ferdinand coming close, but it was schemer Gascoigne who turned scorer in the forty-ninth minute to make it 2-0. Four minutes later, Stuart Pearce blasted in a third goal after a well-worked free-kick from 20 yards out. Unfortunately, Gascoigne was again yellow carded and therefore was ruled out of the crucial return fixture in The Netherlands, much to the annoyance of his manager!

13 October 1993	The Netherlands 2 England 0
Rotterdam	Attendance 47,634

England Team: D. Seaman (Arsenal), P. Parker, T. Dorigo, C. Palmer, T. Adams, G. Pallister, D. Platt, P. Ince, A. Shearer, P. Merson, L. Sharpe. Substitutes: A. Sinton for Palmer, I. Wright for Merson.
Norway had already won England's group and the result of this penultimate qualifying game would decide who would finish second. And it started off at a furious pace. England came under pressure from the first whistle, but hit back with a string of counter-attacks. David Platt headed just wide, Tony Adams had a shot cleared off the line and Tony Dorigo struck a post with a 35-yard free-kick on twenty-five minutes.

Two minutes before half-time, England were fortunate to have a Frank Rijkaard goal ruled out for offside, even though replays showed his effort was legitimate. With England holding the Dutch quite comfortably, and the game locked at 0-0, Platt was fouled by Ronald Koeman as he raced in on goal. The German referee failed to apply the rule of sending him off for a professional foul, awarding a direct free-kick instead. Dorigo's drive was charged down, with defending players clearly encroaching. Minutes later, just past the hour mark, 'Lucky' Koeman took an identical free-kick outside England's penalty area. His first shot was blocked, but it was ordered to be retaken because of encroachment (amazing). The same player then netted with his second attempt.

England hit back strongly, and Paul Merson fired a free-kick against a post but, soon after, Dennis Bergkamp scored a match-winning second goal for The Netherlands, despite using his arm to control the ball. In the meantime, Taylor was in an apoplectic mood on the touchline, berating the officials and referee as the significance of the result sank in. Later on, Dutch goalkeeper Ed de Goey twice saved low down to deny Merson and Platt. It wasn't to be, and this defeat saw the last-but-one nail hammered into manager Taylor's coffin.

17 November 1993	San Marino 1 England 7
Bologna	Attendance 2,378

England Team: D. Seaman, L. Dixon, S. Pearce, P. Ince, G. Pallister, D. Walker, S. Ripley (Blackburn Rovers), D. Platt, L. Ferdinand, I. Wright, A. Sinton.
Manager Graham Taylor's last game in charge ended in farce and embarrassment when England conceded their quickest goal in international football to the minnows from San Marino. Part-timer Davide Gualtieri pounced on a Stuart Pearce back-pass to score after just nine seconds. Needing to win by at least seven clear goals to have any chance of qualifying for the World Cup finals in America, England never really recovered from this early humiliation and a scrappy display was lifted only by Ian Wright's four-goal haul, albeit against very weak opposition. Wright scored in the thirty-fourth, forty-sixth, seventy-eighth and ninetieth minutes, Paul Ince netted twice in the twenty-second and seventy-third minutes, and Les Ferdinand was on target seven minutes before half-time. In the end, this lopsided 7-1 win was irrelevant, as The Netherlands beat Poland 3-1 to clinch a place in the USA.

The attendance in Bologna, fractionally under 2,400, was the lowest an England team had played in front of at senior level for 110 years, since February 1883 when just 2,000 fans saw them beat Wales 5-0.

1994 World Cup Fact File

- Countries taking part: 24 (divided into six groups of 4).
- Final: Brazil 0, Italy 0 (Brazil won 3-2 on penalties).
- Final venue: Rose Bowl, Los Angeles, California (attendance 94,194).
- Leading scorer: Hristo Stoichkov (Bulgaria) and Oleg Salenko (Russia), 6 goals each.
- Roger Milla (Cameroon), aged 42 years 39 days, set a world record when he played against Russia.

- Fifteen players were shown red cards, and 227 received yellow cards.
- Andrés Escobar was shot and killed in Medellín, Colombia, soon after returning from the World Cup. It is widely believed that his murder was carried out after the own goal he conceded against the USA, supposedly causing gambling losses to several powerful drug lords at the time.
- The attendances reached an all-time World Cup high with a total of 3,567,415 spectators watching the 52 matches, giving an average of 68,604.

New Manager, New Hope, and Football Comes Home

Lawrie McMenemy was one of the favourites to take over the mantle as England's team manager from Graham Taylor, but in the end the FA plumped for fifty-year-old Terry Venables. As a player, Venables made a total of 649 League and Cup appearances for four London clubs: Chelsea, Tottenham Hotspur, Queens Park Rangers and Crystal Palace. He also represented England at schoolboy, youth, under-23, amateur and full international level, and had previously managed Palace, QPR, Barcelona and Spurs.

The England national football team was, at this juncture, at a low point. Venables, though not at the time of his appointment active in the game, seemed to have the presence and charisma that could reignite some patriotic pride and achievement. He was appointed manager on 28 January 1994.

However, the appointment coincided with Venables coming under scrutiny and censure in connection with several of his business dealings. The Football Association struggled to identify an alternative candidate. Their discomfort with his soiled reputation for probity was articulated in their appointment of him as England 'coach' rather than under the traditional title of 'manager'. In January 1996, Venables decided that he was going to leave the England job after the European Championships that summer, as he wanted to concentrate on clearing his name in connection with off-the-field business dealings.

As hosts, England did not have to qualify for Euro '96 and, before the tournament started, Venables saw his team compete in nineteen non-competition matches, winning nine, drawing eight and losing only two: 3-1 to Brazil in the Umbro Cup and 1-0 to the Republic of Ireland in Dublin. Those nine wins were against Denmark (1-0), Greece (6-0), the USA (2-0), Nigeria (1-0), Japan (2-1), Switzerland (3-1), Bulgaria (1-0), Hungary (3-0) and China (also 3-0). Draws were played out with Norway (0-0 on two occasions), Romania (1-1), Uruguay (0-0), Sweden (3-3), Colombia (0-0), Portugal (1-1) and Croatia (0-0).

During his first fifteen months in charge, 'TV' brought into the team almost thirty new players; among them the Neville brothers from Manchester United, Gareth Southgate, the Channel Island duo of Matt Le Tissier and Graeme Le Saux and the Liverpool duo of Robbie Fowler and Steve McManaman.

During Euro '96, there were certainly plenty of highs and lows (mostly highs) and excited crowds packed themselves inside Wembley Stadium. Venables' team won three, drew one and lost one of their five games. They beat Scotland 2-0 (with a stunning Paul Gascoigne goal) and The Netherlands 4-1 (when the SAS – Shearer and Sheringham –

were superb) and drew with Switzerland 1-1 in Group A, before knocking out Spain (on penalties, thanks to goalkeeper David Seaman) in the quarter-finals.

Then, with the whole nation cheering them on towards their first major final for thirty years, it all went wrong when foes Germany won 6-5 on penalties after a 1-1 scoreline in the semis. Sadly, it was Gareth Southgate's spot-kick that resulted in England's downfall. This result was a real sickener for everybody associated with England.

After the disappointment of that the semi-finals defeat – and it was bitter disappointment – Venables left his job, replaced by another former Tottenham Hotspur star, Glenn Hoddle, who officially took office on 2 May 1996. Alan Shearer spoke highly of Venables' tenure as England manager, stating, 'The best England's team I played in was the one under Terry in 1995/96. His knowledge and tactical know-how were spot-on and he knew how to get the best out of his players. We responded to him, believed in him and played some outstanding football, especially in Euro '96.'

Hoddle Takes Charge, Disappointment in France

Glenn Hoddle's first game as England manager was the 1998 World Cup qualifier against Moldova in Chişinău on 1 September 1996. This team did him proud by winning 3-0: David Seaman, Gary Neville, Gary Pallister, Gareth Southgate, Pearce, debutant David Beckham, Paul Ince, Paul Gascoigne (substitute David Batty), debutant Andy Hinchcliffe, Nicky Barmby (substitute Matt Le Tissier) and Alan Shearer. Gazza, Shearer and Barmby scored the goals. Five weeks later, Poland were eclipsed 2-0 at Wembley and a month after that, Georgia were defeated by the same score in Tbilisi to complete a hat-trick of qualifying wins.

Unfortunately, 1997 didn't start off too well for Hoddle, who suffered his first qualifying defeat, a 1-0 reverse against Italy. This, in fact, was England's first home defeat in World Cup football in forty-eight years... They played their first qualifier against Northern Ireland in November 1949. But after a 2-0 friendly win over Mexico, England got back on track. They then recorded a 2-0 home victory over Georgia, followed up soon afterwards with another 2-0 qualifying win, this time over Poland – this after beating South Africa 2-1 in an Old Trafford friendly.

By now, Hoddle was chopping and changing his line-up quite considerably. Besides those mentioned earlier, he also gave debuts to goalkeeper David James and the Manchester United midfielder pairing of Nicky Butt and Paul Scholes.

After beating Italy 2-0 and France 1-0, and losing to 1-0 to Brazil in the Tournoi de France in June 1997, England continued their World Cup qualification campaign with a 4-0 victory over Moldova, followed by a goalless draw with Italy, which guaranteed them a place in the 1998 World Cup finals in France. Over 81,000 fans packed into the Stadio Olimpico in Rome to see a resolute England produce a tremendous display to thwart the home side – Southgate and Adams at the heart of the defence, and Beckham, Ince (with his head heavily bandaged) and Batty in midfield, all performing superbly.

21

The 1998 World Cup Qualifying Matches

1 September 1996   Moldova 0 England 3
Chisinau   Attendance 13,503

*England Team: D. Seaman, G. Neville (Manchester United), S. Pearce, P. Ince, G. Pallister,
G. Southgate (Aston Villa), D. Beckham (Manchester United), P. Gascoigne, A. Shearer,
N. Barmby (Middlesbrough), A. Hinchcliffe (Everton). Substitute: D. Batty for Gascoigne,
M. Le Tissier (Southampton) for Barmby.*
David Beckham made his full debut for England, but his neat and tidy performance was
surpassed by his Manchester United teammate Gary Neville, who set up two of the goals
that saw off Moldova. Right-back Neville fed in Nick Barmby, who opened the scoring on
twenty-four minutes. After Paul Gascoigne's looping header had made it 2-0 just ninety
seconds later, Neville's pass freed Alan Shearer, who tucked away goal number three just
past the hour mark. Andy Hinchcliffe also made his debut for England in this encounter.

9 October 1996   England 2 Poland 1
Wembley   Attendance 74,663

*England Team: D. Seaman, G. Neville, S. Pearce, P. Ince, G. Southgate, A. Hinchcliffe,
D. Beckham, P. Gascoigne, A. Shearer, Ferdinand, S. McManaman (Liverpool). Substitute:
G. Pallister for Southgate.*
Two goals by Alan Shearer saw off a resilient Polish side, who had surprisingly grabbed
an early lead through Marek Citko. This was Glen Hoddle's first home match in charge,
and it began disastrously when the visitors took the lead in the seventh minute. At that
point, memories of 1974 came flooding back. However, England composed themselves,
did the basics and gradually gained control of the game before half-time, courtesy of a
brace from hot-shot Shearer, who struck in the twenty-fourth and thirty-eighth minutes.
The second half saw a better England performance, but Poland were desperately unlucky
not to equalise late on when the England's rearguard back-pedalled.

9 November 1996   Georgia 0 England 2
Tbilisi   Attendance 47,840

England Team: D. Seaman, S. Campbell (Tottenham Hotspur), A. Hinchcliffe, P. Ince, T. Adams, G. Southgate, D. Beckham, P. Gascoigne, L. Ferdinand, T. Sheringham, D. Batty. Substitute: I. Wright for Ferdinand.
For this next match in Tbilisi, England's manager Glenn Hoddle made four changes, bringing in Sol Campbell, Tony Adams, David Batty and Teddy Sheringham. After soaking up early pressure from the home team, England scored on the counter-attack on fifteen minutes. Paul Gascoigne fed the ball to Les Ferdinand, who in turn passed to Sheringham, whose precise lob over the 'keeper with his right foot was spot on. So, following a tricky start, England were in the driving seat, leading 1-0.

David Beckham almost scored again in the thirty-first minute with a strike from 30 yards but the ball just went over the crossbar. After an appalling tackle by Murtaz Shelia on Gascoigne, the England midfielder punished the Georgian by letting his football do the talking. He started an attack, and quickly got the ball up to Sheringham, who found Ferdinand. The Newcastle striker kept control under pressure from Kakhaber Tskhadadze, before thumping an unstoppable shot into to the back of the net with nine minutes of the first half remaining. Thereafter, England comfortably held their two-goal lead and should have scored more as the midfield continually orchestrated the play.

12 February 1997   England 0 Italy 1
Wembley   Attendance 75,055

England Team: I. Walker (Tottenham Hotspur), G. Neville, S. Pearce, P. Ince, S. Campbell, G. Le Saux (Blackburn Rovers), D. Beckham, D. Batty, A. Shearer, M. Le Tissier, L. Ferdinand, S. McManaman. Substitutes: P. Merson for McManaman, I. Wright for Batty.
Minus goalkeeper David Seaman and centre-back Tony Adams, England, it must be said, did not play at all well against a defensively minded, close-marking and strong-tackling Italian side, and were undone by a ninth-minute goal by Gianfranco Zola, then of Chelsea, following a wonderful, 40-yard pinpoint pass from Alessandro Costacurta. Les Ferdinand and Matt Le Tissier had good chances to equalise, but generally opportunities in front of goal were few and far between, thanks to a well-organised Italian defence. This, of course, was Glenn Hoddle's first defeat as England manager.

30 April 1997   England 2 Georgia 0
Wembley   Attendance 71,206

England Team: D. Seaman, G. Neville, Le Saux, S. Campbell, T. Adams, D. Batty, D. Beckham, P. Ince, A. Shearer, T. Sheringham, R. Lee (Newcastle United. Substitute: G. Southgate for Adams, J. Redknapp (Liverpool) for Ince.

Against Georgia, manager Glenn Hoddle was able to start with the SAS – Alan Shearer and Teddy Sheringham – for the first time since the European Championships, and they proved to be the match-winners. England began well but missed several early chances and then hit the crossbar. It looked as if the match would remain goalless at half-time, but a strong, purposeful attack led to the breakthrough. Shearer, given space, volleyed the ball hard and straight into the area for strike partner Sheringham to head home in the forty-second minute – the SAS were back, in style.

Georgia made several changes in personnel and tactics at half-time. They started the second half well, hitting the English crossbar, but were beaten when the SAS combined again for England's second goal; Sheringham setting up Shearer in the very last minute to seal a hard-earned victory. This wasn't the greatest of games by a long way, but England did enough to secure the points. And they knew, as did the fans, that they would have to improve tenfold if they were to qualify for the 1998 World Cup finals.

31 May 1997   Poland 0 England 2
Chorzów   Attendance 33,376

England Team: D. Seaman, G. Neville, G. Le Saux, S. Campbell, G. Southgate, D. Beckham, P. Ince, P. Gascoigne, A. Shearer, T. Sheringham, R. Lee. Substitutes: P. Neville (Manchester United) for Beckham, D. Batty for Gascoigne.
It was once again the SAS show as England registered a 2-0 victory over the Poles to clinch a place in the 1998 World Cup finals in France. Alan Shearer converted Paul Ince's cross at the far post to put England ahead in the fifth minute. But the following forty minutes were hit and miss, and right on the half-time whistle, Shearer even missed a penalty, striking the woodwork with his low, right-footed shot – a rare occurrence this. The action improved after the break, but it wasn't until the ninetieth minute that England clinched victory, Rob Lee setting up Sheringham to finish off the resilient Poles. This was England's first win on Polish soil since 1966 … and it was worth waiting for!

10 September 1997   England 4 Moldova 0
Wembley   Attendance 74,102

England Team: D. Seaman, G. Neville, P. Neville, D. Batty, G. Southgate, S. Campbell, D. Beckham, P. Gascoigne, L. Ferdinand, I. Wright, P. Scholes (Manchester United). Substitutes: S. Ripley for Beckham, N. Butt (Manchester United) for Ripley, S. Collymore (Aston Villa) for Ferdinand.
There was not a dry eye among the 74,000-plus spectators as Elton John's 'Candle in the Wind' was played over the PA system in an unscheduled but apt mark of respect to Princess Diana, who had been tragically killed in a car crash in France ten days earlier. A sea of flickering candles illuminated tear-stained faces in the dark stands as voices took up the refrain. Many held up St George flags with 'We love you Diana' daubed in black

marker pen, and all the England players wore black crosses pinned over their hearts. The minute's silence was impeccably observed by the patriotic crowd, its conclusion seeming to represent the flicking of a switch as cheers for the departed princess roared the England's team into action. Swept along on a tidal wave of emotion, England simply couldn't and wouldn't lose this game. And they didn't, whipping the Moldovans 4-0. Quite what the visitors made of it all, I don't know.

Two goals by Ian Wright and one each from the two Pauls – Scholes and Gascoigne – boosted the nation's spirits and put England on the brink of qualification. After prodding and probing for almost half an hour, England took the lead when David Beckham's perfect cross found his United teammate Scholes, who got his ginger top to the ball to send it across 'keeper Denis Roumanenco and into the far corner of the net on twenty-eight minutes. England had been made to toil hard for their lead, and Moldova didn't give in easily. It took Wright's goal fifty-eight seconds after the restart to avert a potentially awkward night. Fed by Gascoigne, the striker escaped his marker Oleg Fistican and blasted the ball left-footed inside the near post. Great goal.

The Arsenal striker, producing perhaps his best performance in a Three Lions shirt, caused problems all night for the visitors' defence, and it was his pass that found Gascoigne to put away goal number three with a minute remaining. An emotional Gazza pointed to the heavens as he scored. Wright duly finished things off by sprinting away in added time to make it four. 'Diana was in our thoughts and we were determined to play to our full capabilities,' Wright said afterwards.

11 October 1997	**Italy 0 England 0**
Rome	**Attendance 81,200**

England Team: D. Seaman, D. Beckham, G. Le Saux, S. Campbell, T. Adams, G. Southgate, P. Gascoigne, D. Batty, I. Wright, T. Sheringham, P. Ince. Substitutes: N. Butt for Gascoigne.

England produced an excellent display in Rome against a very useful and strong Italian side, and as a result qualified for the 1998 World Cup finals in France. Gareth Southgate and Tony Adams were like rocks at the back; David Beckham, Paul Gascoigne, David Batty and Paul Ince (with his cut hand swathed in bloodstained bandages) worked overtime in midfield, and Ian Wright and Teddy Sheringham gave the Italians problems throughout the ninety minutes. 'Pleased and satisfied, to a certain extent, to have qualified,' said manager Glenn Hoddle.

Pre-World Cup Action

Before venturing across the Channel to compete in the World Cup, England fulfilled seven more non-competitive internationals. They beat Cameroon 2-0 and Portugal 3-0, both at Wembley, drew 1-1 with Switzerland in Berne, played out a 0-0 draw with Saudi

Arabia, and lost 2-0 at home to Chile. Meanwhile, in the King Hassan II Cup, staged in Casablanca, they beat the host country Morocco 1-0, but succumbed 4-3 on penalties to Belgium, when the Leeds United goalkeeper Nigel Martyn was furious with himself for not stopping at least two of the converted spot-kicks he faced.

Into the team now came the teenage Liverpool striker Michael Owen, who scored his first senior goal in the victory over Morocco. And he would go on to become a star performer for club(s) and country over the next decade. England had been drawn with Colombia, Romania and Tunisia in Group G, and immediately the press confirmed that this could the year. However, ardent supporters, those who travelled everywhere (known as the Barmy Army) thought otherwise – as did a handful of former players, who agreed that it would be tough, with no easy matches in their group and Romania perhaps the best-equipped of the three other countries.

Glenn Hoddle's twenty-two-man squad for France '98 was:

Goalkeepers: Tim Flowers (Blackburn Rovers), Nigel Martyn (Leeds United), David Seaman (Arsenal). Full-backs: Graeme Le Saux (Chelsea), Gary Neville (Manchester United). Defenders: Tony Adams (Arsenal), Sol Campbell (Tottenham Hotspur), Rio Ferdinand (West Ham United), Martin Keown (Arsenal), Gareth Southgate (Aston Villa). Midfielders: Darren Anderton (Tottenham Hotspur), David Batty (Newcastle United), David Beckham (Manchester United), Paul Ince (Liverpool), Robert Lee (Newcastle United), Steve McManaman (Liverpool), Paul Scholes (Manchester United). Forwards/ strikers: Les Ferdinand (Tottenham Hotspur), Paul Merson (Middlesbrough), Michael Owen (Liverpool), Alan Shearer (Newcastle United), Teddy Sheringham (Manchester United).

NB: *Placed on standby (in reserve) for the trip to France were versatile defender Phil Neville and midfielder Nicky Butt (both from Manchester United) and strikers Dion Dublin (Coventry City) and Ian Wright (Arsenal).*

Manager Hoddle caused controversy in omitting Paul Gascoigne from the squad and bringing in faith healer Eileen Drewery to be a part of the England coaching staff. This led to the team being dubbed 'The Hod Squad.'

Despite suffering a 2-1 defeat at the hands of Romania, England qualified for the second round from a tough group, courtesy of 2-0 wins over Tunisia and Colombia. But then, when all looked to be going well, and after playing some decent attacking football against Argentina, England lost 4-3 on penalties to the South American country. This was very depressing for all concerned, and it took quite a while for the dust to settle on yet another disappointing end to a competition a lot of people sincerely believed England could and should have done well in.

22

The 1998 World Cup in France

15 June 1998   England 2 Tunisia 0
Marseille   Attendance 54,587

England Team: D. Seaman, D. Anderton, G. Le Saux, S. Campbell, G. Southgate, T. Adams, P. Scholes, D. Batty, P. Ince, A. Shearer, T. Sheringham. Substitute: M. Owen for Sheringham.

England got their World Cup campaign off to a winning start with a solid performance against Tunisia in the Stade Vélodrome. It was the first time since 1982 that they had won their opening World Cup game. Manager Glenn Hoddle had left Paul Gascoigne out of his squad, replacing him with Paul Scholes, and the Manchester United player had a fine game, scoring to seal victory in the last minute with an excellent, curling shot. Earlier, both Scholes and Teddy Sheringham had been denied by excellent saves from Tunisia's goalkeeper Chokri El Ouaer. But he was beaten, at last, in the forty-second minute by Alan Shearer's downward header from Graeme Le Saux's free-kick from the left. Michael Owen was introduced as a late substitute to become the third youngest player to participate in the World Cup. This useful performance proved that there is life after Gazza.

Unfortunately, once again, the hooligan element of England supporters fought a running battle with the Marseille police and rival fans on the eve of this opening encounter. Disgraceful.

22 June 1998   England 1 Romania 2
Toulouse   Attendance 37,440

England Team: D. Seaman, G. Neville, G. Le Saux, D. Batty, T. Adams, S. Campbell, D. Anderton, P. Ince, P. Scholes, A. Shearer, T. Sheringham. Substitute: D. Beckham for Ince.

After producing a pretty good display in their opening Group G game against Tunisia, England's progress faltered against Romania. Glenn Hoddle was forced to make one change, drafting in Gary Neville in place of the injured Gareth Southgate, allowing Sol

Campbell to switch into the middle to partner Tony Adams. After dominating the first half-hour, England lost Paul Ince (injured) and David Beckham came on as a substitute. Continuing to hold the upper hand, England suddenly fell behind on forty-seven minutes, when Coventry City's Viorel Moldavon linked up with Gheorge Hagi to score from 8 yards. This goal certainly stunned Hoddle's men, and it took them quite awhile to regain their composure. After a few near misses, they finally drew level through Michael Owen on eighty-three minutes. However, with the game heading for a draw, and with play entering the final minute of normal time, Romania's Dan Petrescu capitalised on a mistake by Graeme Le Saux to squirt the ball through 'keeper David Seaman's legs and into the net. With Romania back in front, England's heads dropped. But they responded quickly, and Owen almost grabbed an equaliser with an effort against a post in added time. This was a horrible result and Hoddle blamed it on 'schoolboy errors'.

26 June 1998   England 2 Colombia 0
Lens   Attendance 41,275

England Team: D. Seaman, G. Neville, G. Le Saux, D. Beckham, T. Adams, S. Campbell, D. Anderton, P. Ince, A. Shearer, M. Owen, P. Scholes. Substitutes: R. Lee for Anderton, D. Batty for Ince, S. McManaman for Scholes.
Needing to progress at least into the knockout stage, England went one better, rekindled their fire and, with a smart performance, duly defeated a neat and tidy Colombian side by two clear goals. After some enterprising play, Darren 'Sicknote' Anderton finally made his mark, firing England ahead on twenty minutes from Michael Owen's low cross. Brimming with confidence, Hoddle's team pressed forward and as Paul Scholes deliberately broke up the wall, David Beckham banged home a free-kick to make it 2-0 on the half-hour. Defenders Sol Campbell and Tony Adams, along with Alan Shearer, Scholes and Owen, all came close to adding to the score as the Colombians began to tire. Next up, Argentina...

30 June 1998   England 2 Argentina 2
Etienne   (After extra time, England lost 4-3 on penalties)
                                                  Attendance 30,589

England Team: D. Seaman, G. Neville, G. Le Saux, D. Beckham, T. Adams, S. Campbell, D. Anderton, P. Ince, A. Shearer, M. Owen, P. Scholes. Substitutes: D. Batty for Anderton, P. Merson for Scholes, G. Southgate for Le Saux.
England were never outplayed or outfought in this last sixteen encounter, yet they went out of the World Cup without technically losing. And, once again, it was the tyranny of penalties that ended their dream. As in Italy '90 and Euro '96, history repeated itself in the most callous manner imaginable.

There is no doubt England – who had David Beckham sent off early in the second half for a stupid flick-kick at Diego Simeone – didn't deserve to lose. They matched the

Argentinians kick for kick, tackle for tackle, pass for pass, goal for goal. Paul Ince was a king among lions, and David Batty, whose fateful last penalty kick was saved, played a crucial part in stiffening the resistance of a depleted England in extra time. As *The Telegraph* reporter wrote, 'England win together and lose together. They certainly played as a band of brothers throughout this nerve-shredding encounter. For 120 minutes, France '98 was treated to the best of English football: the class of Alan Shearer and Michael Owen, who both scored, and the resilience inherent in England's teams when faced with adversity.'

Glenn Hoddle's players performed remarkably well, holding one of the favourites for the tournament. Argentina took the lead on six minutes, Gabriel Batistuta converting a penalty after goalkeeper David Seaman had fouled Simeone. England responded quickly and, in the tenth minute, Michael Owen was brought down inside the box, allowing Alan Shearer to level things up with a blockbuster from the spot. And then, with Argentina on the back foot, Owen scored a sensational individual goal – one of best seen in World Cup football – to edge England in front in the sixteenth minute. Argentina came again, and although they didn't create a great deal, they somehow grabbed an equaliser just before half-time, when Juan Veron touched a free-kick to Javier Zanetti, who fired past Seaman. In the second half, England's ten men battled for every ball. Sol Campbell had a goal ruled out because Shearer fouled the 'keeper (no way), and perhaps they had more possession during extra time. But in the end all that effort and commitment came to nothing as Argentina won the penalty shoot-out 4-3. The sequence of spot-kicks went (Argentina first): Sergio Berti 1-0, Shearer 1-1, Hernán Crespo miss, Ince miss, Verón 2-1, Paul Merson 2-2, Marcelo Gallardo 3-2, Owen 3-3, Roberto Ayala 4-3, Batty miss. Carlos Roa saved both kicks from Ince and Batty. And, in fact, it was Roa who prevented England from reaching the quarter-finals.

NB: *For the record, Argentina lost their quarter-final tie with The Netherlands 2-1.*

1998 World Cup Fact File

- Countries taking part: 32 (divided into eight groups of 4).
- Final: France 3, Brazil 0.
- Final venue: Stade de France, Saint-Denis, Paris (attendance 79,954).
- Leading scorer: Davor Šuker (Croatia), 6 goals.
- A record 171 goals were scored in this year's World Cup tournament.
- German midfielder Lothar Matthäus equalled Antonio Carbajal's record by appearing in his fifth World Cup.

Hoddle Leaves

After the summer break, Glenn Hoddle and his coaching staff got down to assessing the opposition for the qualifying stages of the 2000 European Championships, which were scheduled to take place in Belgium and The Netherlands. England were drawn in the same group as Sweden, Poland, Bulgaria and Luxembourg. Although on paper it looked as if it would be a relatively easy passage, things didn't go strictly according to plan. Hoddle came under fire after England got off to a rather poor start in their group, losing to Sweden, drawing with Bulgaria and beating the minnows of Luxembourg 3-0.

It perhaps came as a shock to some when he was axed in early February 1999, seven weeks after his last game as manager – a 2-0 friendly win over the Czech Republic. Howard Wilkinson took charge on a temporary basis. Hoddle departed having managed his country in twenty-eight internationals, seventeen of which were won, six drawn and five lost. Wilkinson presided for just one game – a 2-0 friendly defeat by France at Wembley – when no fewer than seven Arsenal players took the field, four for England (Seaman, Dixon, Adams and Keown) and three for France (Nicolas Anelka, Emmanuel Petit and Patrick Vieira).

Following Wilkinson, the FA appointed Kevin Keegan, who took charge of the team in February 1999, while also still in charge of Fulham. Almost immediately he had to select a team to play Poland in another qualifier match for Euro 2000, and his choice was spot on. He and England celebrated with a 3-1 victory, Paul Scholes claiming a rare (very rare) hat-trick.

A 1-1 friendly draw with Hungary in Budapest preceded four more vital EC qualifiers, in which England didn't play at all well, again. They drew three of them – 0-0 with Sweden, 1-1 with Bulgaria and 0-0 with Poland – and the only spark, if you can call it that, came when they hammered Luxembourg 6-0, with an Alan Shearer hat-trick.

In the first leg of the play-offs, England won 2-0 at Hampden Park. They then lost the second leg 1-0 but qualified on 2-1 aggregate.

Keegan arranged four more friendlies before England left for the finals in June 2000. The team, to be fair, did okay, drawing 0-0 with Argentina, 1-1 with Brazil, beating Ukraine 2-0 and overhauling Malta 2-1. Centre-back Tony Adams had the pleasure of scoring England's last-ever goal at the 'old' Wembley in the victory over Ukraine and the Arsenal star also made sixty appearances for his country at the 'old' Empire Stadium – more than any other England player.

In his first 16 months as England manager, Keegan gave full international debuts to thirteen players, among them Emile Heskey, Frank Lampard and Steve Gerrard. Lampard made his bow against Belgium in October 1999, and Gerrard followed with his against Ukraine in May 2000. Also, during the 1999/2000 season, David Seaman (*v.* Hungary), Alan Shearer (*v.* Sweden) and Paul Ince (*v.* Malta) all collected their fiftieth caps.

Unfortunately, as had so often happened, England failed to deliver in Belgium and The Netherlands. They didn't even make it out of their group, registering only one win – 1-0 over Germany – while losing 3-2 to Portugal and by the same score to Romania (Alan Shearer's last game for his country).

Soon after the start of the 2000/01 Millennium season, England drew 1-1 with France in Paris, before taking on Germany in the first of the qualifying games for the 2002 World Cup and the last international at the 'old' Wembley.

Keegan Quits

For Keegan, the game against the Germans, which took place on a wet, damp, dank day in October, was to be his last in charge. England lost 1-0 to a Dietmar Hamann's long-range goal on fourteen minutes and, after being out-fought, out-run and sometimes out-played, Keegan and his team left the pitch to a chorus of jeers. In the dressing room, Keegan immediately told his players, 'I'm quitting.' It was that simple.

The former Liverpool, Southampton and Newcastle star of the side, who scored twenty-one goals in sixty-three internationals in ten years up to 1982, departed the scene after just eighteen games in charge (seven wins, seven draws and four defeats). The FA put Howard Wilkinson back in control for one World Cup qualifying game – a goalless draw in Finland.

It was all a bit of a mess, and after several names had been bandied around as possible candidates for the vacant manager's job – with Alex Ferguson and Arsène Wenger among them – it was a Swede, Sven-Göran Eriksson, who was finally appointed as England's first 'foreign' manager on 31 October 2000. Some ardent Englishmen were appalled with the FA's decision to choose a 'foreigner'. One of the 1966 World Cup winning team, Jack 'The Giraffe' Charlton, thought it was a 'a terrible mistake', while Gordon Taylor, FA chief executive, said, 'It's a very sad day for English football.'

However, it was announced that Eriksson would like to see his contract out with the Italian club Lazio before taking over the England job, so Peter Taylor was named as caretaker-boss for the next game, a 1-0 friendly defeat in Italy. Things started to go wrong for Lazio in Serie A and, with the fans unhappy, Eriksson chose to move to England early in the New Year, bringing with him his coach Tord Grip.

For his first game in charge – a friendly against Spain at Villa Park – Eriksson gave debuts to full-backs Michael Ball and Chris Powell (the latter at the ripe old age of thirty-one) and midfielder Gavin McCann. He also brought back Ugo Ehiogu after an absence of almost five years, and the Middlesbrough defender said thank you by scoring in a 3-0 win.

Friendly matches meant almost nothing to Eriksson. 'They are training sessions,' he said. His main priority was to make certain that England qualified for the 2002 World Cup. And, over the space of four days in late March, six points were pocketed from a 2-1 win over Finland at Anfield and a 3-1 victory against Albania in Tirana. Michael Owen scored in both games. After a useful 'friendly' performance against Mexico at Pride Park, Derby (won 4-0), England gained their third straight World Cup qualifying win under Eriksson with a 2-0 victory in Athens against Greece. And, before the turn of the year, they registered a pulsating 5-1 win over Germany in Munich and beat Albania 2-0 at St James' Park, Newcastle, before booking a place on the plane nto the Far East with a nail-biting 2-2 draw with Greece at Old Trafford – David Beckham's wonderful last-minute free-kick securing a place in the finals. It was certainly 'Golden Balls Becks' after this stunning effort.

23

The 2002 World Cup Qualifying Matches

7 October 2000   England 0 Germany 1
Wembley   Attendance 76,377

England Team: D. Seaman, G. Neville, G. Le Saux, G. Southgate, T. Adams, M. Keown (Arsenal), D. Beckham, P. Scholes, A. Cole (Manchester United), M. Owen, N. Barmby. Substitutes: R. Parlour (Arsenal) for Beckham, G. Barry (Aston Villa) for Le Saux.
This game was the last at the 'old' Wembley. The demolition of the stadium, built in 1923, had already been announced. Prior to the match, England's line-up was leaked to the media, leading to criticism from manager Kevin Keegan.

Both England and Germany fielded 4-4-2 formations; Keegan selecting centre-back Gareth Southgate, controversially in some quarters, as a defensive midfielder ahead of Paul Ince and Dennis Wise. The only goal of a tight encounter was scored by Dietmar Hamann after fourteen minutes. It came from a free-kick awarded for a foul on Michael Ballack by Paul Scholes some 30 yards out. Unfortunately, David Seaman took some blame for the goal. Thereafter, outstanding German goalkeeper Oliver Kahn stopped efforts from Andy Cole and Tony Adams in the first half, and pulled off a terrific save from David Beckham's free-kick in the second. This was not the start England wanted, and at the final whistle Keegan quit as manager. Under-21 coach Howard Wilkinson was appointed caretaker-manager for the next game in Finland.

11 October 2000   Finland 0 England 0
Helsinki   Attendance 36,210

England Team: D. Seaman, P. Neville, G. Barry, D. Wise, M. Keown, G. Southgate, R. Parlour, P. Scholes, A. Cole, T. Sheringham, E. Heskey (Leicester City). Substitutes: W. Brown (Manchester United) for Barry, S. McManaman for Sheringham.
This was not a great game. Finland defended resiliently, England lacked penetration and a draw was a fair result. After four days of disruption within the England camp, the backroom staff followed Keegan out of the door, temporarily replaced by Brian Kidd

and Stuart Pearce. Further trouble followed when players Beckham, Gerrard, Adams and Le Saux all withdrew due to injuries. Temporary manager Wilkinson called up the Manchester United duo of Wes Brown and Teddy Sheringham and named Martin Keown as captain. Early in the game, Sheringham, in a one-on-one situation with Finland's goalkeeper Antti Niemi, was pulled down. The challenge looked to be a clear sending off offence, but French referee Alain Sars produced only a yellow card.

England dominated the first half and continued to run the show after the break, but chances were few and far between. In fact, David Seaman did not have a shot to save until the seventy-second minute. With time running out, England thought they had scored when Ray Parlour struck the bar; the ball appeared to have crossed the line but the French referee waved play on, much to England's disgust. As full time approached, Dennis Wise had a penalty appeal turned down. Wilkinson said, 'A point here is okay by me.'

24 March 2001	England 2 Finland 1
Anfield	Attendance 44,262

England Team: D. Seaman, G. Neville, C. Powell (Charlton Athletic), S. Gerrard (Liverpool), R. Ferdinand (Leeds United), S. Campbell, D. Beckham, P. Scholes, A. Cole, M. Owen, S. McManaman. Substitutes: R. Fowler (Liverpool) for Cole, N. Butt (Manchester United) for Owen, E. Heskey for McManaman.

Phew… England just about deserved to win this closely fought encounter. An own-goal by Gary Neville in the twenty-sixth minute gave the Finns the lead. The Manchester United player couldn't avoid Riihilahti's flick-on from a corner, and the ball flew past Seaman off his knee. England pressed forward and, two minutes before half-time, Neville's teasing cross from the right was touched on by Andy Cole to Michael Owen, who scored from close range. Five minutes into the second half, England took the lead. Steve 'Shaggy' McManaman started the move, Paul Scholes carried it on and David Beckham finished off. Later on, Owen struck a post as England came close to adding to their goal tally.

28 March 2001	Albania 1 England 3
Tirana	Attendance 18,034

England Team: D. Seaman, G. Neville, A. Cole (Arsenal), N. Butt, R. Ferdinand, S. Campbell, D. Beckham, P. Scholes, A. Cole (Manchester United), M. Owen, S. McManaman. Substitutes: W. Brown for Campbell, T. Sheringham for Owen, E. Heskey for McManaman.

This was not an easy game; far from it. England had to fight all the way to register this important win. After almost an hour and a quarter without a goal, the crowd saw four come along in the last sector. Michael Owen put England ahead in the seventy-third minute, and Paul Scholes added a second twelve minutes later. Then, within the space thirty seconds, right at the end of the game, substitute Altin Rraklli (Albania) and then Andy Cole, with his first goal in thirteen internationals, made the final score 3-1.

Goalscorer Owen said, 'It was tough out there at times, but we deserved to win.' Left-back Ashley Cole made his senior debut for England, while no less than seven Manchester United players were involved the action during the course of the ninety minutes.

6 June 2001	Greece 0 England 2
Athens	Attendance 29,365

England Team: D. Seaman, P. Neville, A. Cole, S. Gerrard, R. Ferdinand, M. Keown, D. Beckham, P. Scholes, R. Fowler, M. Owen, E. Heskey. Substitutes: N. Butt for Scholes, A. Smith (Leeds United) for Fowler, S. McManaman for Heskey.

No one expected Sven-Göran Eriksson to be on the verge of breaking records in only his fifth game in charge, but history – a weighty and unwanted companion at the best of times for England managers – showed that only Walter Winterbottom had won his first four games in charge. If ever a manager looked so untroubled standing on the threshold of such a record – meaningless though it was – it was Eriksson.

England did not have it all their own way in Athens – far from it. They found the Greeks a hard nut to crack, and it wasn't until the sixty-fourth minute that the breakthrough came. Phil Neville made ground in midfield and passed to Emile Heskey. His miskick squirted through to Paul Scholes, who scored from 6 yards. David Beckham clinched the win with a splendid 28-yard curler past Antonios Nikopolidis in the eighty-seventh minute. Some reports give the attendance at this game as 45,000 – no way.

1 September 2001	Germany 1 England 5
Munich	Attendance 62,788

England Team: D. Seaman, G. Neville, A. Cole, S. Gerrard, S. Campbell, R. Ferdinand, D. Beckham, P. Scholes, M. Owen, N. Barmby, E. Heskey. Substitutes: O. Hargreaves (Bayern Munich) for Gerrard, J. Carragher (Liverpool) for Scholes, S. McManaman for Barmby.

This was a magnificent victory by England. Michael Owen blasted in a stunning hat-trick as Sven-Göran Eriksson's men came from behind to thrash Germany on their own patch. This emphatic result immediately sent shockwaves through the international game, as Germany had only ever lost one World Cup qualifier at home in their history, but suddenly they were torn apart by an England team playing slick football with a clinical edge up front. Owen's treble obviously made the headlines, but there were heroes all over the pitch for England, with captain David Beckham and rejuvenated goalkeeper David Seaman outstanding.

The Germans took the lead on six minutes when hesitancy between Rio Ferdinand and Sol Campbell allowed Carsten Jancker to bundle Oliver Neuville's header over the line. But if England's defenders looked nervous, then the German duo of Thomas Linke and Jens Nowotny seemed nothing short of petrified, and experienced goalkeeper Oliver Kahn looked far from happy. Indeed, after twelve minutes, with Khan caught horribly out of position, Owen equalised from Nicky Barmby's knockdown from Beckham's teasing cross.

At the other end of the pitch, Seaman silenced his critics with a brilliant, one-handed save to turn away Jörg Böhme's low shot and, soon afterwards, Sebastian Deisler fluffed his shot when completely unmarked in front of goal. That proved to be just the second warning that Eriksson's side needed. And Germany were punished in the forty-fifth minute when Ferdinand headed down a Beckham cross for Steven Gerrard to unleash an unstoppable 25-yard drive beyond Kahn's despairing grasp. England went into their dressing room with high spirits, but few could have predicted the astonishing second-half blitz that was to follow.

Owen gave England a vital two-goal cushion when he neatly tucked his low shot inside Kahn's near post, after Emile Heskey had superbly headed down another Beckham cross two minutes after the resumption. The Liverpool star was 'red hot', uncontrollable, and he did not have to wait long for his hat-trick. Gerrard sent him scampering clear with a superb through ball, and the hungry striker ignored Heskey's call and blasted home a sensational shot into the top left-hand corner. On a night when some of England's finest triumphs were remembered, the timing of Owen's clinching goal – in the sixty-sixth minute – was pleasantly significant (World Cup glory).

Heskey's moment did arrive, though, as the big striker put the seal on England's brilliant win seventeen minutes from time. Paul Scholes squared the ball into an empty German penalty area to Heskey, who held off Marko Rehmer's challenge to complete Liverpool's three-man contribution to the scoring. The floodgates had long since been opened, but now the exit doors were thrown open too as thousands of disgruntled German fans headed home in disbelief. Indeed, after all the prematch criticism aimed at England's No. 1, David Seaman, and the claims heralding Kahn as the world's No. 1, the home side's 'keeper was left with egg on his face – or should that be five eggs. Comparitively, Seaman hardly put a foot (or hand) wrong.

The England supporters stayed right where they were, pinching themselves and wondering whether it was all a dream. Munich's Olympic Stadium all of a sudden became festooned with Union Jacks, and red and white flags. A great night and early morning was had by all.

3 September 2001	England 2 Albania 0
St James' Park, Newcastle	Attendance 51,046

England Team: D. Seaman, G. Neville, A. Cole, S. Gerrard, R. Ferdinand, S. Campbell, D. Beckham, P. Scholes, E. Heskey, M. Owen, N. Barmby. Substitutes: J. Carragher for Gerrard, R. Fowler for Heskey, S. McManaman for Barmby.

Sven-Göran Eriksson, having told his players to forget Munich, saw his team struggle in front of a near full-house at Newcastle to break down an obdurate, tightly organised Albanian defence. It took a sharp piece of opportunism by Michael Owen, inspired by a glorious pass from Paul Scholes, to bring England a goal on the stroke of half-time, but still Eriksson's attack laboured against opponents who were never going to be dismissed as lightly as the Germans in their previous match. In fact, it took a piece of late magic from Robbie Fowler to make the scoreline look more respectable against the eighty-sixth ranked country in the world. Before kick-off, a one-minute silence was observed in respect of football commentator Brian Moore, who had died forty-eight hours earlier.

6 October 2001	England 2 Greece 2
Old Trafford	Attendance 66,009

England Team: N. Martyn (Leeds United), G. Neville, A. Cole, S. Gerrard, R. Ferdinand, M. Keown, D. Beckham, P. Scholes, E. Heskey, R. Fowler, N. Barmby. Substitutes: J. Cole (West Ham United) for Barmby, S. McManaman for Cole, T. Sheringham for Fowler.
David Beckham's stunning late equaliser on his home ground booked England a place in the 2002 World Cup finals. Colin Malam wrote in *The Telegraph*, 'Cometh the hour, cometh the man. There was only one minute of stoppage time left when the England captain salvaged his team's fading hopes of qualifying automatically for next year's World Cup finals.' A potential banana-skin of a play-off against Ukraine was looming when Beckham, who played his heart out, managed to curl one of his lethal free-kicks past Antonios Nikopolidis, Greece's heroic goalkeeper. Old Trafford simply erupted. What a goal, what a finish.

Angelos Charisteas had given the visitors the lead in the thirty-second minute. Nigel Martyn, deputising for David Seaman, had no chance of saving the full-back's low, well-struck shot as he cut in from the right. It took quite a while for England to recover from that shock goal, but recover they did. Halfway through the second half, substitute Teddy Sheringham, who had replaced Robbie Fowler just ten seconds earlier, looped a header into the net from Beckham's finely delivered free-kick – the fastest-ever England goal by a substitute.

Everyone knew that England needed to match Germany's result against Finland to win Group 9. But they were unrecognisable as the side that had won so convincingly in Munich five weeks before. In fact, Sven-Göran Eriksson's men looked set to throw it all away when, just ninety seconds later, after some awful defending in general and by Rio Ferdinand in particular, Demis Nikolaidis put Greece back in front with a smart finish after Nikolaos Dabizas had flicked on Christos Patsatzoglou's free-kick. Then came a quite amazing finale. Sheringham conned the referee into awarding a free-kick 20 yards from goal. Up stepped Beckham – bang – 2-2. England had done it, just, as Germany could only manage a draw. 'We don't want any more of these cliffhangers,' said Eriksson.

Problems for Eriksson

Prior to their last three World Cup qualifying matches, England lost 2-0 to The Netherlands at White Hart Lane, when Eriksson used three goalkeepers and twenty-two players during the ninety minutes, and afterwards drew 1-1 with Sweden at Old Trafford, when eighteen players were called into action this time. Well, Eriksson did say that he wanted to have a look at as many players as possible.

Some news that concerned Eriksson, however, was the fact that two of his key players were injured in Champions League matches. The influential David Beckham broke a bone in his left foot playing for Manchester United against Deportivo de La Coruña, and his clubmate Gary Neville joined him on the injured list when he was forced off in the semi-final against Bayer Leverkusen. Kieron Dyer (Newcastle) was also a doubt, as was Liverpool's Steven Gerrard, who was struggling with a groin problem. Thankfully, Beckham and Gerrard proved their fitness, although not Neville.

Before naming his squad to travel to the Far East, Eriksson was able to have another look at more possibilities in three extra friendlies played over a period of three and a half months (February–May). England drew 1-1 with The Netherlands in a return fixture in Amsterdam (when Aston Villa debutant Darius Vassell equalised with a terrific scissor-kick), lost 2-1 to Italy at Elland Road, Leeds, and beat Paraguay 4-0 at Anfield, when Vassell scored again.

Players who appeared in those friendlies, hoping to be allocated a ticket on the plane to the Far East, included full-backs Danny Mills and Wayne Bridge, versatile defender Wes Brown, midfielders Joe Cole, Danny Murphy and Owen Hargreaves, and winger Trevor Sinclair. In the end they were all chosen, ready to face Argentina, Nigeria and Sweden in Group F.

Eriksson's twenty-five-man squad for the 2002 World Cup in Japan and South Korea was:

Goalkeepers: David James (West Ham United), Nigel Martyn (Leeds United), David Seaman (Arsenal). Full-backs: Ashley Cole (Arsenal), Danny Mills (Leeds United), Wayne Bridge (Southampton). Defenders: Wes Brown (Manchester United), Sol Campbell (Arsenal), Rio Ferdinand (Leeds United), Martin Keown (Arsenal), Gareth Southgate (Middlesbrough). Midfielders: David Beckham (Manchester United), Nicky Butt (Manchester United), Joe Cole (West Ham United), Kieron Dyer (Newcastle United), Steve Gerrard (Liverpool), Owen Hargreaves (Bayern Munich), Danny Murphy (Liverpool), Paul Scholes (Manchester United), Trevor Sinclair (West Ham United). Forwards: Robbie Fowler (Leeds United), Emile Heskey (Liverpool), Michael Owen (Liverpool), Teddy Sheringham (Tottenham Hotspur), Darius Vassell (Aston Villa).

NB: Eriksson named the Manchester United brothers Gary and Phil Neville, full-back Chris Powell of Charlton Athletic and striker Kevin Phillips of Sunderland as standby reserves.

For the World Cup in the Land of the Rising Sun, England were given an island base near to Kobe, Japan. To get acclimatised to the weather conditions, two pre-tournament warm-up matches were arranged against South Korea in Seogwuipo and Cameroon in Kobe. Both games ended in draws, 1-1 and 2-2 respectively. England started the competition with an untidy 1-1 draw with Sweden, Sol Campbell netting his country's first goal in Japan.

24

The 2002 World Cup in Japan & South Korea

2 June 2002   England 1 Sweden 1
Saitama   Attendance 52,271

*England Team: D. Seaman, D. Mills, A. Cole, P. Scholes, S. Campbell, R. Ferdinand,
D. Beckham, D. Vassell, E. Heskey, M. Owen, O. Hargreaves. Substitutes: K. Dyer for
Beckham, J. Cole for Vassell.*
England began their World Cup campaign with an unconvincing draw against a Sweden
team who dominated the second half and could easily have snatched victory – only
goalkeeper David Seaman kept his side in the match. Sol Campbell opened the scoring for
England with a powerful header in the twenty-fourth minute, but Niclas Alexandersson
deservedly equalised for the Swedes after fifty-nine minutes, following a Danny Mills
blunder, who failed a chest pass back to Seaman. This was not a great game by any
means. England's passing went to pot and they lost their shape. Owen Hargreaves and
Paul Scholes worked hard in midfield, but Beckham was not fully fit and was substituted
by Dyer after an hour. He never looked fit either. Next up, Argentina.

7 June 2002   England 1 Argentina 0
Sapporo   Attendance 35,927

*England Team: D. Seaman, D. Mills, A. Cole, N. Butt, R. Ferdinand, S. Campbell,
D. Beckham, P. Scholes, E. Heskey, M. Owen, O. Hargreaves. Substitutes: T. Sheringham
for Heskey, W. Bridge for Owen, T. Sinclair for Hargreaves.*
On a night when all of Sven-Göran Eriksson's players showed great composure and
resilience under pressure, David Beckham stood out head and shoulders above the rest.
Presented with a penalty chance just before half-time, after Michael Owen had been fouled
by Mauricio Pochettino (who would become Southampton's manager in January 2013),
Beckham displayed the type of character that has been his hallmark since recovering from
the ignominy of his dismissal against the same opponents four years earlier, smashing the
ball past goalkeeper Pablo Cavallero. England had bowed out of the previous World Cup

on penalties to the Argentinians. This time they had the chance of gaining sweet revenge. And they took it.

There was no chance at all of Michael Owen taking the penalty. It was Beckham's job and he loved it. Argentina tried their best – or worst – to distract 'Golden Balls'. Goalkeeper Cavallero marched over to Beckham and indicated where he should place his shot. What arrogance. Beckham just blanked him. Next to try and distract the Manchester United star was Diego Simeone, whose play-acting had led to Beckham's red card in 1998. He was put firmly in his place by Paul Scholes and Nicky Butt. With the England fans nervously quiet, Beckham strode forward and put four years of hurt into one kick, sending the ball hard and low, and dead straight into the net as Cavallero dived to his right. The goal triggered off a tidal wave of jubilation throughout the Sapporo Dome. For all their posturing at the end, Argentina could not argue with the result. England had won despite Marcelo Bielsa's men having 65 per cent of possession. 'We scored, they didn't,' said Scholes.

Without doubt, this was a victory for the players, who performed with great maturity and discipline, both tactical and temperamental. David Seaman was superb in goal, brilliantly saving Gabriel Batistuta's header, holding onto an Ariel Ortega cross with Juan Sorín's studs almost in his face, and finally keeping out an effort from Mauricio Pochettino. Eriksson and England were now within one point of reaching the knockout stage, a remarkable achievement given that top nations such as France, Argentina and possibly Germany all faced elimination. England needed only a draw against Nigeria in their next game to guarantee a last sixteen meeting with Denmark, Senegal, Uruguay or France. All of a sudden, the England football team was full of Far Eastern promise. Could it last?

12 June 2002	England 0 Nigeria 0
Osaka	Attendance 44,864

England Team: D. Seaman, D. Mills, A. Cole, N. Butt, R. Ferdinand, S. Campbell, D. Beckham, P. Scholes, E. Heskey, M. Owen, T. Sinclair. Substitutes: W. Bridge for Cole, T. Sheringham for Heskey, D. Vassell for Owen.

After producing such an excellent all-round performance against Argentina five days earlier, England laboured to an uninspiring, somewhat cautious, goalless draw against Nigeria, yet the vital point gained was enough to put Sven-Göran Eriksson's men into the last sixteen. There were relatively few highlights in a rather drab encounter. After Nigeria's trio of Ifeanyi Udeze, Benedict Akwuegbu and Julius Aghahowa had threatened early on, Jay-Jay Okocha's powerful free-kick on thirty minutes was fumbled by David Seaman who, thankfully, 'got away with his error'. Two minutes before half-time, Paul Scholes' fierce drive was palmed onto the post by the diving Vincent Enyeama, and late on Teddy Sheringham missed an open goal from Michael Owen's flick-on, while Ashley Cole's freak shot struck the Nigerian crossbar. However, it must be said that the real highlight of the afternoon for England fans was not their team's performance but the fact that Sweden had knocked out fierce rivals Argentina in the other group game. Say no more.

Next up for Sven's men were the vulnerable Danes, with a place in the quarter-finals awaiting the winners.

15 June 2002   England 3 Denmark 0
Niigata   Attendance 40,582

England Team: D. Seaman, D. Mills, A. Cole, N. Butt, S. Campbell, R. Ferdinand, D. Beckham, P. Scholes, E. Heskey, M. Owen, T. Sinclair. Substitutes: T. Sheringham for Heskey, K. Dyer for Scholes, R. Fowler for Owen.

Some awful, comical defending by the Danes made this a 'stroll in the park' for England, who equalled their best-ever score in World Cup finals with a comfortable victory in front of 10,000 travelling fans in Niigata. It must be said, as well, that England produced some smart finishes, comfortably clinching a quarter-final place before half-time, courtesy of three mistakes.

Martin Laursen showed the Danes' collective edginess by conceding a needless corner after five minutes. From David Beckham's flag-kick, goalkeeper Thomas Sørensen, caught in no man's land, watched the ball soar over his head and into Rio Ferdinand's path, 6 yards out. The centre-back should have scored, but fluffed his header back towards Sørensen. Instead of diving on the ball, however, the Danish 'keeper snatched at it – not once, not twice, but three times – before seeing it bobble over the line.

The scoreboard showed England 1-0 up, and that quickly became 2-0 when, in the twenty-second minute, the ball broke to Trevor Sinclair down the left. He slid a pass across the face of the box to Nicky Butt, whose elaborate flick should have been cut out by Laursen. Instead, the ball went through his legs. Michael Owen pounced to steer it into the bottom-right corner.

The Danes were killed off just before half-time by Emile Heskey, whose 20-yard drive sped under Sørensen's body. Another boob. England eased off in the second half. The Danes played a bit better but, overall, this was an easy victory for Sven's improving team. Next on the agenda: a Friday morning match against mighty Brazil.

21 June 2002   England 1 Brazil 2
Shizuoka   Attendance 47,436

England Team: D. Seaman, D. Mills, A. Cole, N. Butt, S. Campbell, R. Ferdinand, D. Beckham, P. Scholes, E. Heskey, M. Owen, T. Sinclair. Substitutes: T. Sheringham for Cole, D. Vassell for Owen, K. Dyer for Sinclair.

Unfortunately, England failed to live up to prematch expectations and never really looked like beating the Samba Men, even after their opponents were reduced to ten men when Ronaldinho was undeservedly sent off by Mexican referee Ramos Rizo in the fifty-eighth minute for a foul on Danny Mills. Sven-Göran Eriksson's men were second best for long periods and, in the end, could well have conceded two or three more goals. In fact, Brazil had twice as many efforts on goal than England.

Following a mistake by centre-half Lúcio da Silva, England surprisingly took the lead in the twenty-third minute thanks to a wonderful piece of marksmanship by Michael Owen. But after that they never really threatened, and conceded goals either side of the interval. Two and a half minutes into added time at the end of the first half, out-of-sorts David Beckham jumped high, near the halfway line, to avoid a 'sandwich'. The ball broke free, and when Paul Scholes missed his midfield challenge, Brazil gained possession, putting together two swift passes to send the influential Rivaldo through to equalise, with a cracking left-footed drive out of the reach of goalkeeper David Seaman.

Five minutes after the resumption, England gave away a foul 40 yards from goal. There seemed no danger whatsoever as Ronaldinho, more in hope than anything else, lofted his free-kick towards England's penalty area. However, to everyone's amazement, even the Brazilians, Seaman, seemingly in no-man's land, completely misjudged the flight of the ball, and as he struggled to regain his composure, it was in the back of his net. A bad, bad mistake.

After this setback, England simply ran out of steam and ideas as the game progressed, failing to make the extra man count. In fact, it looked as if Brazil had eleven players on the pitch, not England. If the truth be known, a line-up featuring Darius Vassell, Trevor Sinclair and Danny Mills – they all played a part, I'll give them that – was never going to win the World Cup. Reaching the quarter-finals was a fair reflection of this team's overall ability.

The heat and humidity certainly got to the players in Japan, and there is no doubt that at least four were carrying injuries. Taking on the best opposition in world football was a tough call in the end, and England, found wanting, simply couldn't manage it. So, it was all hands to the pump for manager, coaches and players as preparations began for the 2004 European Championships in Portugal, while the 2006 World Cup, four years away, was scheduled to take place in Germany.

2002 World Cup Fact File

- Countries taking part: 32 (divided into eight groups of 4).
- Final: Brazil 2, Germany 0.
- Final venue: International Stadium, Yokohama (attendance 69,029).
- Leading scorer: Ronaldo Luís Nazário de Lima (Brazil), 8 goals.
- Brazil won a record seven matches during this tournament.
- Turkey's Hakan Şükür scored the fastest goal in World Cup finals, netting after just eleven seconds' play against South Korea.

Euro 2004 Ahead of the Next World Cup

After a warm-up 1-1 friendly draw with Portugal at Villa Park, England won their first Euro 2004 qualifying match 2-1 in Bratislava against Slovakia. They followed up with a 2-2 home draw against Macedonia, but were then booed off the pitch by their fans after losing 3-1 in a friendly to Australia at Upton Park, home of West Ham United. This was, without a shadow of doubt, a diabolical performance – one of England's worst for many years – and Eriksson took a lot of stick for once again using twenty-two different players on the night, leaving another five sitting, rather frustrated, on the bench. Wayne Rooney, aged seventeen years, 111 days, had his senior debut, becoming the youngest player ever to win a full England cap (at that time – February 2003).

However, Eriksson's men picked themselves up and won their next five qualifiers – beating Liechtenstein 2-0 in Vaduz, Turkey 2-0 at the Stadium of Light, Sunderland, Slovakia 2-1 in the return game at Middlesbrough, Macedonia 2-1 in Skopje and Liechtenstein, again, 2-0 at Old Trafford. This left them needing just one point from the last game against Turkey in Istanbul to qualify. They achieved their goal, claiming a 0-0 to top the group.

In the middle of these qualifying matches, and to keep the momentum flowing, England played and won four friendlies; defeating South Africa 2-1 in Durban, Serbia and Montenegro by the same score at Leicester (when John Terry won his first cap) and Croatia 3-1 at Ipswich. But they ended 2003 rather disappointingly by losing 3-2 at Old Trafford against Denmark when right-back Glen Johnson made his debut and five Chelsea players were involved in the action.

Before the Euro Championships, Eriksson arranged four more friendly matches, three of them against potentially strong opponents. England remained unbeaten, drawing 1-1 with Portugal in Faro, beating Sweden 1-0 in Gothenburg, while drawing 1-1 with Japan and beating Iceland 6-1 in a summer tournament staged at the City of Manchester (Eastlands) Stadium. Again, Eriksson utilised twenty-two of the twenty-three players he named in his squad for the game against Iceland.

The Euro 2004 finals started in June. In their first match in Lisbon, England were leading 1-0 against France after ninety minutes, but ended up losing to two dramatic Zinedine Zidane goals in injury time. Victories over Switzerland (3-0) and Croatia (4-2) followed, meaning that Eriksson's team qualified for the quarter-final, where they would play the hosts, Portugal, in Lisbon.

In front of a passionate home crowd, Michael Owen gave England an early lead, but Hélder Postiga equalised to take the tie into extra time. While Sol Campbell had what looked like a perfectly good winning header, it was disallowed and no further goals were scored. England, as usual, lost on penalties (6-5).

NB: By this time, Paul Scholes had played in his sixty-sixth and final international, having established a record of being substituted thirty-eight times.

Build Up Commences

Regardless of the antipathy to manager Eriksson expressed by some in the English media, the players had total confidence in him and threatened to strike during one media-driven campaign to oust him. He was also backed by the official England Fan organisations, and this led to the FA renewing and even extending the Swede's contract by two further years to include the 2008 European Championships.

After an early season 3-0 victory in a friendly against Ukraine at Newcastle, England got their World Cup qualifying campaign underway in September 2004. Drawn in Group 6 with Austria, Azerbaijan, Northern Ireland, Poland and Wales, they started off with a 2-2 draw with the Austrians, having led 2-0 at one time in Vienna. In their second game, they beat a stubborn Polish side 2-1 in Chorzów, courtesy of an own-goal, followed by a 2-0 victory over Wales at Old Trafford, and then edged home 1-0 against plucky Azerbaijan in Baku – Michael Owen's twenty-second-minute goal deciding the tight match. After a 1-0 friendly defeat at the hands of Spain in Madrid (when goalkeeper Paul Robinson saved a penalty) and a goalless draw with The Netherlands at Villa Park, England's fifth World Cup qualifier resulted in a comfortable 4-0 win over Northern Ireland, also at the home of Manchester United.

They then ran up four successive wins: a 2-0 victory over Azerbaijan at St James' Park, Newcastle; a 2-1 success over the USA at Soldier Field, Chicago (when Fulham's giant defender Zat Knight became the fiftieth black player to win a full England cap); a 3-2 triumph over Colombia in the Giants Stadium, East Rutherford, New Jersey, on their American tour; and a 1-0 qualifying victory over Wales at the Millennium Stadium. Joe Cole bagged the winner in the fifty-fourth minute to topple the resilient Welsh.

After a 4-1 friendly reverse in Denmark in early September 2005 – their heaviest defeat in twenty-five years since losing by the same score against Wales in May 1980 – England, against all the odds, surprisingly lost their return qualifier with Northern Ireland 1-0 at Windsor Park, Belfast. This was the first time the Irish had beaten an England's team since 1972. In fact, this defeat was one of only five suffered by England during Eriksson's tenure. Although it was the first defeat in a World Cup or European Championship qualifying match under Eriksson, it brought his position under unprecedented pressure, and he was criticised both by supporters and by BBC commentators for his alleged lack of charisma and tactical awareness. With harsh criticism still ongoing, England pulled off an excellent 3-2 win over Argentina in Geneva in mid-November, scrambled to a 1-0 victory over Austria in their penultimate qualifying game – which saw David Beckham controversially sent off. Despite the absence of the suspended Beckham, and Sol Campbell and Steven Gerrard through injury, they claimed a 2-1 win over Poland at Old Trafford in their final qualifier, Frank Lampard striking in the eighty-first minute.

As a result of that last victory, England finished top of group with twenty-five points (eight wins and a draw), one more than Poland, with Austria a distant third.

25

The 2006 World Cup Qualifying Matches

4 September 2004   Austria 2 England 2
Vienna   Attendance 48,453

England Team: D. James, G. Neville, A. Cole, S. Gerrard, J. Terry, L. King, D. Beckham, F. Lampard, A. Smith, M. Owen, W. Bridge. Substitutes: J. Carragher for Gerrard, J. Cole for Bridge, J. Defoe for Smith.

Goalkeeping errors were plentiful in this encounter, and two calamitous mistakes by David James cost England victory in Vienna. In the twenty-fourth minute, James' opposite number, Alex Manninger – the ex-Arsenal 'keeper known for a neurotic intensity that made Woody Allen look calm – contrived to help England into a lead. He stupidly broke the rule by picking up a back pass, David Beckham took the free-kick and Frank Lampard tapped home. England doubled their lead in the sixty-fourth minute when Steven Gerrard netted with a delightful 25-yard chip. Then it was time for Mr James to take centre stage inside the Ernst Happel Stadium.

At this juncture, with around twenty-five minutes remaining, Austria were looking far worse than their eighty-ninth world ranking signified. But, suddenly, out of the blue, they burst into life. In the seventy-first minute their euphoria was mixed with disbelief when a speculative long-range shot from Roland Kollman, slithered underneath James's body and into the net: 2-1. Two minutes later, the ground erupted when Andreas Ivanschitz equalised with a 25-yarder, the ball slithering through James' fingers as he dived across his line. Several England players put their hands to their faces ... They couldn't believe what had happened in the space of 120 seconds. This was a game James will never forget.

After the opening set of qualification matches, Group 6 looked a good deal tighter than anyone expected. England's next game was against Poland in Chorzów, and they had just three days to sharpen up at both ends of the field or else.

8 September 2004
Chorzów

Poland 1 England 2
Attendance 38,120

England Team: P. Robinson, G. Neville, A. Cole, S. Gerrard, J. Terry, L. King, D. Beckham, F. Lampard, J. Defoe, M. Owen, W. Bridge. Substitutes: J. Carragher for Neville, O. Hargreaves for Beckham, K. Dyer for Defoe.

Sven-Göran Eriksson made two changes to his line-up after the disappointing draw in Austria. David James was dropped in favour of Paul Robinson, and Alan Smith was also axed. Jermain Defoe was brought in to lead the attack, and after failing to convert a relatively easy chance on twenty minutes, he turned brilliantly inside the penalty area to put England ahead eight minutes from half-time.

The lively Maciej Żurawski equalised for Poland with a powerful 15-yard finish three minutes after the restart, before England claimed the winner on fifty-seven minutes when Arkadiusz Głowacki, finding Michael Owen on his tail, deflected Ashley Cole's cross past his own goalkeeper, Jerzy Dudek. Both Wayne Bridge and Owen came close to adding to the score late on.

This was a vital, morale-boosting win for England, which left them on four points from their opening two games. Defoe's performance also gave Eriksson a pleasant dilemma, knowing that Wayne Rooney would soon be available for selection after a foot injury.

9 October 2004
Old Trafford

England 2 Wales 0
Attendance 65,224

England Team: P. Robinson, G. Neville, A. Cole, N. Butt, S. Campbell, R. Ferdinand, D. Beckham, W. Rooney, M. Owen, J. Defoe, F. Lampard. Substitutes: O. Hargreaves for Beckham, L. King for Rooney, A. Smith for Defoe.

David Beckham netted with a quite spectacular strike to secure England a comfortable World Cup qualifying victory over Wales. England's first attack in the fourth minute produced a goal, Frank Lampard's shot flying into the net off the heel of Michael Owen. Beckham put the icing on the cake when he curled a shot high into the top right-hand corner of Paul Jones' goal with twelve minutes remaining. Jones, in fact, was quite outstanding, producing excellent saves from Owen, Wayne Rooney and Beckham, whose silly late booking ruled him out of England's game in Azerbaijan. Apart from that, there was little to complain about for England boss Sven-Göran Eriksson, who recalled Rooney and Sol Campbell, as well as bringing back Rio Ferdinand following his eight-month ban for missing a drug test.

13 October 2004   Azerbaijan 0 England 1
Baku   Attendance 14,899

England Team: P. Robinson, G. Neville, A. Cole, N. Butt, S. Campbell, R. Ferdinand, J. Jenas, W. Rooney, M. Owen, J. Defoe, F. Lampard. Substitutions: S. Wright-Phillips for Jenas, J. Cole for Rooney, A. Smith for Defoe.

In really atrocious conditions, England's stand-in captain Michael Owen led from the front by netting the game's only goal in the twenty-first minute of a rather scrappy encounter. Deputising for the injured and suspended David Beckham, the Liverpool striker stole in unmarked at the back post to head Ashley Cole's deep cross past Jahangir Hasanzade from 8 yards. This narrow victory strengthened England's position at the top of Group 6. Azerbaijan rarely threatened, Emin Guliyev firing in their only worthwhile effort at goal as early as the eleventh minute. England's goalkeeper Paul Robinson hardly touched the ball with his hands.

26 March 2005   England 4 Northern Ireland 0
Old Trafford   Attendance 65,239

England Team: P. Robinson, G. Neville, A .Cole, S. Gerrard, R. Ferdinand, J. Terry, D. Beckham, F. Lampard, M. Owen, W. Rooney, J. Cole. Substitutions: K. Dyer for Beckham, O. Hargreaves for Gerrard, J. Defoe for Rooney.

England turned on the style in the second half at Old Trafford, striking four goals in fifteen minutes to end Northern Ireland's stubborn resistance in a very entertaining World Cup qualifier. The men in green had frustrated England throughout the first half with some dogged defending, although Wayne Rooney did hit a post. Irish 'keeper Maik Taylor was quite outstanding, saving superbly from David Beckham, Frank Lampard, Rooney and Michael Owen.

However, after the interval, England took charge. Joe Cole set the ball rolling in the forty-sixth minute. The midfielder collected a careless pass from Tony Capaldi before curling the ball home from 20 yards. Five minutes later, Owen added a second from close range after Lampard had surged into the penalty area, and the unfortunate Chris Baird turned Rooney's cross into his own net to make it 3-0 ninety seconds later. The inspirational Lampard's shot flew off the head of the unlucky Colin Murdock in the sixty-second minute for England's fourth. England were impressive in killing off the Irish once the deadlock was broken, and boss Sven-Göran Eriksson admitted he was delighted to see his side take another giant stride towards the World Cup in Germany.

30 March 2005   England 2 Azerbaijan 0
St James' Park   Attendance 49,046

England Team: P. Robinson, G. Neville, A. Cole, R. Ferdinand, J. Terry, S. Gerrard, D. Beckham, F. Lampard, M. Owen, W. Rooney, J. Cole. Substitutes: L. King for Ferdinand, J. Defoe for Beckham, K. Dyer for Rooney.

England suffered forty-five minutes of frustration before goals from Steven Gerrard and David Beckham finally clinched a hard-earned, yet well-deserved, victory over gutsy opponents. Azerbaijan survived a first-half siege, and even came close to going ahead through Gurban Gurbanov before England broke the deadlock after fifty-one minutes, Gerrard scoring at the far post from Wayne Rooney's cross. Eleven minutes later, Beckham raced clear to add a second. England dominated proceedings after that, with Rooney and Frank Lampard both hitting the woodwork.

However, Sven-Göran Eriksson's side never threatened to emulate Poland's 8-0 thrashing of Azerbaijan, and a stupid second-half booking for Michael Owen ruled him out of the next qualifier against Wales in Cardiff.

3 September 2005   Wales 0 England 1
Millennium Stadium   Attendance 70,715

England Team: P. Robinson, L. Young, A. Cole, R. Ferdinand, J. Carragher, D. Beckham, F. Lampard, S. Gerrard, S. Wright-Phillips, J. Cole, W. Rooney. Substitutions: K. Richardson for Gerrard, J. Defoe for Wright-Phillips, O. Hargreaves for J. Cole.

Joe Cole's second-half winner sank Wales and kept England on course for World Cup qualification. Cole broke the deadlock after fifty-four minutes when his shot from Shaun Wright-Phillips' cross was deflected past 'keeper Danny Coyne by defender Danny Gabbidon. Although England dominated throughout, goalkeeper Paul Robinson still needed to produce a brilliant save to prevent John Hartson from giving Wales the lead. Meanwhile, goalscorers Cole and Wayne Rooney were both guilty of bad misses. England, fielding a five-man midfield, had Charlton's Luke Young at right-back in place of the injured Gary Neville.

Midfielder Owen Hargreaves came off the bench in the seventy-sixth minute (for Joe Cole) to equal the record set by Teddy Sheringham and Keiron Dyer for most substitute appearances for England – twenty-one in total.

7 September 2005   Northern Ireland 1 England 0
Belfast   Attendance 13,930

England Team: P. Robinson, L. Young, A. Cole, R. Ferdinand, J. Carragher, D. Beckham, S. Gerrard, F. Lampard, S. Wright-Phillips, W. Rooney, M. Owen. Substitutions: J. Cole for Wright-Phillips, J. Defoe for Gerrard, O. Hargreaves for Lampard.

This was a shock result, as Northern Ireland put a dent in England's World Cup hopes with a one-goal victory at Windsor Park. The Leeds United striker David Healy fired home Steve Davis' pass after seventy-three minutes to give Lawrie Sanchez's side their first victory over England in thirty-three years. It capped a nightmare England display, in which a petulant Wayne Rooney picked up another yellow card and, as a result, was ruled out of the next qualifier against Austria. David Beckham, perhaps England's best player, hit the bar with a free-kick, and Michael Owen came close with a late diving header. Nothing more to be said; this was a horror show.

8 October 2005	England 1 Austria 0
Old Trafford	Attendance 64,822

England Team: P. Robinson, L. Young, J. Carragher, J. Terry, S. Campbell, S. Gerrard, D. Beckham, F. Lampard, J. Cole, P. Crouch, M. Owen. Substitutions: L. King for Cole, K. Richardson for Owen, R. Ferdinand for Campbell.

David Beckham became the first player to be sent off twice for England as they stuttered to victory against Austria at Old Trafford. Beckham was shown two yellow cards in the space of two minutes in the second half, both for fouls on Andreas Ibertsberger.

Playing a 4-4-2 system, England took the lead in the twenty-fifth minute with a Frank Lampard penalty, awarded after Paul Scharner fouled Michael Owen. But while their display was far from assured, England avoided having to take part in the play-offs by qualifying for the finals in Germany after hearing the news that The Netherlands had registered an important victory over the Czech Republic in Group 1. The result of England's next game against Poland, also at Old Trafford, would confirm who would finish up as winners and runners-up in Group 6.

12 October 2005	England 2 Poland 1
Old Trafford	Attendance 65,467

England Team: P. Robinson, L. Young, J. Carragher, L. King, R. Ferdinand, J. Terry, F. Lampard, J. Cole, S. Wright-Phillips, M. Owen, W. Rooney. Substitutions: P. Crouch for Wright-Phillips, J. Jenas for Owen, A. Smith for Cole.

After this competent performance, no one could honestly accuse England of easing through to the World Cup finals. This was, by far, their most impressive showing in Group 6, which they topped thanks to Frank Lampard's eightieth-minute decider. Sven-Göran Eriksson's side showed enterprise, flair and a lot of endurance to cope with a rather unexpected equaliser following Michael Owen's thirty-third goal for his country.

England, aiming to be one of the top seeds at Germany in 2006, played very well overall. Several players had outstanding games, none more so than Tottenham's Ledley King, who despite an uncertain opening, was par excellence as the holding player in a five-man midfield that was minus both Steve Gerrard and the suspended David Beckham. England attacked boldly and frequently, but they had to wait until the forty-fourth minute before taking the lead, Owen diverting Joe Cole's cross-shot past 'keeper Artur Boruc. But then, completely out of the blue, the Poles drew level in stoppage time at the end of the first half. Kamil Kosowski created enough space on the right to deliver the perfect cross for Tomasz Frankowski to volley past Paul Robinson. England, though, were confident throughout the second period and, in the eightieth minute, Cole flipped a pass to Owen, who in turn crossed for Lampard to thump home his tenth goal for his country. Good stuff.

Germany Here We Come

Before setting off for Germany, and with criticism from within the media still rife, Sven-Göran Eriksson saw his players score eleven goals in three friendly matches, beating Uruguay 2-1 at Anfield, Hungary 3-1 at Old Trafford (the day when Theo Walcott, at the age of 17 years, 75 days, became England's youngest-ever senior player, taking over the mantle from Rooney) and Jamaica 6-0, also at the latter stadium. But there was something in the air … and when the FA declared that Eriksson was to be 'released' at the end of the 2006 World Cup tournament, the official England Fan organisation undertook an unprecedented 'Save Our Sven' campaign, which was also engaged in by several British newspapers. The decision was made, however, and Eriksson's tenure was terminated, costing the FA a whole year of penalty payment damages that saw the Swede unemployed for twelve months at the FA's considerable expense.

In 2006, Eriksson was recorded saying he would be willing to quit as manager to take charge of Aston Villa if England won the World Cup, after being duped into believing that a wealthy Arab would buy the Birmingham club and wanted him as manager. The wealthy 'Arab' was, in fact, the 'Fake Sheikh' Mazher Mahmood, an undercover reporter for the *News of the World*. On 23 January 2006, the Football Association announced that Eriksson would officially leave his job when the World Cup was over, and it was thought that the *News of the World* allegations played a part in this decision. This was later denied by both parties, with Eriksson explaining that there was a prior arrangement to terminate his contract immediately after the World Cup. The announcement that Eriksson was to depart from the job as England's team coach was met with extensive protests. Following a lengthy period of public and media speculation as to his successor, the FA announced on 4 May 2006 that Steve McClaren, Eriksson's assistant, would take over the reins for the start of the 2006/07 season.

Meanwhile this was Eriksson's twenty-two-man squad for the 2006 World Cup:

Goalkeepers: Scott Carson (Liverpool), David James (Manchester City), Paul Robinson (Tottenham Hotspur). Full-backs: Wayne Bridge (Chelsea), Ashley Cole (Arsenal), Gary Neville (Manchester United). Defenders: Sol Campbell (Arsenal), Rio Ferdinand (Manchester United), John Terry (Chelsea). Midfielders: David Beckham (Real Madrid), Michael Carrick (Manchester United), Joe Cole (Chelsea), Stewart Downing (Middlesbrough), Steven Gerrard (Liverpool), Owen Hargreaves (Bayern Munich), Jermaine Jenas (Tottenham Hotspur), Frank Lampard (Chelsea), Aaron Lennon (Tottenham Hotspur). Forwards:

Peter Crouch (Liverpool), Michael Owen (Newcastle United), Wayne Rooney (Manchester United), Theo Walcott (Arsenal). Goalkeeper Carson was a late replacement for the injured Rob Green, and in reserve for Germany, Eriksson named full-back Luke Young (Charlton Athletic), midfielder Nigel Reo-Coker (West Ham United) and strikers Jermain Defoe (Tottenham Hotspur and Andrew Johnson (Crystal Palace).

More Disappointment and Another New Manager

The surprise inclusion in Eriksson's squad was young Arsenal winger Theo Walcott, who had not made a single Premiership appearance for the Gunners following his £5 million (rising to £12 million) transfer from Southampton in March 2006.

England were drawn in Group B of the 2006 World Cup finals alongside Paraguay, Sweden and Trinidad & Tobago, and although they didn't play brilliantly – the press indicated that the performances were far from satisfactory – they did enough to finish top of the pile by beating Paraguay 1-0, Trinidad & Tobago 2-0 and drawing 2-2 with the Swedes. Next up it was Ecuador and, again playing well below par, England scraped through with a David Beckham trademark free-kick. This set up a tie with Portugal as Eriksson once again came face to face with his nemesis, Luiz Felipe Scolari. But it all went wrong in Gelsenkirchen. Wayne Rooney was sent off for stamping on defender Ricardo Carvalho and, as a result, the Portuguese held on for a goalless draw before winning the penalty shoot-out 3-1. With Beckham off injured and Rooney red-carded, this meant that two of the best spot-kick takers were missing. What is it with England when it comes to kicking a dead ball towards goal from 12 yards? This was Eriksson's third successive exit in a major tournament quarter-final and, in his farewell speech, he wished England well and singled out Rooney for special praise, advising the press not to blame the youngster's dismissal for England's exit.

Eriksson improved England's FIFA World ranking from seventeenth place in January 2001 to fifth in July 2006, reaching fourth during the 2006 World Cup, and he was also rated by the FA as England's second most successful manager, behind Sir Alf Ramsey. He is also one of only four men – Ramsey, Terry Venables and current head coach Roy Hodgson being the others – to have never failed to guide England into the last eight of a major international tournament. Under Eriksson, England achieved the highest point percentage in major tournament matches of all time, losing only three competitive games (excluding extra time) and achieved top qualifying place in all three International tournaments. Only Brazil matched England's record of reaching the quarter-final in tournaments in 2002, 2004, and 2006. And, coincidentally, the same manager, Luiz Felipe Scolari, knocked England out of all three of these tournaments – first with Brazil and then twice with Portugal. Eriksson is also the only England manager never to have led his team out at either the old or the new Wembley Stadium. The old one was closed for redevelopment the same month that the FA asked him to take over (October 2000), and he resigned before the new ground was opened.

As England manager, Eriksson awarded over twenty-five players their first cap: among them, Aaron Lennon, Peter Crouch, Jermain Defoe, Stewart Downing, Rob Green, Scott Parker, goalkeeper Paul Robinson, Rooney, Terry, Upson, Walcott and Shaun Wright-Phillips.

26

The 2006 World Cup in Germany

10 June 2006	England 1 Paraguay 0
Hessen, Frankfurt	Attendance 47,710

England Team: P. Robinson, G. Neville, A. Cole, S. Gerrard, R Ferdinand, J. Terry, D. Beckham, F. Lampard, P. Crouch, M. Owen, J. Cole. Substitutions: S. Downing for Owen, O. Hargreaves for J. Cole.

Let's be honest, England stuttered to victory in their opening Group B game against a strong Polish side in Frankfurt. Carlos Gamarra's third-minute own-goal following David Beckham's left-wing free-kick decided the contest, which was far from being a classic. The first half was dominated by England, but it was a different story after the break as Paraguay threatened more and more. A cautious England put themselves under unnecessary pressure. Frank Lampard came closest to extending the lead with two long-range efforts, as the South Americans pressed for a draw, which they perhaps deserved. England coach Sven-Göran Eriksson was certainly happier with the points gained than the performance produced.

15 June 2006	England 2 Trinidad & Tobago 0
Nuremburg	Attendance 40,848

England Team: P. Robinson, J. Carragher, A. Cole, S. Gerrard, R. Ferdinand, J. Terry, D. Beckham, F. Lampard, P. Crouch, M. Owen, J. Cole. Substitutions: W. Rooney for Owen, S. Downing for J. Cole, A. Lennon for Carragher.

From England's point of view, this match was fraught with nervous tension, but in the end it was the result that mattered most of all – a 2-0 victory thanks to two goals in the final seven minutes of play. Prior to the introduction of substitutes Wayne Rooney and Aaron Lennon in the fifty-eighth minute, England had been par average; John Terry even had to kick the ball off his own goal line. But during the last half-hour, they finally clicked into gear as Sven-Göran Eriksson told his men to go for the Soca Warrior's jugular.

On eighty-three minutes, skipper David Beckham crossed high towards the far post where the 6-foot 7-inch Peter Crouch was lurking. The giant striker rose confidently above Brent Sancho and powered a header into the top left corner. Trinidad & Tobago's line was finally broken. Steven Gerrard sewed up the win in the ninety-second minute.

The Liverpool star cut in from the edge of the penalty area before firing a left-footer into the top left corner of Shaka Hislop's net.

This win meant that England were guaranteed a place in the knockout round of the World Cup, having squeezed out maximum points from two games in Group B.

20 June 2006   England 2 Sweden 2
Cologne   Attendance 44,901

England Team: P. Robinson, J. Carragher, A. Cole, O. Hargreaves, R. Ferdinand, J. Terry, D. Beckham, F. Lampard, M. Owen, W. Rooney, J. Cole. Substitutions: P. Crouch for Owen, S. Campbell for Ferdinand, S. Gerrard for Rooney.

Sweden twice came from behind to deny England victory in an eventful if scrappy final Group B game in Cologne. With ten seconds remaining, England led 2-1 against a team that had not beaten since May 1968. But a long throw from Sweden's left was missed by Sol Campbell, allowing Henrik Larsson to nip in and touch the ball into the far corner of Paul Robinson's net. For England, who needed at least a draw to top the group and play Ecuador in the round of sixteen, the drama began after just two minutes. Striker Michael Owen, unchallenged, fell to the floor apparently badly injured. He was rolled off the pitch and substituted with Peter Crouch. Later it was confirmed that Owen would not play again at the 2006 World Cup. He was flown home.

Sweden pressured an unsettled England early on with aerial balls, especially from corners, and it was these sorts of direct tactics that would, in the end, produce two second-half goals for the Scandinavians. England, who had 55 per cent of the play during the whole game, were dominant before half-time, and took the lead on thirty-three minutes. Joe Cole, on the left, collected a high clearance on his chest 35 yards from goal and, as the ball dropped, he volleyed it first time on a high dipping trajectory towards the scrambling Andreas Isaksson, who could only paddle it over the line via an upright. Six minutes after the interval, the Swedes drew level. From one of their twelve corner-kicks, Marcus Allbäck, on the left edge of the 6-yard box, flicked on Tobias Linderoth's cross. The ball somehow looped behind him, soared over the top of the defence and into the net. England hit back and, after two near misses, regained the lead with five minutes remaining. Joe Cole's measured chip to the far post was met full on by Steven Gerrard, whose powerful header flew past Isaksson. But then came the late drama, when Henrik Larsson stabbed home Sweden's second equaliser with virtually the last kick of the game.

25 June 2006   England 1 Ecuador 0
Stuttgart   Attendance 51,694

England Team: P. Robinson, O. Hargreaves, A. Cole, M. Carrick, R. Ferdinand, J. Terry, D. Beckham, F. Lampard, W. Rooney, S. Gerrard, J. Cole. Substitutions: A. Lennon for Beckham, S. Downing for Gerrard, J. Carragher for J. Cole.

David Beckham became the first England player to score at three World Cups, as his free-kick earned his country a quarter-final tie against Portugal. Beckham, defying illness, stepped up to curl the ball home from 30 yards on the hour mark, but England made hard work of beating Ecuador. Indeed, the ambitious South Americans could have gone in front early on, Carlos Tenorio's shot deflecting off Ashley Cole and onto the bar following a mistake by John Terry. Frank Lampard then missed two fine chances as England did just enough to win.

Next up for Sven-Göran Eriksson's side would be Portugal, who knocked out The Netherlands in their last sixteen game.

1 July 2006	England 0 Portugal 0 (England lost 3-1 on penalties)
Gelsenkirchen	Attendance 51,927

England Team: P. Robinson, G. Neville, A. Cole, O. Hargreaves, R. Ferdinand, J. Terry, D. Beckham, F. Lampard, W. Rooney, S. Gerrard, J. Cole. Substitutions: A. Lennon for Beckham, J. Carragher for Lennon, P. Crouch for J. Cole.
This quarter-final encounter was the second between England and Portugal in successive major tournaments and, once again, it was decided by a penalty shoot-out. In fact, it had been ten years since England's only shoot-out victory – against Spain in the 1996 European Championship – whereas Portugal's first at senior level had resulted in a 6-5 victory over England some two years earlier, in the European Championship in Lisbon. This was a scrappy game of half-chances on a very humid afternoon.

With David Beckham going off injured early in the second half, and then Wayne Rooney being sent off for a stamp on defender Ricardo Carvalho just past the hour mark, England did well to hold out for a draw and take the tie to a penalty shoot-out. However, minus two key penalty takers, there was an air of inevitability. The best England could hope for was a long-awaited victory from the spot, but recent history did nothing to raise hopes of that prospect ever coming to fruition. For Rooney, it was particularly frustrating, as he had left the field with a broken left foot against Portugal in 2004 when playing on top of his game. This time around, he had been struggling to recapture his form while recovering from a broken right foot. This dismissal in Gelsenkirchen was silly, and there is no doubt whatsoever that Argentine referee Horacio Elizondo was urged on by several Portuguese players, including Rooney's Manchester United teammate Cristiano Ronaldo, to take action. He did just that, and probably cost England the match.

Portugal went first in the shoot-out, Sabrosa Simão opening the scoring with a crisp, low drive to Robinson's right. Frank Lampard and Hugo Viana then missed with their 12-yard efforts before Owen Hargreaves tied things up for England. Armando Petit (Portugal) and Steven Gerrard both fluffed their kicks, allowing Hélder Postiga to fire Portugal 2-1 in front. Jamie Carragher had the chance to make it 2-2 but missed, enabling an arrogant, smiling Ronaldo to convert the winning penalty. That made it 3-1 to Portugal, whose excellent goalkeeper Ricardo Pereira saved all of England's three 'missed' kicks. So it was over and out, beaten from the spot yet again. When, if ever, will it all end?

2006 World Cup Fact File

- Countries taking part: 32 (divided into eight groups of 4).
- Final: Italy 1, France 1 (after extra time), Italy won 5-3 on penalties.
- Final venue: Olympiastadion, Berlin (attendance 68,668).
- Leading scorer: Mirolsav Klose (Germany), five goals. This was the lowest number of goals scored by a tournament's top marksman since six players tied on 4 goals each in 1962.
- Ronaldo (Brazil) scored his record sixteenth goal in World Cup finals.
- Zinedine Zidane collected his record sixth card in World Cup finals.
- Four players were sent off in The Netherlands-Portugal game, all dismissed by former player Valentin Ivanov.
- There were a record twenty-eight red cards shown during the tournament.

New Brush Sweeps Clean ... Not Quite

During the 2006/07 season, under manager Steve McClaren, England played eleven matches – four friendlies and seven European Championship qualifiers, four of which they won. In the non-competitive games, England beat Greece 4-0 (helped by two goals from Peter Crouch), drew 1-1 with The Netherlands in Amsterdam, and likewise with Brazil at Wembley, but lost 1-0 to Spain at Old Trafford. In their Euro 2008 qualifiers, they defeated Andorra 5-0 at home (two more goals here for Crouch) and 3-0 away, and won 1-0 in Macedonia (Crouch again on target) and 3-0 in Tallinn against Estonia. They had to settle for draws against Israel 0-0 in Tel Aviv and Macedonia 0-0 in the return fixture, but lost 2-0 to Croatia in Zagreb. Players came and went, and among the new faces introduced at senior level by McClaren were Joey Barton, goalkeepers Scott Carson and Ben Foster, and Micah Richards.

Into season 2007/08 and England began by losing 2-1 at home to Germany before recording successive 3-0 European Championship qualifying victories over Israel, Russia and Estonia, all at home, only to lose 2-1 against the Russians in Moscow. There followed a 1-0 friendly win in Austria, but then came horror and dismay, when Croatia visited Wembley for the final, yet crucial, EC qualifier. Having fought back from 2-0 down to draw level, Carson, England's goalkeeper, let slip a long-range shot from Niko Kranjčar to present the visitors with a 3-2 victory. This was McClaren's last game in charge. He departed to be replaced by Italian Fabio Capello, who took office on 14 December 2007.

Before the end of the season, Capello was able to assess his playing strength to a certain degree when England played four friendlies. They beat Switzerland 2-1 and the USA 2-0, both at Wembley, eased past Trinidad & Tobago 3-0 in Port of Spain, but lost narrowly 1-0 to France at Saint-Denis, Paris. Capello's target now was to get England to South Africa for the 2010 World Cup finals.

27

The 2010 World Cup Qualifying Matches

6 September 2008
Barcelona

Andorra 0 England 2
Attendance 12,276

England Team: D. James, G. Johnson, A. Cole, G. Barry, J. Terry, J. Lescott, T. Walcott, F. Lampard, W. Rooney, J. Defoe, S. Downing. Substitutions: D. Beckham for Lampard, E. Heskey for Defoe, J. Cole for Downing.

Two goals by second-half substitute Joe Cole gave England a vital three points in this, the first match in their World Cup qualifying group at the Estadi Olímpic Lluís Companys Stadium in Barcelona. At times the play was scrappy, and in truth England's performance was rather laboured, but this game was a potential banana skin and in the end Fabio Capello was delighted with the three points.

Andorra set their stall out from the start, defending in numbers, having no intention of attacking, simply hoping to frustrate England for as long as they could. For the first forty-five minutes they succeeded, and England, infuriatingly, could fathom a way through or round a packed defence. Predictably, they enjoyed the bulk of possession but too many players were off form. Wayne Rooney missed a sitter; Frank Lampard's shot was touched around a post by Andorra's veteran goalkeeper Luis Koldo. Thankfully, Capello changed things at half-time, bringing on the extra power of Emile Heskey and the more direct skills of Cole, for Jermaine Defoe and Stuart Downing respectively. That move paid dividends.

Within four minutes of the restart England went ahead at last. Lampard's free-kick was side-footed by Joleon Lescott on to Cole, who volleyed home, much to the visitors' relief and delight. Six minutes later, it was game over as Rooney sent a delightful pass through to Cole, who once again scored with the minimum of fuss. The Chelsea midfielder certainly made a huge impact, and his presence gave his manager some food for thought with the big game against Croatia coming up. In the meantime, England left Spain with the job done after what was overall a poor match.

10 September 2008   Croatia 1 England 4
Zagreb   Attendance 35,218

England Team: D. James, W. Brown, A. Cole, J. Terry, R. Ferdinand, F. Lampard, J. Cole,
G. Barry, T. Walcott, W. Rooney, E. Heskey. Substitutions: M. Upson for Terry, J. Jenas for
J. Cole, D. Beckham for Walcott.

After all the prematch build up – with much talk of revenge for the defeat by Croatia at
Wembley almost a year previous – England certainly did the business, but it was Arsenal
prodigy Theo Walcott who stole the limelight. This was the night when the travelling
supporters witnessed what was probably England's best performance on the road since
battering Germany 5-1 in 2001. And they not only blitzed Croatia, they shattered the
thirty-five-game unbeaten run of the home team.

   A couple of shaky moments from goalkeeper David James caused a flutter or two, but
England should have had a penalty on twenty minutes when Emile Heskey was pulled
over by Josip Šimunić when moving in on a Walcott cross. That incident seemed to spur
England on and, within five minutes, they deservedly took the lead. Rio Ferdinand found
Wayne Rooney who, in turn, tried to find Walcott. A lucky rebound off a defender saw
the ball eventually bounce kindly for the winger. He wasted no time, confidently drilling
his shot across goal and into the far corner of the Croatian net. It was a great finish. There
were very few scares for England prior to the break, and they went into the dressing
looking composed and confident.

   England's cause was helped no end when Robert Kovač was sent off in the fifty-second
minute for elbowing Joe Cole in the head. Taking full advantage of an extra man against
ten, England drove forward and, in the fifty-ninth minute, a lovely move involving
Rooney, Heskey and Frank Lampard, which allowed Walcott to make it a double. For
the second time, the Arsenal winger wasted no time in drilling his shot into the far corner.
Four minutes later, it got even better for England when Jermaine Jenas, substituting for
Joe Cole, pulled the ball back from the right for Rooney to nonchalantly stroke home.

   Croatia managed to conjure up a goal in the seventy-eighth minute, when Mario
Mandžukić broke away to beat James with a side-footer from 12 yards. But back came
England, and 'Man of the Match' Walcott completed his hat-trick on eighty-three minutes,
firing home from 13 yards after more good work by Rooney. There's no denying it … this
was a superb win.

11 October 2008   England 5 Kazakhstan 1
Wembley   Attendance 89,107

England Team: D. James, W. Brown, A. Cole, S. Gerrard, R. Ferdinand, M. Upson,
T. Walcott, F. Lampard, E. Heskey, W. Rooney, G. Barry. Substitutions: D. Beckham for
Walcott, J. Defoe for Rooney, S. Wright-Phillips for Barry.

A month after England's sensational win in Croatia, almost a full house at Wembley
expected another goal glut against Kazakhstan. But England have a habit of following a

good performance with a disappointing one, and only a late flurry spared their blushes against moderate opponents. On one of those infuriating nights when the result was better than the performance, England struggled to get going in a forgettable first half. Their performance was disjointed and lacklustre, and they made Kazakhstan look a reasonable outfit. In fact, the visitors' debutant winger Tanat Nusserbayev looked the best player on the field in the opening forty-five minutes.

But once Rio Ferdinand had scored the opening goal with a 6-yard header on fifty-two minutes, it was virtually one-way traffic through to the final whistle, although three of England's goals came inside the last quarter of an hour. Aleksandr Kuchma, under pressure from Wayne Rooney following Frank Lampard's free-kick, conceded an own-goal in the sixty-fourth minute to put England two up. Surprisingly, against the run of play, Zhambyl Kukeyev drilled in a 12-yard shot to reduce the deficit four minutes later. Rooney then buried an 8-yard header from Theo Walcott's cross on seventy-six, following up ten minutes later with England's fourth goal, a tap-in from David Beckham's free-kick. Jermain Defoe finished things off with a last-minute drive from 18 yards after being set up by Emile Heskey.

15 October 2008	Belarus 1 England 3
Minsk	Attendance 29,585

England Team: D. James, W. Brown, W. Bridge, S. Gerrard, R. Ferdinand, M. Upson, T. Walcott, F. Lampard, E. Heskey, W. Rooney, G. Barry. Substitutions: D. Beckham for Rooney, S. Wright-Phillips for Walcott, P. Crouch for Heskey.

England made it four wins out of four, and fourteen goals scored, with another excellent performance, which put them in complete control of their World Cup group. It was always going to be a tricky fixture in Minsk, but Fabio Capello's players were up for this one and, with Steven Gerrard and Wayne Rooney outstanding, they produced a solid performance.

Making a positive start to the match, England took the lead on eleven minutes. Gerrard, who was given more freedom to attack in this game, took a Rooney pass in his stride before banging home a 25-yard shot past goalkeeper Yuri Zhevnov. This was a fine goal – one Gerrard's best. However, Belarus showed plenty of fighting spirit, and got back on terms in the twenty-eighth minute when Pavel Sitko stooped to head home from 5 yards after a mix-up between Wes Brown and Walcott following a cross from the left.

Five minutes into the second half, England regained the lead when Rooney glided in Emile Heskey's cross after a quick throw-in by Wayne Bridge. After a relaxed spell, England picked up the pace again and added a third goal in the seventy-fourth minute. Rooney, dummying his marker superbly, darted forward, collected Gerrard's pass, produced a clever feint and finished with a cool chip. This clearly showed what a superb player he is … on his day.

1 April 2009   England 2 Ukraine 1
Wembley   Attendance 87,548

England Team: D. James, G. Johnson, A. Cole, G. Barry, R. Ferdinand, J. Terry, A. Lennon, F. Lampard, P. Crouch, W. Rooney, S. Gerrard. Substitutions: P. Jagielka for Ferdinand, D. Beckham for Lennon, S. Wright-Phillips for Crouch.

This match was always going to be a difficult one for England, and so it proved. But even though Fabio Capello's men didn't fire on all cylinders, they still managed to record a valuable win in their quest for World Cup qualification. To be blunt, this was a disjointed game all round, with both sides cancelling each other out, as they have done so often over the years.

After a fairly even passage of play, Peter Crouch broke the deadlock in the twenty-ninth minute. Frank Lampard's corner found John Terry's head. The ball went across the face of the goal, where Crouch volleyed home from 3 yards to keep up his impressive international scoring record. From then on, it was anyone's game. There were a few chances here and there, and in the seventy-fourth minute Andriy Shevchenko took one for Ukraine, toeing the ball home from close range after a free-kick, conceded by Terry, had bounced off Glen Johnson. Back came England, and with five minutes remaining, Terry scored the winner from 4 yards, after Gerrard had headed on David Beckham's free-kick. At last, it was good to hear some noise from the England supporters inside the new Wembley – they certainly played their part in that late winning goal.

6 June 2009   Kazakhstan 0 England 4
Almaty   Attendance 23,665

England Team: R. Green, G. Johnson, A. Cole, D. Batty, J. Terry, M. Upson, S. Gerrard, F. Lampard, E. Heskey, W. Rooney, T. Walcott. Substitutes: D. Beckham for Johnson, S. Wright-Phillips for Walcott, J. Defoe for Heskey.

Despite enduring a long, hard League season, the England players went into this important qualifying group game against Kazakhstan in a confident mood. With five wins out of five behind them, England were expected to win in Almaty, and win well. But after thirty minutes of some rather disjointed and sluggish football on a difficult surface, they looked far from happy. They were also facing a Kazakhstan side fired up from the start and roared on by a frenzied crowd. The home side should have taken the lead in the first minute, as Glen Johnson's sloppiness let in Zhambyl Kukeyev down the left wing. His cross found Sergei Ostapenko, but through a combination of a desperate dive from goalkeeper Robert Green and a typically gutsy challenge from John Terry, the ball was kept out. Chances after that were few and far between, until Gareth Barry silenced the home fans with a headed goal in the thirty-eighth minute. Ashley Cole and Steven Gerrard worked a short corner on the left, Gerrard drove over a superb cross from the byline to the far post where Barry, timing his run to perfection, sent a clever header into the far corner, with goalkeeper Aleksandr Mokin flat-footed. A minute into added time at the end of the half, Emile Heskey popped the ball home from close range after a clever deflected lob by Gerrard had been clawed away by Mokin.

Kazakhstan never really threatened again. It was all England, in effect, and it was certainly game over in the seventy-second minute when Rooney made it 3-0, netting with an overhead kick after Mokin had saved his first effort. Five minutes later, Frank Lampard put the icing on the cake by thumping in a penalty following Rinat Abdulin's tug on Heskey.

10 June 2009	England 6 Andorra 0
Wembley	Attendance 57,897

England Team: R. Green, G. Johnson, A. Cole, D. Beckham, J. Terry, J. Lescott, S. Gerrard, F. Lampard, P. Crouch, W. Rooney, T. Walcott. Substitutes: W. Bridge for Cole, A. Young (Aston Villa) for Gerrard, J. Defoe for Rooney.

If the start England made against Kazakhstan in the previous match was rather moderate, or even poor in some respects, then this one against Andorra was terrific – just what manager Fabio Capello wanted. Right from the off, England stroked the ball around with precision on Wembley's lush surface, keeping possession and continually probing for openings. In the first three minutes, they could have scored three goals as the pace and the sharpness of their play carved Andorra's defence apart.

Wayne Rooney was brilliant on the night, and his turn and chip after just thirty seconds was worthy of a goal. But all credit to Jesús Koldo, Andorra's veteran goalkeeper, who made an excellent tip-over save. Theo Walcott produced another Koldo save soon afterwards, while a stretching Rooney struck a post. The 'keeper, making his last international appearance, looked as though he was going to end on a high, but England were not to be denied and, in the fourth minute, Glen Johnson crossed perfectly to the far post for Rooney to guide his header under the diving custodian.

Just before the half-hour mark, Frank Lampard doubled England's lead with a 12-yard drive and, ten minutes later, Rooney scored his second of the night with a clinical 8-yard side-foot volley. Although having the lion's share of the play and powering in shots and headers at will, England had to wait until the last quarter of an hour before running in three more goals. Jermain Defoe scored with a 7-yard header, and bagged his second and England's fifth soon afterwards, with a close-range tap-in after the ball had rebounded to him off a defender following David Beckham's free-kick. Peter Crouch poked home the sixth goal on eighty minutes. During the game, England had twenty-five attempts on goal to Andorra's one on a night when the final scoreline could easily have been 10-0.

9 September 2009	England 5 Croatia 1
Wembley	Attendance 87,319

England Team: R. Green, G. Johnson, A. Cole, G. Barry, J. Terry, M. Upson, A. Lennon, F. Lampard, E. Heskey, W. Rooney, S. Gerrard. Substitutes: J. Milner for Lennon, J. Defoe for Heskey, D. Beckham for Gerrard.

All the prematch questions as to whether England could qualify for the 2010 World Cup in South Africa by beating Croatia were answered emphatically with a scintillating performance at Wembley. England, full of determination, shot out of the blocks like greyhounds, pinning the Croatians in their own half. It took just seven minutes to unlock the visitors' defence. Aaron Lennon's pace had already frightened the Croatians and, when the nippy Spurs winger cut inside and zipped across the edge of the penalty area, Josip Šimunić's clumsy challenge gave the referee no option but to award a penalty. This was exquisitely dispatched by Frank Lampard with an exact replica of his spot-kick against Slovenia four days earlier.

That was just the start England wanted, and they kept up the momentum throughout the first half, but in the end had to settle for just two. The second came in the eighteenth minute, just after Gareth Barry had seen his rocket shot saved by Vedran Runje. Steven Gerrard found Lennon on the right, and then his cross to the far post was met by the Liverpool captain, who scored with a glorious header.

In a basically one-sided second half, Lampard made it 3-0 with a 12-yard header on fifty-nine minutes. Gerrard also used his head to bag a fourth in the sixty-seventh minute and, although Eduardo da Silva pulled a goal back for Croatia with a tap-in on seventy-one minutes, Rooney's 13-yard drive, after a poor clearance, rounded things off in the seventy-eighth minute. South Africa here we come.

10 October 2009	Ukraine 1 England 0
Dnipropetrovsk	Attendance 30,885

England Team: R. Green, G. Johnson, A. Cole, M. Carrick, J. Terry, R. Ferdinand, A. Lennon, F. Lampard, W. Rooney, E. Heskey, S. Gerrard. Substitutes: D. James for Lennon, C. Cole (West Ham United) for Heskey, J. Milner for Gerrard.

In a cauldron of hostility, England finally lost their 100 per cent record in the World Cup group qualifying matches – beaten by a Ukraine side desperate for victory to enhance their chances of making the play-offs. Unfortunately, everything that could go wrong for England did. They were beaten by a single deflected goal by Serhij Nazarenko in the twenty-ninth minute, the ball fizzing into the net of Ashley Cole.

England were reduced to ten men as early as the fourteenth minute when goalkeeper Rob Green was sent off for bringing down Artem Milevskiy. The referee initially showed the red card to Rio Ferdinand, but changed his mind after consulting his linesman. Former Chelsea striker Andriy Shevchenko stepped up to take the kick against David James, who took over between the posts, Aaron Lennon going off. The Ukrainian, however, missed from the spot, despite sending the England 'keeper the wrong way.

Frank Lampard and Carlton Cole had chances to equalise in the second half, although Ukraine also had opportunities to increase their lead. In the end, it was a disappointing night for England, who would now face Belarus at Wembley in their final group game, hoping to put this defeat behind them.

14 October 2009   England 3 Belarus 0
Wembley   Attendance 76,897

England Team: B. Foster (Manchester United), G. Johnson, W. Bridge, G. Barry, J. Terry, R. Ferdinand, A. Lennon, F. Lampard, P. Crouch, G. Agbonlahor (Aston Villa), S. Wright-Phillips. Substitutes: J. Milner for Bridge, D. Beckham for Lennon, C. Cole for Agbonlahor.

England closed out their qualifying campaign with an emphatic victory over Belarus at Wembley. There were several good individual performances, certainly by goalkeeper Ben Foster, defenders John Terry and Rio Ferdinand, and Gareth Barry, and England certainly played solidly and effectively as a unit to win their group by six clear points.

The opening goal came as early as the fourth minute when Peter Crouch slid in with his long leg to convert Gabby Agbonlahor's low left-wing cross. Frank Lampard, Agbonlahor (twice) and Crouch should have doubled the score before Shaun Wright-Phillips eventually made it 2-0 in the fifty-ninth minute, with a 20-yard shot that took a slight deflection. Crouch completed the scoring with a quarter of an hour remaining, knocking in a rebound from 5 yards after Carlton Cole's powerful shot had been parried out by goalkeeper Yuri Zhevnov. All England had to do now was to produce this form in South Africa.

Capello's Boys

Before heading to the World Cup, England played four more friendlies. They lost 1-0 to Brazil in Qatar, beat Egypt 3-1, and Mexico also by 3-1, both at Wembley, before defeating Japan 2-1 in Graz, Austria. Manager Capello, by this time, knew which players he would be naming in his squad for South Africa – and he hinted that there would be at least a couple of surprises.

Capello's twenty-three-man squad that went to the 2010 World Cup was:

Goalkeepers: Rob Green (West Ham United), Joe Hart (Manchester City), David James (Portsmouth). Full-backs: Ashley Cole (Chelsea), Glen Johnson (Liverpool), Stephen Warnock (Aston Villa). Defenders: Jamie Carragher (Liverpool), Michael Dawson (Tottenham Hotspur), Ledley King (Tottenham Hotspur), John Terry (Chelsea), Matthew Upson (West Ham United). Midfielders: Gareth Barry (Manchester City), Michael Carrick (Manchester United), Joe Cole (Chelsea), Steven Gerrard (Liverpool), Frank Lampard (Chelsea), Aaron Lennon (Tottenham Hotspur), James Milner (Aston Villa), Shaun Wright-Phillips (Manchester City). Forwards: Peter Crouch (Tottenham Hotspur), Jermain Defoe (Tottenham Hotspur), Emile Heskey (Aston Villa), Wayne Rooney (Manchester United).

NB: *Dawson was a late replacement for the injured Rio Ferdinand, and six players were named as standby reserves: left-back Leighton Baines (Everton), midfielders Tom Huddlestone (Tottenham Hotspur) and Scott Parker (West Ham United), wide men Adam Johnson (Manchester City) and Theo Walcott (Arsenal), and striker Darren Bent (Sunderland).*

28

The 2010 World Cup in South Africa

12 June 2010
Rustenburg

England 1 USA 1
Attendance 38,646

England Team: R. Green, G. Johnson, A. Cole, S. Gerrard, L. King, J. Terry, A. Lennon, F. Lampard, E. Heskey, W. Rooney, J. Milner. Substitutes: J. Carragher for King, P. Crouch for Heskey, S. Wright-Phillips for Milner.

This was certainly not the best of starts by England. Their opening Group C game was fairly even, although England did have eighteen shots on target against eleven by the USA. There were quite a few positives, but also plenty of negatives as the Americans played pretty well throughout.

England, in fact, began superbly, looking sharp and confident with Emile Heskey a dangerous front man. Indeed, it was his brilliant pass from Frank Lampard's touch inside in the fourth minute that sent the whole of England, at home and in South Africa, wild with delight. Steven Gerrard, rampaging into the box, took the ball in his stride before tucking it neatly past Tim Howard. It was just the start England wanted, and fittingly it was their new skipper who provided the moment. For a while, the Americans looked rattled and the omens looked good for England, who retained possession well, creating chances in the process. But the Yanks proved to be no pushovers, and with a well organised and hard working set of players, they gradually got into the game. The narrow pitch suited their style and, with Aaron Lennon struggling to find width and Wayne Rooney marked tightly, it was down to Heskey to pose the greatest threat up front.

However, in the fortieth minute came a moment that England, and particularly goalkeeper Robert Green, will never forget. Fabio Capello's midfielders were sloppy in allowing Clint Dempsey far too much time and space to turn several times before firing in a low speculative shot from 25 yards. It looked an easy save for Green to make, but the West Ham 'keeper allowed the ball to evade his attempted two-handed block, and it crept over the line for an awful goal. It is common knowledge that England fans have endured their fair share of such calamitous goalkeeping moments over the years, and this one, for sure, will never be forgotten. As the England players trooped off at the interval, there were several heads bowed low. In a rather disappointing second half, it was the USA who came closest to winning the match, Green pushing a drive from Josmer Altidore onto a post, while Heskey did miss a good chance at the other end. Algeria next ... what could England come up with against the Africans?

18 June 2010	England 0 Algeria 0
Wes-Kaap, Cape Town	Attendance 64,100

England Team: D. James, G. Johnson, A. Cole, G. Barry, J. Carragher, J. Terry, A. Lennon, F. Lampard, E. Heskey, W. Rooney, S. Gerrard. Substitutes: P. Crouch for Barry, J. Defoe for Heskey, S. Wright-Phillips for Lennon.

England's loyal band of travelling supporters have had to endure some pretty poor performances over the years, and this goalless encounter against one of minnows of the 2010 World Cup, Algeria, must rank with the best (or worst) of them. From the off there was little real effort or even cohesion in England's play and, for the first thirty minutes, the team rarely strung two passes together. The first touch, so crucial at this level (or any other level for that matter), was missing, and more worrying at the time was the fact that so many players constantly gave the ball away and were even second to virtually every loose ball. The Algerians simply couldn't believe their luck, having acres of space in which to enjoy their football.

One of England's most influential stars, Wayne Rooney, looked a pale shadow of the player everyone knew he could be. Was he injured, was he tired? Unknown. He missed with a clear header late on – his only chance in a poor game. Frank Lampard put in two good efforts and Steven Gerrard one, but opposing goalkeeper Raïs M'Bohli was rarely troubled. Fussy Uzbekistan referee Ravshan Irmatov could have awarded both teams a penalty. Algeria had 52 per cent of the play, and created eleven chances, yet only one was on target. After two nonplus draws, England knew they had to beat Slovenia in the last group game to qualify for the next phase. It was a scenario no one expected, but perhaps it would, at last, bring the best out of Capello's men.

23 June 2010	England 1 Slovenia 0
Port Elizabeth	Attendance 36,893

England Team: D. James, G. Johnson, A. Cole, G. Barry, M. Upson, J. Terry, J. Milner, F. Lampard, J. Defoe, W. Rooney, S. Gerrard. Substitutes: E. Heskey for Defoe, J. Cole for Rooney.

At long last, England got their World Cup challenge up and running with this narrow yet thoroughly deserved victory over plucky Slovenia at the Nelson Mandela Bay Stadium in Port Elizabeth. Fabio Capello's men – playing in all red – produced a far better display than they did in their first two group matches, and after all the trials and tribulations of the previous ten days or so, it was very satisfying, especially for the travelling supporters, to see England play well. They rose to the challenge splendidly.

Right from the start there was a lot more urgency and determination, but if the truth be known, there was a certain amount of nervousness during the opening quarter of an hour. However, the players themselves were all up for this one, there's no doubting this. Capello made three changes from the Algeria game. He introduced Matthew Upson alongside John Terry, brought back wide midfielder James Milner, who looked much sharper than he did against the Americans, and played Jermain Defoe up front with Wayne Rooney, yet he continued to use Steven Gerrard on the left.

Although still fractionally under par by his standards, Rooney looked much more like his old self, making some strong runs and smart touches, while goalkeeper David James pulled off two fine saves, one of them quite superb from the dangerous Valter Birsa.

After a Frank Lampard free-kick had been saved by the brilliant Samir Handanović in the Slovenia goal, England took the lead in the twenty-third minute. Glen Johnson, Lampard and Gareth Barry forged a passing routine, which led to Milner crossing brilliantly into the danger zone where Defoe, timing his run to perfection, volleyed home right-footed from 20 yards. Handanović later produced a stunning save from Gerrard; he also denied Defoe and Terry, while Lampard fired over. At the other end of the field, Terry, defending this time, threw everything he had to block an effort from Milivoje Novakovič. It was Germany next on the hit list.

27 June 2010	England 1 Germany 4
Bloemfontein	Attendance 40,510

England team: D. James, G. Johnson, A. Cole, G. Barry, J. Terry, M. Upson, J. Milner, F. Lampard, J. Defoe, W. Rooney, S. Gerrard. Substitutes: S. Wright-Phillips for Johnson, J. Cole for Milner, E. Heskey for Defoe.
This was horrible. Yet, it could have been a completely different story if Frank Lampard's goal had been allowed. The ball was almost a yard over the line ... Everyone knew that except the assistant referee.

There's no doubt that when all ten England outfield players play well, they can match, or even beat, any team in the world. But against the Germans, sadly, only three produced the goods, and some of the defending was atrocious. There were warning signs almost immediately after the referee started the game, and after just three minutes, Mesut Özil, clean through, was denied by David James. England worked hard, there's no denying that, but far too many passes went astray, especially in the first ten minutes, while the Germans were spot in with theirs. Özil and Bastian Schweinsteiger bossed the midfield for long periods. England's creative department, by comparison, stuttered, with Frank Lampard the only one likely to breach the German defence.

Germany took a deserved lead in the twentieth minute. A long goal kick by 'keeper Manuel Neuer travelled the whole length of the pitch without an England player touching the ball. Miroslav Klose easily held off Matthew Upson's feeble challenge and slotted it past James. This was an awful goal to concede from England's point of view. In response, Wayne Rooney fired high and wide, and Gareth Barry had a low shot saved. Passes continued to go amiss and, at times, England's display was embarrassing. With the back four being run ragged by the speedy German forwards, England fell two behind on thirty-two minutes, just after Defoe had just hit the bar. Messrs Özil, Klose and Müller walked through England's static defence; the latter fed the unmarked Podolski wide on the left. His first touch was poor but he had ample time, and space, for a second touch, and this time it was lethal, in off the far post, James being left helpless. To their credit, England didn't collapse. They came back, albeit not altogether convincingly, but on thirty-four minutes, from James Milner's ball into the box, Neuer saved well from Lampard.

With England struggling overall, they grabbed a lifeline in the thirty-seventh minute. After a short corner, Steven Gerrard put in a superb cross that was met by Upson, who headed home. Suddenly it was game on. The Germans were looking far less assured. In the thirty-ninth minute came the turning point of the whole game. After a scramble on the edge of the penalty area, the ball broke for Lampard, whose chip over Neuer struck the bar and bounced down over the line. Unfortunately for the disbelieving England players, the German goalkeeper grabbed the ball and delivered it downfield with the referee waving play on. It was an abysmal error by the linesman and the referee and once again the bad luck hit England. We all know about Geoff Hurst's seemingly dubious but allowed goal in 1966, this effort was different – the ball was certainly over the line. Having said all that, Germany could, and should, have been three or four goals clear come half-time.

After the interval, England showed more determination, Milner and Gerrard firing over and wide respectively. Then, on fifty-two minutes, it was more bad luck for England when Lampard's terrific 30-yard free-kick almost broke the crossbar. This was followed by a Gerrard shot, which was saved. Defoe almost forced an equaliser, and Milner should have done better when well placed, but he sent his shot far too close to Neuer. In the sixty-seventh minute, Germany settled the contest. Lampard's free-kick was blocked, and when Barry lost possession, Germany broke away quickly. With England's defence all at sea and labouring (only Glen Johnson was in a good position), it was easy for Schweinsteiger to feed Müller, who comfortably picked his spot past the stranded James. And three minutes later, it got even worse for England. Özil beat Barry to a 50/50 ball, and sprinted forward before slipping the perfect pass into the path of Müller, who once again scored with consummate ease.

England, to their credit, fought on and, in fact, created a handful of chances late on; Gerrard bringing a fine save out of the impressive Neuer. But, in all fairness, Germany, with a young, strong and very talented team, outplayed England for at last seventy-five minutes. It was a bad defeat, and Capello and his deflated England squad flew home after yet another ultra-disappointing World Cup. What of the manager? He'd certainly made a lot of selection and tactical mistakes in South Africa and, as a result, the Football Association immediately met to discuss his – and the team's – performances in depth.

2010 World Cup Fact File

- Countries taking part: 32 (divided into eight groups of 4).
- Final: Spain 1, The Netherlands 0 (after extra time).
- Final venue: Soccer City, Johannesburg (attendance 84,490).
- Leading scorer: Thomas Müller (Germany), five goals.

More Euro Disappointment

In what many considered a surprising move, on 2 July 2010, the FA announced that Fabio Capello would remain as England manager for the foreseeable future. Contemplating what might have been in South Africa, especially if Frank Lampard's 'goal' had been awarded, he was somewhat pessimistic when he named his team for the first friendly international of the 2010/11 season against Hungary at Wembley, bringing in defender Phil Jagielka and forwards Adam Johnson and Theo Walcott, neither of whom had been at the World Cup. England won 2-1, to set things up nicely for the first batch of 2012 European Championship qualifiers, which saw them beat Bulgaria 4-0 at home and Switzerland 3-1 in Basel, and draw 0-0 with Montenegro 0-0 at Wembley.

After a home friendly defeat by France (2-1) and victory in Denmark (2-1), England beat Wales 2-0 in their fourth EC qualifier in Cardiff before being held 1-1 in another friendly by Ghana. Then it was back to trying to qualify for the EC in Ukraine, and England ended the season with a 2-2 draw in the return fixture with Switzerland. Once the players had been up and running with their respective club sides at the start of the 2011/12 season, it was once again into three more EC qualifiers, and England continued to make good, sound headway; beating Bulgaria 3-0 in Sofia, Wales 1-0 at Wembley and drawing 2-2 with Montenegro in Podgerica. That brought their overall points-tally to eighteen out of a possible twenty-four. They were on their way. Capello looked happy; so did the fans, although the press still had their doubts.

In November 2011, England won two home friendlies, against Spain and Sweden (both 1-0). But then, before the next encounter against The Netherlands at Wembley, Capello resigned on 8 February 2012, after the FA had taken the captaincy away from John Terry. The Italian had given debuts to more than twenty players, including goalkeepers Joe Hart and Chris Kirkland, full-backs Leighton Baines, Kieran Gibbs and Kyle Walker, defenders Gary Cahill, Phil Jagielka, Joleon Lescott and Chris Smalley, midfielders Tom Cleverley, Tom Huddlestone and James Milner and forwards Gabby Agbonlahor, Andy Carroll, Carlton Cole, Daniel Sturridge, Danny Welbeck and Ashley Young. With Capello gone, under-21 manager Stuart Pearce took charge of team for the game against the Dutch, which England lost 3-2, putting up a stout performance against a very useful side.

FA Appoint Hodgson

It had been widely reported in the British press that then-Tottenham Hotspur boss Harry Redknapp was favourite to take over as England manager. However, the FA chairman, David Bernstein, stated that, despite there being a shortlist of candidates, Roy Hodgson was the only one approached for the position. On 1 May 2012, Hodgson was officially appointed as England's new manager, agreeing a four-year contract. Having already managed in Italy, Switzerland, Sweden, Denmark, the UAE and Finland, as well as bossing Blackburn Rovers, Bristol City, Fulham and Liverpool, Hodgson, aged sixty-four and in charge of Premiership side West Bromwich Albion at the time, became the oldest manager ever appointed by the FA.

He immediately engendered controversy when he left former captain Rio Ferdinand out of his first senior squad; sternly defending his decision by stating his omission was down to 'footballing reasons', citing Ferdinand's lack of appearances for the national team, his last cap having come in June 2011. And, in fact, there were also concerns over his fitness. Ferdinand's club manager Sir Alex Ferguson agreed with Hodgson, saying that at the Euros, 'You play something like a game every four days. Rio Ferdinand couldn't do that.' Speculation, however, hinted that Ferdinand was not selected due to Hodgson not wanting both the Manchester United defender and John Terry in the same dressing room, with Terry due to undergo trial in July for allegedly racially abusing Ferdinand's brother, Anton.

After injury forced centre-back Gary Cahill to withdraw from his squad, Hodgson elected to pick full-back Martin Kelly ahead of Ferdinand, and his explanation for leaving Ferdinand out was simple: 'When it came to bringing another player in, I wasn't going to bring in a player of Rio's age, class, background and experience to be a cover player. I had to be convinced, if I was going to take Rio in my twenty-three, he'd be one of the first names on the team sheet. I couldn't be convinced that would be the case.'

Hodgson's opening game was a friendly in late May in Oslo. England won 1-0, recording their first victory over Norway for thirty-two years. Hodgson's second game in charge, and his first at Wembley, was against Belgium in early June. England ran out 1-0 winners courtesy of a first-half Danny Welbeck strike. Although the team didn't enjoy the higher percentage of possession, there were signs they would be a tough unit to beat.

Prior to Euro 2012, Hodgson named Ray Lewington, Gary Neville and Dave Watson to his coaching team, with the latter looking after the goalkeepers. Hodgson's Euro squad was hit by injuries, but the team battled well in their opening group match, holding France to a 1-1 draw. After a scare, Sweden were defeated 3-2 in their second game and in their final group fixture, Wayne Rooney returned from suspension to score the only goal to beat co-hosts Ukraine 1-0. Combined with Sweden's shock 2-0 victory over France, the result meant England qualified as group winners, with France runners-up.

In the quarter-finals, England took on Italy and, after a goalless 120 minutes, Hodgson's team lost 4-2 on penalties – another spot-kick nightmare. Praised for being well-organised and hard to beat, England either met or exceeded their expectations. Under Hodgson's management, England rose to third in the FIFA World Rankings, their highest-ever position since the rankings were introduced in 1992.

Qualification A Priority

Less than two months after being eliminated by Italy at Euro 2012, England played them again in a friendly in Berne, Switzerland, recording a 2-1 win, with Jermain Defoe coming off the bench to score the winner in the seventy-ninth minute.

England were drawn in Group H of the European zone of qualification for the 2014 FIFA World Cup, alongside Moldova, Montenegro, Poland, San Marino and Ukraine. Hodgson's England started their qualification campaign on 7 September 2012 with a convincing 5-0 away win over Moldova; Frank Lampard scoring twice – his first within three minutes from the penalty spot. In their second qualifier, four days later, England drew 1-1 to Ukraine

Moving on, in October 2012, England recorded a second 5-0 win, this time at home against the minnows San Marino, and followed up with a 1-1 draw away in Poland. England then lost 4-2 in a friendly in Sweden in mid-November 2012 – Hodgson's first defeat as manager. Leading 2-1 with twenty-three minutes to go, England were bowled over by home striker Zlatan Ibrahimović, who scored in the seventy-seventh, eighty-fourth and ninetieth minutes to take his tally to four and win the game for his country.

In another friendly at Wembley on 6 February 2013, England beat Brazil 2-1, their first win against the South American side for twenty-three years. Hodgson's side then resumed its World Cup qualifying campaign on 22 March by thumping San Marino 8-0 at the Stadio Olimpico. The goals came from seven different scorers and included a brace for Jermain Defoe, an own goal and a first England goal for Daniel Sturridge. This win was England's biggest since beating Turkey 8-0 in October 1987, and it vastly improved their goal difference ahead of their tough away tie against Montenegro in March. That match finished 1-1 after the hosts cancelled out Wayne Rooney's sixth-minute goal, leaving England trailing Montenegro by two points in the group.

Halfway through October 2013, England beat Poland 2-0 at Wembley, with goals from Rooney and Steven Gerrard, to qualify for the 2014 World Cup finals. Hodgson said after the match, 'Seeing England reach the 2014 World Cup in Brazil is my proudest moment in football.' However, following that win over the Poles, the England manager was criticised after information leaked from the dressing room about him referring to a joke about a monkey and an astronaut at half-time in the qualifier win.

29

The 2014 World Cup Qualifying Matches

7 September 2012
Chişinău

Moldova 0 England 5
Attendance 10,102

England's team: J. Hart, G. Johnson, J. Lescott, J. Terry, L. Baines, J. Milner, F. Lampard, T. Cleverley, A. Oxlade-Chamberlain, S. Gerrard, J. Defoe. Substitutes: T. Walcott for Oxlade-Chamberlain, M. Carrick for Gerrard, D. Welbeck for Defoe.

England's qualifying Group H campaign began without a hitch, as two first-half goals from Frank Lampard helped them to a straightforward win against Moldova in Chişinău. A confident Lampard fired home from the spot in the third minute after Tom Cleverley's shot had been handled inside the box by Simeon Bulgaru. The Chelsea midfielder followed up with a second goal in the twenty-ninth minute, ghosting in unnoticed to steer home Glen Johnson's superb flight cross from the right. Jermain Defoe made it 3-0 on thirty-two minutes after some delightful build-up play by the hard-working James Milner and Alex Oxlade-Chamberlain.

With Moldova under the cosh, and although dominating the play, England had to wait until the seventy-fourth minute before adding a fourth goal through Milner – his first for his country at senior level – the Aston Villa midfielder netting with a well-struck shot from 18 yards after Theo Walcott, Cleverley and Danny Welbeck had done the spadework. Everton's left-back Leighton Baines rounded things off with a fifth goal in the eighty-third minute, his free-kick leaving 'keeper Stanislav Namaşco flat-footed after deflecting off the top of the Moldovan wall.

Even allowing for the weak opposition, this was good, solid performance by Roy Hodgson's team, who had no less than twenty-eight attempts at goal (eleven of them on target). Now it was on to Wembley with a visit from Ukraine in their second Group H match. Everyone knew that this would be a much sterner test, yet the England players, at this juncture, were not short of confidence and it was a game they knew they could win. However, the fixture proved to be a lot tougher than anyone expected.

11 September 2012   England 1 Ukraine 1
Wembley   Attendance 68,681

England Team: J. Hart, G. Johnson, P. Jagielka, J. Lescott, L. Baines, F. Lampard,
S. Gerrard, J. Milner, T. Cleverley, A. Oxlade-Chamberlain, J. Defoe. Substitutes: R. Bertrand
(Chelsea) for Baines, D. Welbeck for Cleverley, D. Sturridge for Oxlade-Chamberlain.
England, who had Steven Gerrard sent off very late on, fought back from a goal down
to earn a crucial point. Frank Lampard efficiently converted an eighty-seventh-minute
penalty, his twenty-sixth for his country, which took him past former skipper Bryan
Robson's tally in the all-time scoring list.

The impressive Yevhen Konoplyanka had given the visitors the lead in the thirty-ninth
minute after Joleon Lescott's juvenile error. Despite having the lion's share of the possession,
England's passing (once again) left a lot to be desired, with the midfield players giving the ball
away far too often and, indeed, far too cheaply. Danny Welbeck, on as a substitute, saw his
chipped cross handled by Yevhen Khacheridi to set up Lampard's spot-kick equaliser. Tom
Cleverley and Welbeck, along with Ukraine's Oleg Husiev, all struck the woodwork in what
was an interesting encounter. 'We can play better than this, much better,' said Lampard, while
manager Hodgson admitted that this was 'a poor performance by us'.

Steven Gerrard was dismissed for two yellow cards, which automatically ruled him out
of England's next qualifying game against San Marino. Glen Johnson would also miss the
match following his second booking in as many games.

12 October 2012   England 5 San Marino 0
Wembley   Attendance 85,865

England Team: J. Hart, K. Walker, G. Cahill, P. Jagielka, L. Baines, T. Walcott, M. Carrick,
T. Cleverley, A. Oxlade-Chamberlain, D. Welbeck, W. Rooney. Substitutes: A. Lennon for
Walcott, A. Carroll (Liverpool) for Rooney, J. Shelvey (Liverpool) for Carrick.
England were expected to win this game comfortably … and they did. But realistically
the scoreline should have been far greater, possibly into double figures. It was a one-sided
contest from start to finish as England dominated proceedings. Indeed, Roy Hodgson's
team had thirty-three attempts at goal to just one by San Marino. After a lot of possession
and continuous attacking activity, Wayne Rooney, with a thirty-fifth-minute penalty, finally
broke the deadlock. Danny Welbeck was felled in the area by goalkeeper Aldo Simoncini,
who was shown a yellow card for his misdemeanour. Two minutes later, Simoncini was
lucky not to see red. He raced out of his area and clattered into Theo Walcott, who was
carried off and taken to hospital. Aaron Lennon was brought on as his replacement.

Eight minutes before half-time, Welbeck added a second goal. Tom Cleverley's pass was
knocked into the danger zone by Lennon for the lively Manchester United striker to flick
nonchalantly into the net – a replica of his goal scored against Sweden in the European
Championships. Surprisingly, however, it was not really until the last quarter of the game
that England, at long last, hit top form.

On as a substitute for Michael Carrick and making his international debut, Liverpool's Jonjo Shelvey picked out Leighton Baines with a pinpoint aerial cross. The left-back headed the ball into the penalty area, where Rooney curled in a beauty. This was Rooney's thirty-first goal for his country, taking him ahead of Alan 'Big Al' Shearer, Nat Lofthouse and Tom Finney. Welbeck then smartly popped in his second goal of the evening in the seventy-first minute, after some smart work down the right between Kyle Walker and Cleverley, before teenager Alex Oxlade-Chamberlain bagged number five in the seventy-sixth minute to complete a nap hand. This final goal came after some brilliant approaches involving Baines, Welbeck and Cleverley. The ball eventually fell to Oxlade-Chamberlain, who created history by finding the net with an exquisite chip over Simoncini. It was the first time a father (Mark Chamberlain *v.* Luxembourg in 1982) and son (Alex) had both scored for England. 'There will be far stronger opposition ahead – don't get carried away,' said one ardent supporter.

17 October 2012	Poland 1 England 1
Warsaw	Attendance 43,430

England Team: J. Hart, G. Johnson, P. Jagielka, J. Lescott, A. Cole, J. Milner, M. Carrick, S. Gerrard, T. Cleverley, W. Rooney, J. Defoe. Substitutes: A. Oxlade-Chamberlain for Rooney, D. Welbeck for Defoe.

Roy Hodgson's side were on course for all three points, which would have been a generous reward for a mediocre display, after Wayne Rooney's header (off his shoulder really) from Steven Gerrard's corner had given them a thirty-first-minute lead. But the hosts hit back after the break and Kamil Glik equalised with twenty minutes remaining to earn the battling Poles a deserved point in this delayed World Cup qualifier.

In a game played twenty-four hours after the scheduled encounter was washed away in a Warsaw deluge, England struggled to exert any supremacy on a sodden pitch. It was no surprise when Glik took advantage of a rare misjudgement by Manchester City goalkeeper Joe Hart to head in a right-wing corner from Ludovic Obraniak. Goalkeeper Przemysław Tytoń produced three fine saves to keep Poland in the match, although he was also fortunate when two other efforts missed the woodwork by inches.

England – wearing dark blue shirts and light blue shorts – were hoping for a victory that would have given them control of a potentially very tight qualifying group, but in the end they had to settle for a draw, which left them only a point clear at the top. Skipper Gerrard and left-back Ashley Cole won their ninety-ninth full caps in this game, although Cole blotted his copybook by receiving a yellow card for ungentlemanly conduct in the thirty eighth minute.

22 March 2013   San Marino 0 England 8
Stadio Olimpico, Serravalle   Attendance 4,922

England Team: J. Hart, K. Walker, C. Smalling (Manchester United), J. Lescott, L. Baines, A. Oxlade-Chamberlain, F. Lampard, T. Cleverley, A. Young, W. Rooney, J. Defoe. Substitutes: S. Parker (Tottenham Hotspur) for Lampard, D. Sturridge for Rooney, L. Osman (Everton) for Cleverley.

The minnows of San Marino, who had lost fifty internationals in succession, were completely outplayed by England as manager Roy Hodgson fielded his ninth different centre-back pairing of Chris Smalling and Joleon Lescott. So much were England in control, they had twenty-eight attempts at goal to San Marino's one.

After Alessandro Della Valle's twelfth-minute own-goal (from Leighton Baines' well-driven cross from the left) had unlocked the visitors' defensive door. Now it was a case of how many times could England find the net? Alex Oxlade-Chamberlain made it 2-0 in the twenty-eighth minute. Brilliant inter-passing between Wayne Rooney (winning his eighty-seventh cap) and Alex Oxlade-Chamberlain carved open the San Marino defence, allowing the latter to fire home a fierce shot, the goal taking him past his father's total of one for England. Oxlade-Chamberlain also had a hand in England's third goal in the thirty-fifth minute. Rooney's chip to the far post was headed across goal by the Arsenal youngster, allowing the predatory Jermain Defoe a simple tap-in from 2 yards out.

Manchester United's Ashley Young netted goal number four in the thirty-ninth minute. He exchanged passes with Leighton Baines before blasting home a tremendous shot from fully 25 yards out, which absolutely flew into the top corner leaving goalkeeper Aldo Simoncini helpless. It was a goal worthy of beating a much better side than San Marino. Frank Lampard then got on the scoring charts in the forty-second minute. Rooney dummied the pass to leave the Chelsea midfielder free to continue his rich vein of scoring with an excellent side-footed finish: 5-0.

The half ended with England totally and utterly dominant in every facet of the game. The big question everyone was asking was simple: would they ease off in the second half, or go flat out for a big win?

Well, they continued to play football, retaining possession at will and, in the fifty-fourth minute, England were awarded a free-kick just outside the 18-yard box following a foul on Tom Cleverley. Despite the presence of Baines, Rooney made it clear that he, and only he, was going to take the kick. And he duly delivered, curling his shot over the wall and into the bottom corner of the net, with goalkeeper Simoncini nowhere to be seen.

Soon afterwards, Rooney was replaced by substitute Daniel Sturridge who, after striking the woodwork, added a seventh goal in the seventieth minute. Defoe and Young combined well again, and when Young delivered a perfect chipped cross, Sturridge was there to head home at the far post for his first England goal. Then Defoe struck again with thirteen minutes remaining, tapping the ball home, unchallenged, after some brilliant play between 'Man of the Match' Oxlade-Chamberlain and right-back Kyle Walker. This was England's first eight-goal victory since beating Turkey at Wembley in 1987. Would things be this easy against Montenegro? No, certainly not.

26 March 2013   Montenegro 1 England 1
Podgorica   Attendance 12,120

England Team: J. Hart, G. Johnson, C. Smalling, J. Lescott, A. Cole, S. Gerrard, M. Carrick, J. Milner, T. Cleverley, D. Welbeck, W. Rooney. Substitute: A. Young for Cleverley.

England's path to World Cup qualification remained far from guaranteed after Montenegro had battled back to earn a deserved draw. Wayne Rooney got England off to the best possible start, scoring with a header from Steven Gerrard's left-wing corner after just six minutes. This was the Manchester United striker's fifth goal in six games since Euro 2012. He was on fire and in form.

In fact, England dominated the first half, playing some very enterprising and positive football. However, they eventually paid a heavy price for failing to capitalise fully on that superiority, and a dreadful second half display lacked any semblance of composure or cohesion, or indeed firepower. In the end, they had to settle for a draw when, with thirteen minutes remaining, Montenegro scored an equaliser.

The ball was whipped into England's penalty area, where substitute Dejan Damjanović was given a free header, which Hart parried well, pushing it out to the danger zone. However, the ball continued to get ping-ponged about inside the box without a single England player being able – or indeed willing – to make a positive clearance. It proved fatal, as Damjanović finally forced the ball over the line to send the home fans into delirium.

6 September 2013   England 4 Moldova 0
Wembley   Attendance 61,607

England Team: J. Hart, K. Walker, G. Cahill, P. Jagielka, A. Cole, F. Lampard, S. Gerrard, J. Wilshere (Arsenal), T. Walcott, R. Lambert (Southampton), D. Welbeck. Substitutes: L. Baines for Cole, J. Milner for Lambert, J. Barkley (Everton) for Wilshere.

In the four days leading up to this crucial game, three key players dropped out of the England squad with injuries: Wayne Rooney, Daniel Sturridge and Glen Johnson. But manager Roy Hodgson was still able to select a team that proved far too strong for the relatively poor Moldovan side, which simply wasn't at the races. In fact, England had twenty-three goal attempts (thirteen on target) against just two by their opponents.

From the kick-off there was a purpose about England. Steven Gerrard, looking bright and breezy, and obviously back to his forceful best and eager for possession, started to make some surging runs from the midfield. Taking a page out of the skipper's book, the rest of the team followed suit. All knew their jobs and gradually settled into destroying their opponents' defences. Southampton striker Rickie Lambert, playing in only his second full international, shot over early on from a good position after Ashley Cole's smart dash down the left. After Kyle Walker's low cross flew across goal without anyone near enough to touch it home, England took the lead on twelve minutes, with skipper Gerrard smashing the ball into the bottom corner of Stanislav Namasco's net from 20 yards after being teed up by Frank Lampard. Lambert then made it two when goalkeeper Namaşco inexplicably spilled the ball onto his head 2 yards out from Theo Walcott's shot.

Unfortunately, in-form Danny Welbeck picked up a yellow card late in the first half, which ruled him out of the next vital qualifier in the Ukraine. But he didn't let that worry him unduly, and he added a third in injury-time at the end of the first half, slipping through the middle to pick up Lambert's pass before rounding Namaşco to tap-into an empty net. The Manchester United striker went on to grab England's fourth goal five minutes into the second half, when a flowing move allowed him to break into the box to delicately chip the ball over the onrushing Moldovan 'keeper. On the hour, Everton midfielder Ross Barkley came on for his senior debut, replacing Arsenal's Jack Wilshere. One reporter wrote, 'This was a solid victory, well deserved and most welcome.' I agree.

10 September 2013	**Ukraine 0 England 0**
Kiev	**Attendance 69,890**

England Team: J. Hart, K. Walker, G. Cahill, P. Jagielka, A. Cole, F. Lampard, S. Gerrard, J. Wilshere, J. Milner, T. Walcott, R. Lambert. Substitutes: A. Young for Wilshere, T. Cleverley for Walcott.

This hard-earned draw took Roy Hodgson's side closer to the 2014 World Cup finals, but if they play as badly as this in Brazil, they will get well and truly slaughtered. *The Daily Telegraph*'s reporter, Henry Winter, wrote, 'On this dispiriting evidence, England won't get the ball off the kids on Copacabana beach let alone Spain or Brazil at Maracana.' In truth, this was one ugly performance, which highlighted many technical flaws. But at the same time, it was also undeniably one sweet qualifying point at the home of their Group H rivals.

With every single midfielder continually losing possession, and Rickie Lambert isolated in attack, England looked second-class going forward and, in the end, were totally indebted to Gary Cahill and Ashley Cole, masterful figures of defiance in defence, for this draw. It was, in some respects, a real dogged performance, and Hodgson's men did just about enough to avoid defeat. Now it was all down to themselves – two wins from two home games, both in front of near full houses at Wembley, would see them through to Brazil. Bring it on.

11 October 2013	**England 4 Montenegro 1**
Wembley	**Attendance 83,807**

England Team: J. Hart, K. Walker, G. Cahill, P. Jagielka, L. Baines, F. Lampard, S. Gerrard, A. Townsend, D. Welbeck, W. Rooney, D. Sturridge. Substitutes: J. Milner for Gerrard, J. Wilshere for Townsend, M. Carrick for Lampard.

England manager Roy Hodgson sprang a huge surprise by selecting the in-form and pacy Tottenham Hotspur right winger Andros Townsend for his senior debut against Montenegro. Eyebrows were raised by many when they learned of Townsend's inclusion, but boy, what a great choice it turned out to be … The young man had a blinder.

Right from the start, England looked sharp, competitive and up for the fight. There was plenty of passing from all quarters, some great awareness and movement by the front men, and generally each and every player looked lively. And this is how it was throughout the game, with few taking an occasional breather here and there.

Unfortunately, despite having the majority of the play, the first half was goalless, but once Wayne Rooney had made the breakthrough in the forty-eighth minute, there was never any doubt that England would win.

A brilliant positive run down the right by Townsend – he made several of these during the game – left defenders trailing in his wake. As his cross came over, it was deflected towards the advancing Danny Welbeck, who drilled in a low shot from 18 yards. Goalkeeper Vukašin Poleksić blocked the ball, but the rebound was superbly controlled by Wayne Rooney, who then turned superbly before shooting under the body of the diving keeper. Pouring forward in numbers, England had two more chances before going two up in the sixty-second minute, when Branko Bošković miscued his clearance past his own 'keeper.

Then, soon after Stevan Jovetić had smashed a stunning pile-driver against Joe Hart's crossbar, Montenegro snatched a surprise goal with twenty minutes remaining. Fatos Bećiraj was allowed to fire in a speculative ground shot towards his target. The ball was certainly going well wide until the alert Dejan Damjonović stuck out a foot to deflect it wide of the helpless England goalkeeper. This setback seemed to inspire England to greater things, and in the seventy-eighth minute Townsend, who had been terrific, crowned a fine display by thumping home goal number three from 20 yards. What a way to celebrate your debut. It was almost his last contribution, as Hodgson took him off and the player left to a deserved standing ovation. With ninety-three minutes on the clock, and Spanish referee Alberto Mallenco, who had a very good match by the way, ready to call time, Daniel Sturridge took James Milner's pass in his stride, attacked the defenders, as he had done all night, and was brought down inside the box by Ivan Kecojević. After picking himself up, Sturridge, as cool as you like, side-footed the ball home from the spot to add a little more icing on top of the cake.

England did everything right on the night. Everyone played their part, what more could you ask for – a win over Poland? Yes, of course. One down, one to play ... Brazil here we come.

15 October 2013   **England 2 Poland 0**
Wembley   **Attendance 85,186**

England Team: J. Hart, C. Smalling, G. Cahill, P. Jagielka, L. Baines, M. Carrick, S. Gerrard, A. Townsend, D. Welbeck, W. Rooney, D. Sturridge. Substitutes: J. Milner for Townsend, J. Wilshere for Sturridge, F. Lampard for Carrick.

The scene was set, the table laid, the spectators were seated, the atmosphere was electric, everything was ready, and England – on a high after that fine win over Montenegro – took on Poland for a place in the 2014 World Cup finals in Brazil. All that was left for Roy Hodgson's players to do was to go out and win their final Group H game. Thankfully, on a night when passion and commitment were the two keywords and, indeed, vital factors, they did just that and they did it in fine style too, beating the Poles 2-0.

There's no doubt it was a hard-earned yet fully deserved victory, achieved inside a nervous and tension-packed stadium that contained around 20,000 vociferous Polish supporters. Roy Hodgson's men played exceedingly well, knowing what was at stake, and showing their mettle with a gutsy, resilient performance. They had eighteen attempts at goal, while Poland managed just six, four by the impressive and dangerous Robert Lewandowski.

After a couple of near misses, and some nail-biting moments, Wayne Rooney finally broke the deadlock with a smartly taken headed goal shortly before half-time. Michael Carrick fed Leighton Baines down the left. His cross was inch-perfect, and the Manchester United striker to rose majestically to send a fantastic header wide of Arsenal's goalkeeper Wojciech Szczęsny and into the net. It was going to take a superb goal to beat the in-form Szczęsny, and this was certainly worthy of that accolade.

Nerves continued to jangle, both on and off the pitch, and with both sets of defenders coming under pressure, Townsend, Rooney, Welbeck and Daniel Sturridge for England, and Lewandowski twice for Poland, all went close with good efforts. With just two minutes left to play, James Milner lobbed a pass that was collected by England captain Steve Gerrard as he darted purposefully into the penalty area. The Liverpool man, who was winning his 107th cap, showed great determination, commitment and composure as he brought the ball under control before delicately chipping it over the onrushing Szczęsny to clinch victory. What joy ... The England bench and fans inside Wembley went absolutely wild. And I know, for sure, that the celebrations went on long into the night...

Two Defeats, World Cup Draw

Amazingly, after qualifying for the 2014 World Cup, England contrived to lose their next two internationals – both at home – going down 2-0 to Chile and 1-0 to arch-rivals Germany. In fact, it was the first time England had lost two games in succession at Wembley since 1977. But manager Roy Hodgson was not too downhearted, saying, 'We certainly learnt a lot from these two games. We played against very good opponents and I know now what will be required to succeed, even win a game, in Brazil.'

In his first two seasons in charge (May 2012 to May 2014), Hodgson handed senior debuts to some twenty players, including goalkeepers Jack Butland, Celtic's Fraser Forster and John Ruddy, full-backs Ryan Bertrand and Carl Jenkinson, defender Steven Caulker, midfielders Jordan Henderson, Alex Oxlade-Chamberlain, Leon Osman, Jack Rodwell and Jonjo Shelvey, the Southampton trio of Rickie Lambert, Adam Lallana and Jay Rodriguez and wingers Raheem Sterling, Andros Townsend and Wilfried Zaha. When capped against Italy in Switzerland in 2012, Butland, standing 6 feet 4 inches tall, became England's youngest-ever goalkeeper at the age of 19 years, 158 days.

On 6 December 2013, the draw was made in Brazil for the first phase of the World Cup, and England – unseeded – received no favours, coming out in the pot with Costa Rica, Italy (with Mario Balotelli) and Uruguay (who will be relying on a certain Luis Suarez and Diego Forlan) in a what is regarded as a tough Group D.

On hearing the draw, Wayne Rooney said, 'It will be tough but it's not a disaster. We have to beat the best if we are to become champions. Get out of the group and who knows.' Midfielder Jack Wilshere admitted, 'Okay, it's a tough group, but so what? If we want to win the World Cup, we will have to play the top teams anyway!'

For former player and manager Glenn Hoddle, however, the draw was excellent. 'The tougher the opposition the better England play. We know that both Italy and Uruguay are good sides and don't give too much away – but there's a lot worse out there and we are better when we are up against it,' he said. Ex-England striker Alan Shearer also agreed: 'It will be a tough challenge, knowing that their first game against Italy will take place in the Amazon rainforest with 99 per cent humidity.' Another former skipper, Ray Wilkins, said, 'Suarez is going to have a tough end to the season with Liverpool, I'm sure of that. I might have a word with John Terry as Chelsea meet the Merseysiders on April 26.'

For the experienced midfield duo of Steven Gerrard and Frank Lampard, both of whom have over 100 caps under their belts, this for certain, will be their last major tournament. It could also be a swan song in World Cup football for other centurions – Ashley Cole, Michael Carrick James Milner and even Jermain Defoe. And if chosen there is no doubt they will be determined to do well in Brazil.

England encountered two friendlies at Wembley against Denmark on 5 March and Peru on 30 May, followed by further non-competitive matches against Ecuador on 4 June and Honduras on 7 June, both in Miami before starting their World Cup campaign on 14 June with opening Group D encounter against Italy, followed by games against Uruguay five days later and Costa Rica on 24 June.

Hodgson's twenty-three-man squad to travel to Brazil would, it seemed, be chosen from an initial list of forty, which could be:

Goalkeepers: Fraser Forster, Ben Foster, Joe Hart, John Ruddy. Full-backs: Leighton Baines, Ashley Cole, Kieran Gibbs, Glen Johnson, Luke Shaw, Kyle Walker. Defenders: Gary Cahill, Michael Dawson, Phil Jagielka, Chris Smalling*, John Terry. Midfielders: Ross Barkley, Michael Carrick, Tom Cleverley, Steven Gerrard, Jordan Henderson, Adam Johnson, Phil Jones*, Frank Lampard, Adam Lallana, James Milner, Leon Osman, Alex Oxlade-Chamberlain, Jack Rodwell, Jack Wilshere, Ashley Young. Forwards: Gabby Agbonlahor, Saido Berahino, Jermain Defoe, Ricky Lambert, Jay Rodriguez, Wayne Rooney, Raheem Sterling, Daniel Sturridge, Andros Townsend, Theo Walcott, Danny Welbeck.
* *Utility players.*

2014 World Cup Fact File

- Countries taking part: 32 (divided into eight groups of 4).
- Final venue: Estádio do Maracanã, Rio de Janeiro.
- The first hat-trick in Brazil will be the fiftieth in World Cup finals.
- The host nation, Brazil, will be making their twentieth consecutive appearance in World Cup finals.

England World Cup Facts

- Peter Shilton has played in the most World Cup finals matches (17). Terry Butcher, Bobby Charlton, Ashley Cole, Bobby Moore all made 14 appearances, David Beckham 13 and Gary Lineker and Michael Owen 12 each.
- Centre-half Laurie Hughes (Liverpool) made his international debut for England against Chile in Rio de Janeiro in June 1950.
- Of the 203 different players named in the various squads, 158 have actually represented England in World Cup tournaments: 1950–2010.
- Shilton was also the oldest England captain in the World Cup, aged 40 years, 202 days *v.* Italy, July 1990. Shilton also kept a record 10 cleansheets (1982–90).
- The joint highest scoring draw in World Cup finals is 4-4 – England *v.* Belgium in 1954.
- In 1966, England became the third country, after Uruguay (1930) and Italy (1934) to win the World Cup on home soil.
- England players have missed a record seven spot-kicks in three penalty shoot-outs at the end of drawn World Cup final matches.
- Alan Ball (*v.* Poland in 1973) was the first England player to be sent off in any form of World Cup game.
- Ray Wilkins was the first England player to be sent off in World Cup finals, dismissed against Morocco in 1986.